Walt Whitman,
Philosopher Poet

Walt Whitman, Philosopher Poet

Leaves of Grass by Indirection

JOHN W. McDONALD

McFarland & Company, Inc., Publishers
Jefferson, North Carolina, and London

John W. McDonald died in April 2006 after delivering the completed manuscript for this book. The publishers are grateful to Iantha McDonald, his widow, for her generous assistance thereafter.

FRONTISPIECE: Portrait of Walt Whitman by William Thompson Russell Smith (1812–1896). Courtesy Duke University. Photograph by the *Durham Herald-Sun*.

LIBRARY OF CONGRESS CATALOGUING-IN-PUBLICATION DATA

McDonald, John W., 1924–
    Walt Whitman, philosopher poet : Leaves of grass by indirection / John W. McDonald.
      p.   cm.
    Includes bibliographical references and index.

    ISBN-13: 978-0-7864-2388-0
    (softcover : 50# alkaline paper) ∞

    1. Whitman, Walt, 1819–1892. Leaves of grass.   2. Whitman, Walt, 1819–1892 — Philosophy.   3. Philosophy in literature. 4. Determinism (Philosophy)   I. Title.
PS3238.M2 2007
811'.3–dc22   2006025065

British Library cataloguing data are available

Cover photograph: Walt Whitman in 1863 (Feinberg-Whitman Collection, Library of Congress)

Manufactured in the United States of America

McFarland & Company, Inc., Publishers
  Box 611, Jefferson, North Carolina 28640
  www.mcfarlandpub.com

In memory of
Professor E.L. Marilla,
whose enthusiasm
gave me courage

Acknowledgments

Foremost among the many influences which contributed to the writing of this book was that of Professor Peter A. Carmichael, an alumnus of the University of North Carolina of a time when education was at a peak not reached since. As my most beloved teacher at Louisiana State University, he led me into the wonderland of philosophy and gave me a high regard for logic and intellectual integrity. At that university also was Mr. Esmond L. Marilla, professor of English (not American) literature, who sensed the importance of my early Whitman findings and sponsored my candidacy for a Rockefeller Foundation scholarship which enabled me to enter the University of North Carolina as a graduate student in American literature. An inspiring friend and adviser at Chapel Hill was Mr. Robert Linker, professor of Spanish. Librarians at LSU, UNC, Duke University, and Florida Keys Community College deserve my thanks for their courtesies.

Although I have departed almost entirely from earlier Whitman criticism, I have nevertheless profited greatly from the writings of three authors in particular: Gay Wilson Allen, whose 1946 *Walt Whitman Handbook* opened the gates to productive investigations; David S. Reynolds, whose *Walt Whitman's America* (1995) acquainted me more intimately with Whitman; and Horace Traubel, whose *With Walt Whitman in Camden,* filling nine volumes with the records of his almost daily visits to Whitman, provided a multitude of references which support my findings. Though it came to my attention late, *Walt Whitman: An Encyclopedia* (1998), with the stellar editing of LeMaster and Kummings, furnished an overview of Whitman research and thereby gave me assurance that my book stands solidly on its own merits.

More than once, my computer guru, Roger Johnson, rescued me from chaos.

During the early years of the writing (1952–55), I received encouragement and many a free meal from my dear friends Pat and Norman Jarrard, who were fellow students with me at Chapel Hill. My wife, Iantha Smart, whom I met in Chapel Hill, had a practical influence on me: she insisted that I stop revising and helped me type a "final" copy. In the ensuing fifty years, as new evidence forced itself upon me, there have been many other "final" copies, some of which were constructed in the wonderful Chapel Hill studio which Iantha (a frustrated architect) designed and had built for me above the garage.

Table of Contents

Preface

This book had its inception fifty-four years ago. I am eighty-one years old now, in 2006. Then I was twenty-seven, an undergraduate at Louisiana State University. I discovered in the Preface to *Leaves of Grass* an unnoticed tag-end of Whitman's thought and began to unravel what proved to be his philosophy. Yes, his philosophy — he was a philosopher who wrote poetry.

After an unsuccessful effort to publish this book in 1955, I laid the manuscript on the shelf and pursued a life independent of scholarship. Like Whitman, I worked as a printer and became a teacher. For eighteen years I was an independent commercial fisherman on the turquoise waters of the Florida Keys. I owned my own boat, built my own traps, and caught Florida lobster. My wife and I raised three fine children. I retired from fishing in 1989 and returned, though not immediately, to my old love: I began re-editing the book and strengthening its findings.

I have conscientiously reviewed Whitman criticism and emended my text and notes accordingly, bringing the content up to date. The findings have always been, and still are, almost entirely independent of other Whitman criticism.

It is a salient fact that my own philosophy is nearly the same as what I shall prove to have been Whitman's. I hope not many readers will agree with the prejudicial assessment that no doubt will be made — that I simply see in Whitman what I want to see: confirmation of my own beliefs. I have not always suppressed my own philosophical enthusiasms, allowing them, indeed, to assist in the explication of Whitman's meanings.

For objectivity I have tried to avoid stating my own opinions, supplying, instead, statements from various sources, particularly philosophic, which show obvious agreement or disagreement with the ideas of Whitman as discovered in his poems and revealed in his prose and notes and conversations. It would be easier for me, and for the reader, if I said in my own words, "This

1

is so!" But by entering quotations in evidence I hope to make it possible for others to see *why* I think it is so.

In searching for Whitman's meanings I became aware of what I call "echoes." Because they emphasize coincidental similarities of ideas or perhaps even strongly suggest Whitman's indebtedness to other authors, these echoes throw light on Whitman's thought. Sometimes they reveal an indebtedness of Whitman to himself, as earlier and later passages and poems are compared. A valuable revelation of these echoes is the fair proof that Whitman's ideas and images remained remarkably constant.

Sometimes, while the writing was in progress, nuances of meaning, discoveries of new relationships, and suddenly occurring logical insights came so fast that I sometimes felt overwhelmed by an avalanche of evidence.

Through good luck and hard work, I have to a certain measure resurrected parts of Walt Whitman's mind. I hope the reader can share my excitement at being able to enter that mind and logically (or intuitively) wander about.

That you are here — that life exists and identity
That the powerful play goes on,
and you may contribute a verse.

Whitman, "Answer"
in "O Me! O Life!"

Engraved portrait of Walt Whitman, 1871, by William J. Linton.

I

The Unseen Roots

"It lies behind almost every line;
but concealed, studiedly concealed."
— Whitman to Edward Carpenter.

In 1888, after a third of a century of abuse and misinterpretation, an exasperated Whitman said of his critics:

Yet not one of them comprehends — not one of them — not one of them all — (the whole batch who have written, criticized, annulled) — has grasped the truth, the principle: has come into contact with, and prized, what is the first essential. Oh! it is a shallow, shallow brood![1]

In 2005 the real Walt Whitman, philosopher and poet, remains undiscovered. We have not come very far since 1893, when Edmund Gosse summed up by saying: "I am sadly conscious that, after reading what a great many people of authority and of assumption have written about Whitman — reading it, too, in a humble spirit — though I have been stimulated and entertained, I have not been at all instructed.... To me, at least, after all the oceans of talk, after all the extravagant eulogy, all the mad vituperation, he remains perfectly cryptic and opaque."[2]

Horace Traubel says Whitman believed that the "formal-cut" men could not comprehend "Leaves of Grass." "They like portions, beauties, what they would call 'gems' — do not see more." They did not see "the thread connecting all."[3] For Whitman the "roots" of *Leaves of Grass* were of fundamental importance. In a conversation about certain writers (including Matthew Arnold) he complained: "...they do not lift you off your feet — they are without inspiration. They make more fuss over foliage than root, if that may be: think the foliage may be superior to the root — neglect the root."[4]

5

There will be much more evidence about the "roots" in the next few pages. We must be aware of the roots and try to identify them. It does not help much to call Whitman "the poet of democracy" or "the poet of freedom." We must find out why these statements can be made. There is urgent need for an energetic effort to discover what *supports* Whitman's poetry.

Probably no candidate for understanding Whitman has not been haunted and mocked by the closing lines of "Whoever You Are Holding Me Now in Hand":

> Even while you should think you had unquestionably caught me, behold!
> Already you see I have escaped from you.
>
> For it is not for what I have put into it that I have written this book,
> Nor is it by reading it you will acquire it, ...
> For all is useless without that which you may guess at many times and
> not hit, that which I hinted at;
> Therefore release me and depart on your way.

We are baffled by what Whitman calls his "indirections." We should be wise to note, however, that these were not, as they may seem to be, an impish effort by Whitman to throw the reader off. Evidence indicates that he was forced to rely on indirections to convey his deeper meanings. Late in life he declared of *Leaves of Grass*:

> ... it can never be understood but by an indirection.[5]

He at times does refer to his indirections as if they were a sort of game of hide-and-seek which he played to evade the reader's comprehension. In an early review of his own poems he mentioned their "distinct purposes, curiously veiled." "Theirs is no writer," he explained, "to be gone through with in a day or a month. Rather it is his pleasure to elude you and provoke you for deliberate purposes of his own."[6] One might think that Whitman was merely toying with the reader. But the hidden message is far more serious. David Kuebrich wisely perceived: "Whitman asks a great deal of his readers not only because his mystical meanings are ultimately ineffable but also because he intentionally uses a suggestive method which leaves much unsaid."[7]

Whitman told Traubel, "I feel that there is a solid basis for what I have done — a a root-idea justifying all — from the first leaf of all the Leaves to the last leaf— the very last: as there must also be for anything that is yet to come."[8] In 1884, in the course of a long and intimate conversation with Edward Carpenter, Whitman remarked:

> What lies behind "Leaves of Grass" is something that few, very few, only
> one here and there, perhaps oftenest women, are at all in a position to seize.
> It lies behind almost every line; but concealed, studiedly concealed; some

passages left purposely obscure. There is something in my nature *furtive* like an old hen! You see a hen wandering up and down a hedgerow, looking apparently quite unconcerned, but presently she finds a concealed spot, and furtively lays an egg, and comes away as though nothing had happened! That is how I felt in writing "Leaves of Grass." Sloan Kennedy calls me "artful"—which about hits the mark. I think there are truths which it is necessary to envelop or wrap up.[9]

What was this "root-idea" which Whitman so "studiedly concealed," this important something which "lies behind almost every line?" Heed the following note, written by Whitman himself:

Philosophy of *Leaves of Grass:*

Walt Whitman's philosophy—or perhaps metaphysics, to give it a more definite name—as evinced in his poems, and running through them and sometimes quite palpable in his verses, but far oftener latent, and like the unseen roots or sap of trees—is not the least of his peculiarities—one must not say originalities, for Whitman himself disclaims originality—at least in the superficial sense. His notion explicitly is that there is nothing actually new only an accumulation or fruitage or carrying out of the old or its adaptation to the modern and to these new occasions and requirements.[10]

Whitman here again refers to the "roots." His "philosophy" is "like the unseen roots or sap of trees." He used the root metaphor many times, but never more tellingly than in a remark he made at his 71st birthday dinner in response to Robert Ingersoll's praise of his poems:

Colonel Ingersoll justifies fully my method, my tricks—my method of describing and appealing. I felt willing to keep the roots of everything in "Leaves of Grass" underground, out of sight, and let the book work its way. If it grew, in verdure and flowerage, so much the better; but certain important results were to me the main things.[11]

Traubel's report of that birthday celebration gives a quite similar statement by Whitman:

I have kept the roots well underground. "Leaves of Grass," be they what they may, are only in part the fact—for beneath, around, are contributing forces, which do not come out in the superficial exposé.[12]

Analysis of these last several quotations indicates that there is a *key* to *Leaves of Grass*, a "root-idea justifying all," and that this key, this "root-idea," was premeditatedly and intentionally concealed by Whitman and that what he concealed was a philosophy, a kind of metaphysics.

These conclusions seem to be well substantiated, but if we search further, we find Whitman contradicting them. He declares in "Song of Myself," Sec. 12, "I have no chair, no church, no philosophy." Traubel reports a conversation in which a friend, Daniel G. Brinton, said to Whitman, "You give

us no consistent philosophy." To which Whitman replied, "I guess I don't —
I should not desire to do so." Traubel suggested, "Plenty of philosophy but
not *a* philosophy." Whitman agreed, "That's better — that's more the idea."[13]
Later, recalling Brinton's suggestion that his philosophy lacked in definite-
ness, Whitman remarked:

> Well, it is true, I guess — indeed, true without the shadow of a doubt: the
> more I turn it over the more convinced am I. Of all things, I imagine I am
> most lacking in what is called definiteness, in so far as that applies to special
> theories of life and death. As I grow older I am more firmly than ever fixed
> in my belief that all things tend to good, that no bad is forever bad, that the
> universe has its own ends to subserve and will subserve them well. Beyond
> that, when it comes to launching out into mathematics — tying philosophy
> to the multiplication table — I am lost — lost utterly. Let them all whack
> away — I am satisfied: if they can explain they can do more than I can do. I
> am not Anarchist, not Methodist, not anything you can name. Yet I see
> why all the ists and isms and haters and dogmatists exist — can see why they
> must exist and why I must include all.[14]

Whitman had concluded the earlier conversation with Brinton with an
interesting comment about "Passage to India": "There's more of me, the essential ultimate me, in that than in any of the poems. There is no philosophy,
consistent or inconsistent, in that poem — there Brinton would be right — but
the burden of it is evolution — the one thing escaping the other — the unfolding of cosmic purposes."[15] Without knowing how Whitman would have
defined philosophy, one cannot accuse him of a self-contradiction, but it
would seem from this remark that he is confessing, in spite of his protest,
that in a sense "Passage to India" does contain a philosophy. In a footnote to
the 1876 Preface he makes the statement, "(Then probably *Passage to India*
and its cluster, are but freer vent and fuller expression to what, from the first,
and so on throughout, more or less lurks in my writings, underneath every
page, every line, everywhere.)"[16] Here again there is a hint that there is some
mysterious common denominator for the poems. But is it a philosophy? Whitman said of "Passage to India," "There is no philosophy, consistent or inconsistent, in that poem." The following comment by Whitman will help to clear
up the confusion:

> Using the term in its latest and largest, and not at all in its dogmatic and
> scholastic sense, Walt Whitman's poetry is, in its intention, *philosophic*. It is
> beyond the moral law, and will probably therefore always appall many. The
> moral law, it is true, is present, penetrating the verse, like shafts of light.
> But the whole relentless kosmos out of which come monsters and crime and
> the inexhaustible germs of all the heat of sex, and all the lawless rut and
> arrogant greed of the universe and especially of the human race, are also

there. Strange and paradoxical are these pages. They accept and celebrate Nature in absolute faith.[17]

Is not Whitman here once more asserting that the poems are philosophic? The confusion may not be so great as it seems.

Let us take a closer look at the apparently contradictory statements. Whitman has said that "Passage to India" contains "no philosophy." Yet he has spoken of something of which the poem is an expression, something which "more or less lurks in my writings, underneath every page, every line, everywhere."

The important point to be noted is this: that which is "underneath" every page, every line, etc., is, in one sense, not *in* the poems at all. What Whitman could have made clearer was that he did not *preach* a philosophy in his poems. He told Dr. Bucke: "The unspoken meaning of *Leaves of Grass*, never absent, yet not told out — the indefinable animus behind every page, is a main part of the book." And then he hinted, fragmentarily: "Something entirely outside of literature, as hitherto written; outside of art in all departments."[18]

He might have explained that he made *use* of a philosophy in his poems. The philosophy is not in the poems: it "lies behind" them. It is the "roots" of the *Leaves of Grass*. It is "sometimes quite palpable in his verses, but far oftener latent, and like the unseen roots or sap of trees." It is "underground, out of sight." It is "behind almost every line; but concealed, studiedly concealed."

The critics have staggered about in their efforts to reduce Whitman's thought to a system. Some have, in fact, given up altogether. F. O. Matthiessen stated flatly: "No arrangement or rearrangement of Whitman's thoughts ... can resolve the paradoxes or discover in them a fully coherent pattern. He was incapable of sustained logic...."[19] David Daiches dismissed the question with a dispirited remark that "to treat Whitman as a systematic philosopher is an unrealistic and unprofitable procedure."[20] G. W. Allen concluded that we would probably be "wasting our time to search in Whitman's writings for a systematic or professional theory."[21]

The abundant evidence herein presented will show that Whitman, in spite of Matthiessen's insulting pronouncement, was *not* "incapable of sustained logic" and that a search for a systematic philosophy would not be, as Daiches sees it, an "unprofitable procedure" or, as Allen would advise us, a waste of time. Gathered here will be evidence from Whitman's poems and prose and from his notes and quoted remarks, enough evidence to show beyond doubt that a philosophy was the most significant influence in Whitman's thought and in his art.

The quotations already given provide certain clues as to what that philosophy is.

Referring to his "essential ultimate me," Whitman remarked that "the burden of it is evolution — the one thing escaping the other — the unfolding of cosmic purposes." Having asserted that his poetry is "in its intention, *philosophic*," Whitman went on to mention the presence in his poems of "the whole relentless kosmos out of which come monsters and crime and the inexhaustible germs of all the heat of sex, and all the lawless rut and arrogant greed of the universe and especially of the human race." In his third-person note on "Philosophy of *Leaves of Grass*" Whitman stated: "…Whitman himself disclaims originality — at least in the superficial sense. His notion explicitly is that there is nothing actually new only an accumulation or fruitage or carrying out of the old…."

William James speaks of "Determinists … who say that individual men originate nothing, but merely transmit to the future the whole push of the past cosmos…."[22] Need we search further? Have we not already found the key? We have. Whitman had a secret philosophy. This philosophy was called in Whitman's day necessitarianism or necessity or necessarianism. It is now called determinism.

Whitman actually proclaimed his allegiance to determinism in the 1855 Preface when he wrote:

> … no result exists now without being from its long antecedent result, and that from its antecedent, and so backward without the farthest mentionable spot coming a bit nearer the beginning than any other spot.[23]

Interpretation hinges on the word "antecedent," which Whitman uses twice in the statement. Keep this word in mind as you read the following definitions of determinism from six dictionaries chosen at random (they are all I have with me). For clarity, I shall italicize "antecedent" and its plural:

"**determinism** … the doctrine that whatever is or happens is determined by *antecedent* causes." — *The New Century Dictionary*, 1959.

"**determinism** … the theory that all occurrences in nature are determined by *antecedent* causes…." — *Webster's Third New International Dictionary*, 1969.

"**determinism** … a doctrine that acts of the will, occurrences in nature, or social or psychological phenomena are determined by *antecedent* causes." — *Webster's New Collegiate Dictionary*, 1976.

"**determinism** … The philosophical doctrine that every event, act, and decision is the inevitable consequence of *antecedents*…." — *The American Heritage Dictionary*, 1981.

"**determinism** … doctrine that all human actions and historical events are determined by *antecedent* causes and conditions…." — *Collier's Dictionary*, 1986.

"**determinism** … 1. the doctrine that human actions are the necessary results of *antecedent* causes. 2. the doctrine that all events are determined by *antecedent* causes...." — *The World Book Dictionary*, 1990.

Keeping these definitions in mind, reread Whitman's declaration (italics mine):

> ... no result exists now without being from its long *antecedent* result, and that from its *antecedent*, and so backward without the farthest mentionable spot coming a bit nearer the beginning than any other spot.

This is determinism. The quoted definitions make that clear.

One who is aware of the determinist significance of "antecedents" will understand Whitman's poem "With Antecedents." (Discussion of the poem follows Note 49, Chapter V.) Whitman's determinism rings out in the lines,

> I assert that all past days were what they must have been...
> And that to-day is what it must be...

Compare: "Yet I see why all the ists and isms and haters and dogmatists exist — can see why they must exist." Echo: "must"/ "must ... must." Whitman's consciousness of the *inevitability* of all events and all things and all persons pervades *Leaves of Grass*. He believed, as any true determinist believes, that all that happens is all that *can* happen.

For one who reads *Leaves of Grass* with an understanding of determinism and with an awareness that Whitman made conscious use of it in writing his poems, many passages will be raised from a seeming trash heap of jumbled imagery to the level of true poetic art. Whitman has been criticized for his endless lists, his "catalogues." We shall see that they are simply reflections of his determinism.

I want to interject here that most people, including surely most of Whitman's would-be interpreters, feel that determinism rules out free will. Parts of this book will be devoted to resolving this conflict. Chapter II will do so by explaining determinism. Chapter III will be given entirely to the solution of the difficulty of coming to terms with determinism. The last few pages of Chapter V will show that Whitman's support of freedom was compatible with determinism.

The mere mention of determinism would be enough to set the average Whitmanite on the defensive. Nine out of ten Whitman critics, if they heard the word determinism, would latch the doors on their disbelief. But critics are fascinated by paradoxes, and perhaps a few of them, one or two, will be able to appreciate the idea that there is a gigantic, central paradox in the thought of Walt Whitman. Determinism will appear to be the antithesis of what is usually thought of as Whitman's chief message and most cherished belief. He is hailed as the poet of freedom. How contradictory to assign to him the philosophy of determinism! How could one possibly conceive that Whitman would not have rejected this terrible doctrine altogether?

Four critics, to their credit, have come close to setting out in the right direction.

Gay Wilson Allen has been stumbling over the signposts for years. In 1946 in his *Walt Whitman Handbook* he used the phrase "pantheistic determinism" in elucidating some lines by Whitman on "prudence."[24] In 1955, discussing "prudence" in his biography of Whitman, he changed the phrasing to "a kind of moralistic determinism" and varied it with "a kind of mystic determinism."[25] In the same work, discussing Whitman's "To Think of Time," he again found determinism handy as a term of explication: "This cosmic process might be called 'spiritual determinism': 'The threads that were spun are gathered ... the weft crosses the warp.... The pattern is systematic.'"[26] Allen has several times come close to finding the path to the great revelation. In fact he even followed the path once for a little while without knowing it. How close he was in his theory of a "long journey motif" in Whitman! With a slight but revealing change in terminology, the "long journey" becomes the idea of the causal successions of determinism (see Ch. V). But apparently Allen never thought of applying determinism as a general concept for understanding Whitman.

David Daiches recognized Whitman's determinism, but not, regrettably, as determinism. He called it "a sort of cosmic dance":

> Whitman's view of the relationship between the individual, society and the cosmos led him occasionally to see the whole of life as a sort of cosmic dance, in which everyone and everything moves according to its own laws and both fulfills its own destiny and plays its proper part in the general movement. This is an old notion among poets and philosophers, going back to Plotinus and beyond.

Having illustrated with quotations from Plotinus and from Sir John Davies (from whom he appears to have got the "dance" idea), Daiches makes his point by quoting Whitman:

> Embracing man, embracing all, proceed the three hundred and sixty-five resistlessly round the sun;
> Embracing all, soothing, supporting, follow close three hundred and sixty-five offsets of the first, sure and necessary as they.

From these lines from "A Song of the Rolling Earth," he says, "we get a similar picture of the dance of the days and the years and the hours, the stately procession of time in the universe, with its relation to human fate."[27]

How close Daiches *was* to the hidden determinism of *Leaves of Grass*! In the prose quotation above, he exhibits a precise, an ingenious, understanding of the Hegelian import of Whitman's message.

V. K. Chari, failing, like Daiches, to see Whitman's determinism as determinism, perceived it, like Daiches, only in its Hegelian matrix. Chari sensed in *Leaves of Grass* Whitman's immersion in "a vast spiritual continuum": "While merging in the life and motion of the world, the self is also aware of itself as a unique and separate identity, … 'watching and wondering' at the pageantry of life ('Song of Myself,' section 4)."[28]

For an understanding of Whitman's Hegelianism see Ch. IV, Sec. 7, and Ch. V.

Floyd Stovall seems to have been acquainted with Hegel before announcing, in a note to "With Antecedents": "Whitman's philosophy had a place for necessity as well as for freedom." The remainder of the note is devoted to what seems to be a desperate attempt to absolve Whitman of his determinism by explaining its compatibility with freedom: "Necessity is the will of the Absolute. But the Absolute is that which is self-determined, which submits to no law except the law of self. Hence the Absolute is free, for that which is self-determined is free. The individual soul is also self-determined and so identical with the Absolute. The true will of the individual, that is, the rational will, since it is self-determined, is identical with the will of the Absolute, or necessity, and therefore free."[29] I realize now that in earlier drafts I was too severe in stressing the shortcomings of this faltering venture into philosophy. Still, I cannot resist pointing out that if the "individual soul is … self-determined," why need it be identical with the will of the Absolute to be free? If it is self-determined, it is free independently of the Absolute. The whole argument sounds like misconstrued Hegelianism. I know from personal acquaintance with Stovall that he was reluctant to have Whitman called a determinist. This reluctance was due to the fact that he looked upon determinism, as certainly most people, even most well-educated and intelligent people like himself, persist in doing, as something very bad. If he had been less prejudicial, he might well have come to see the overpowering pervasiveness of determinism in his beloved *Leaves of Grass*. I really do not see how he can have believed his own assertion of the compatibility of determinism and freedom and have remained so adamantly opposed (as it seemed to me he definitely was) to the determinist philosophy. But he is at least to be credited for sensing that determinism was somehow involved in the one poem "With Antecedents" even though, alas, he failed to realize that determinism is actually the open sesame to Whitman.

Certainly, as Stovall tried to explain, determinism does not annihilate free will. No one who understands determinism, or who has devoted even for a little while his serious attention to the traditional arguments for and against it, will be so naïve as to conclude that since Whitman so wholeheartedly defended freedom he was logically barred from a belief in determinism. But it is astonishing how nearly totally ignorant of this philosophy are the educated minds of our day. This ignorance, paradoxically, coexists with a growing willingness to treat social ills such as poverty and crime in a determinist context. But as a personal philosophy determinism is brushed aside even with no effort to study it and understand it. It is dismissed as a "terrible" philosophy which "makes man a slave" to "iron law" and relieves him of his moral duty, degrading him to the class of mere animals or indeed lower, to the status of rocks and algae. (Most determinists would not altogether disagree with this harsh analysis. We shall see that Whitman suggested there may be little difference between men and trees [Ch. VI].) Philosophers have written excellent books and excellent parts of books explaining away the horrors; but determinism remains, even in the minds of most well-educated persons, in disrepute.

> It is not only true that most people entirely misunderstand Freedom, but I sometimes think I have not yet met one person who rightly understands it.

With these words Whitman began his little-noticed paragraph headed "FREE-DOM" (see Ch. V). Whitman knew that he was writing poems for readers who would not understand the determinism which underlay those poems. Long ago, he had read his beloved Frances Wright's assessment of determinism as "the most simple and evident of moral truths, and the most darkened, tortured, and belabored by moral teachers" (Ch. IV). He would have agreed with that assessment. It is an indication of his good judgment that he chose to hide his determinism, to refer to it in his poems only indirectly.

Whitman was by no means the only determinist who was reluctant to reveal his belief in determinism. Witness:

Benjamin Franklin, statesman, printer, and, yes, a determinist, ran off a hundred copies of his *Dissertation on Liberty and Necessity*. He gave a few to friends and then, deciding that further dissemination would be unwise, "burnt the rest except one copy." Only four copies are known to have survived, possibly including the one Franklin kept.[30]

Mark Twain agonized over the decision to publish his deterministic treatise *What Is Man?* His wife refused to read it and forbade him to publish it. In 1883 he presented an early version of it before Hartford's Monday Evening Club. "There was not a man there," said Twain, "who did not scoff at it, jeer it, revile it, and call it a lie, a thousand times a lie!"[31] (Whitman: "You shall be treated to the ironical smiles and mockings of those who remain behind you."[32]) In 1906, two years after his wife's death, Mark Twain published *What Is Man?*, anonymously, in an edition of 250 copies, for private distribution.

Thomas Hobbes "humbly beseeched" that his letter discussing determinism be kept in strictest confidence. The letter was later published, without

Hobbes's consent, as a treatise "Of Liberty and Necessity."[33] Leibniz expressed privately the determinist view that "the individual notion of each person involves once for all everything that will happen to him." His friend Arnauld was taken aback at this statement and expressed his horror of it. Leibniz "carefully refrained"[34] from making his opinion public: "I should not like to have it get abroad. For not even the most accurate remarks are understood by everyone."[35] Spinoza never published his *Short Treatise* but circulated it among friends. At the end of the manuscript, he wrote: "…I would beg of you most earnestly to be very careful about communication of these things to others."[36] His determinism led him into beliefs that were heretical. His fellow Jews, endangered by public opinion, excommunicated him. His life was in danger. Stuart Hampshire explains: "…a philosopher must expect to meet bitter sentimental resistance from those whose desires and fears, loves and hates, are tied to the primitive superstitions which represent persons as free and uncaused causes."[37]

Abraham Lincoln. Whitman admired him more than he did any other person. Did he know Lincoln was a determinist? I suspect so but have no evidence that it is so. In 1846 Lincoln was fighting for a seat in the U. S. Congress. He was attacked because of his religious opinions and prepared a handbill defending his views. He did admit that he had been "inclined to believe" in "the Doctrine of Necessity" and had defended the argument "(with one, two or three, but never publicly)." The handbill was published on August 15, 1846, in the *Illinois Gazette*, Lacon, Illinois. Was this his only public reference to his determinist philosophy? It *was* his philosophy, never abandoned, as was attested by William Herndon, his law partner for more than twenty years, in letters reporting their "private conversations." These letters can be found in the book *The Hidden Lincoln*. Note, please, the word "Hidden." For excerpts, and for references for this account, see, below, Ch. IV, Sec. 2.

I think it is clear that any determinist might be reticent about his philosophy. Some of the reasons will be evident later. But there is one very interesting reason Whitman kept his philosophy secret: the simple but astonishing fact is that Epictetus told him to! Whitman wrote in his Common-place Book, and later selected as a sample for inclusion in *Specimen Days*, the following:

> Preach not to others what they should eat, but eat as becomes you and be silent. — Epictetus.[38]

This quotation is taken, in paraphrase, from a section of the *Enchiridion* in which Epictetus advises:

> Never call yourself a philosopher, nor talk a great deal among the unlearned about theorems, but act conformably to them. Thus, at an entertainment, do not talk how persons ought to eat, but eat as you ought. For remember that in this manner Socrates also universally avoided all ostenta-

tion. And when persons came to him and desired to be recommended by him to philosophers, he took and recommended them, so well did he bear being overlooked. So that if ever any talk should happen among the unlearned concerning philosophic theorems, be you, for the most part, silent. For there is a great danger in immediately throwing out what you have not digested. And, if any one tells you that you know nothing, and you are not nettled at it, then you may be sure that you have begun your business. For sheep do not throw up the grass to show the shepherds how much they have eaten; but, inwardly digesting their food, they outwardly produce wool and milk. Thus, therefore, do you likewise not show theorems to the unlearned, but the actions produced by them after they have been digested.[39]

The *Enchiridion*, or handbook, consists of short pieces which convey in miniature the message of the *Discourses*. We shall see in Chapter IV that Whitman read Epictetus at an early age (at sixteen, according to his own recollection) and was profoundly impressed by this Stoic philosopher. "It was like being born again," Whitman reminisced to Traubel.[40] We may suspect that Whitman found the eighth chapter of Book IV of the *Discourses* particularly interesting, for this is the chapter on which the section just quoted from the *Enchiridion* is based. There we find: "…Euphrates was in the right to say, 'I long endeavoured to conceal my embracing the philosophic life, and it was of use to me. For, in the first place, I knew that what I did right I did it not for spectators, but for myself. I had a composed look and walk, all for God and myself.'"[41] Now we begin to see what Whitman's quotation may have meant to him — "Preach not to others what they should eat, but eat as becomes you and be silent." Those who know Whitman well can easily imagine that he himself had, like Euphrates, "a composed look and walk, all for God and myself." Inspiration for Whitman's title "Song of Myself" may have come from this very statement in the *Discourses* of Epictetus. In "Song of Myself" we find other echoes of the Epictetus passages:

> I carry the plenum of proof and everything else in my face,
> With the hush of my lips I wholly confound the skeptic.[42]

It is perhaps not by coincidence that we find in this same chapter of the *Discourses*, a page or two further on, a possible source for Whitman's "root" metaphor:

> First study to conceal what you are; philosophise a little while by yourself. Fruit is produced thus. The seed must be buried in the ground, lie hid there some time, and grow up by degrees, that it may come to perfection. But, if it produces the ear before the stalk hath its proper joints, it is imperfect, and of the garden of Adonis. Now, you are a poor plant of this kind. You have blossomed too soon, the winter will kill you. See what country-

men say about seeds of any sort, when the warm weather comes too early. They are in great anxiety, for fear the seeds should shoot out too luxuriantly; and then, one frost taking them, shows how prejudicial their forwardness was. Beware you too, man. You have shot out luxuriantly, you have sprung forth towards a trifling fame, before the proper season. You seem to be somebody, as a fool among fools. You will be taken by the frost; or rather, you are already frozen downwards, at the root; you still blossom indeed a little at the top, and therefore you think you are still alive and flourishing. Let us, at least, ripen naturally. Why do you lay us open? Why do you force us? We cannot yet bear the air. Suffer the root to grow; then the first, then the second, then the third joint of the stalk to spring from it: and thus nature will force out the fruit, whether I will or not.[43]

In an early manuscript version of Section 41 of "Song of Myself" Whitman wrote:

> Doctrine gets empty consent or mocking politeness,
> It wriggles through mankind, it is never loved or believed,
> The throat is not safe that speaks it aloud.
> I will take a sprig of parsley and a budding rose and go through the whole earth.
> You shall see I will not find one heretic against them.[44]

More than thirty years later he wrote: "I seek less to state or display any theme or thought, and more to bring you, reader, into the atmosphere of the theme or thought — there to pursue your own flight."[45]

Whitman prided himself on his "caution." His phrenological "chart of bumps" showed "Cautiousness" to be large.[46] In a copy of the *Enchiridion* given him by his friend Rolleston in 1881 he wrote: "Be bold — Be bold — Be bold — be not too bold."[47] In 1860 he had published a poem, or rather a collection of fragments, called "Debris." The first two fragments were as follows:

> He is wisest who has the most caution,
> He only wins who goes far enough.
>
> Any thing is as good as established, when that is established that will produce it and continue it.[48]

Did Whitman resolve from the outset to follow the advice of Epictetus about the concealment of one's philosophy? Epictetus had warned him, "Suffer the root to grow."[49] Whitman admitted that he had "felt willing to keep the roots ... underground, out of sight," to "let the book work its way" and "If it grew [echo: "grow"/ "grew"], in verdure and flowerage, so much the better...."[50] The root-growth-fruit symbolism employed by Epictetus gives us a good clue to the mysterious origin of Whitman's unusual title *Leaves of Grass*!

Whitman will show the leaves that spring from the roots, the concealed philosophy. The design on the cover of the 1855 edition displayed not only leaves but an abundance of roots as well. "Each letter in the title looked like a small growing thing, sending its roots into the ground."[51]

In a note Whitman reminded himself, "do not argue at all or compose proofs to demonstrate things. State nothing which it will not do to state as apparent to all eyes."[52] The following lines are obviously a symbolic restatement of those two sentences:

> I will take an egg out of the robin's nest in the orchard,
> I will take a branch of gooseberries from the old bush in the garden, and
> go preach to the world;
> You shall see I will not meet a single heretic or scorner,
> You shall see how I stump clergymen, and confound them,
> You shall see me showing a scarlet tomato and a white pebble from the
> beach.[53]

The egg, the gooseberries, the tomato symbolize the fruits of the philosophy. The white pebble may also be a fruit, a fruit of the earth's geology.

We can take Whitman's root-fruit symbolism to mean that he had resolved that, as Epictetus had advised, he would "not show theorems to the unlearned, but the actions produced by" those theorems or fundamental principles. It will be enough, perhaps he said to himself, if I am able to put into the book the character, the man himself, the man *produced* by the philosophy. One of Whitman's notes reads: "Convey what I want to convey by models or illustrations of the *results* I demand. Convey these by *characters*, selections of *incidents* and *behaviour*[.] This *indirect mode* of *attack* is better than all direct modes of attack[.] The spirit of the above should pervade all my poems."[54] Why need I embarrass myself (perhaps Whitman said) by attempting to explain a philosophy which I know will be only rarely accepted, which only a few will understand? "If you have an earnest desire of attaining philosophy," Epictetus advised, "prepare yourself from the very first to be laughed at, to be sneered by the multitude."[55] If you travel with me, Whitman warns, "You shall be treated to the ironical smiles and mockings of those who remain behind you."[56] (A significant echo here of the line already quoted, "Doctrine gets empty consent or mocking politeness."[57] Notice: "mockings"/ "mocking.")

Remembering Whitman's fondness for Epictetus, we may better understand such passages as the following:

> Speech is the twin of my vision, it is unequal to measure itself,
> It provokes me forever, it says sarcastically,
> *Walt you contain enough, why don't you let it out then?*
> Come now I will not be tantalized, you conceive too much of articulation,

Do you not know O speech how the buds beneath you are folded?
Waiting in gloom, protected by frost,
The dirt receding before my prophetical screams,
I underlying causes to balance them at last,
My knowledge my live parts, it keeping tally with the meaning of all
things,
Happiness, (which whoever hears me let him or her set out in search of
this day.)

My final merit I refuse you, I refuse putting from me what I really am,
Encompass worlds, but never try to encompass me,
I crowd your sleekest and best by simply looking toward you.

Writing and talk do not prove me,
I carry the plenum of proof and every thing else in my face,
With the hush of my lips I wholly confound the skeptic.[58]

We may interpret the symbolism of these lines in this way: The "buds beneath" represent the concealed philosophy. Speech is inadequate to communicate this philosophy. The phrase "protected by frost" is an echo of Epictetus' "one frost taking them," and also of his "the winter will kill you."[59] In another poem Whitman speaks of "Perennial roots, tall leaves," and he promises, "O the winter shall not freeze you delicate leaves...."[60] The line "The dirt receding before my prophetical screams," makes sense only with reference to the symbolism employed by Epictetus, who, it will be recalled, compares the philosopher and his philosophy to the plant which springs from a seed "buried in the ground" to "grow up by degrees." Compare the line in the 1860 version of Whitman's "Roots and Leaves Themselves Alone": "They have come slowly up out of the earth and me, and are to come slowly up out of you."[61] Echo: Epictetus, "up by degrees" /Whitman, "slowly up." "My knowledge my live parts," continues the figure, in the passage quoted above. In that passage "speech" says to Whitman, "Walt you contain enough, why don't you let it out then?" Whitman refuses, answering, "...you conceive too much of articulation./ Do you not know O speech how the buds beneath you are folded?" Whitman will follow the advice of Epictetus and be "for the most part, silent." ("I and mine do not convince by arguments, similes, rhymes,/ We convince by our presence.")[62] "With the hush of my lips ["silent," per Epictetus' advice!] I wholly confound the skeptic." The underlying philosophy must remain concealed. Articulation is inadequate because of the way "the buds beneath ... are folded."

Whitman defends his reticence in "A Song of the Rolling Earth," Sec. 3, declaring:

I swear I see what is better than to tell the best,
It is always to leave the best untold.

But even if he tried, his efforts would be fruitless:

> When I undertake to tell the best I find I cannot,
> My tongue is ineffectual on its pivots....

Edward Carpenter, with deep understanding of Whitman, wrote:

> Whitman refused to address himself to the Brain alone. He saw that with
> regard to the highest truths it is useless to try to seize or impart them that
> way. They must be *felt* as well as thought. To try to *think* them alone, as
> one would prove a syllogism, is a kind of blasphemy. And to create the feel-
> ing, the direct awareness and consciousness of the highest facts, one must
> proceed in another way; one must use the method of indirection....[63]

Whitman understood that there was no way for him to give a poetic definition
of his philosophy. "The best poetic utterance, after all," he wrote, "can merely
hint, or remind, often very indirectly [*sic*], or at distant removes. Aught of
real perfection, or the solution of any deep problem, or any completed statement of the moral, the true, the beautiful, eludes the greatest, deftest poet —
flies away like an always uncaught bird."[64] Poetry can give expression to ideas
which it cannot, remaining poetry, explain. The poet could attempt to explain
his ideas in statements external to the poems, but he would not dare do so.
Whitman underlined the following words in an 1849 (pre–*Leaves of Grass*)
review of Tennyson's *The Princess*, edition of 1848:

> A poet, by becoming openly didactic, would deprive his work of that
> essential quality of suggestiveness by which activity on the part of the reader
> is absolutely demanded....[65]

Another passage, double-bracketed by Whitman on a clipping from an 1851
(pre–*Leaves of Grass*) article, rules out internal poetic explanation:

> The purposes of art are simple, and not speculative; its materials derive
> from nature and tradition, and not from excogitation and analysis....[66]

Ultimately, Whitman's poetry is to be judged by the criterion laid down by
Wellek and Warren:

> Poetry is not substitute-philosophy; it has its own justification and aim.
> Poetry of ideas is like other poetry, not to be judged by the value of the
> material but by its degree of integration and artistic integrity.[67]

To translate: The genius of Walt Whitman lies not in his conveying a philosophy as such to the reader, but in his weaving that philosophy unobtru-
sively into his poems.

But beyond these technical poetic considerations are certain practical reasons that Whitman would have had for suppressing his determinism.

He intended his book not for the learned man but for the average man.

And he knew that there was no way to explain to the average man or woman the intricacies of the philosophic "problem" of freedom.

> To the degraded or undevelopt — and even to too many others — the thought of freedom is a thought of escaping from law — which, of course, is impossible.[68]

These are Whitman's own words! He knew as well as did Schopenhauer that "every uncultured man, following his feeling, ardently defends complete freedom in particular actions."[69] "I have frequently considered," says Hume, "what could possibly be the reason why all mankind, though they have ever, without hesitation, acknowledged the doctrine of necessity in their whole practice and reasoning, have yet discovered such a reluctance to acknowledge it in words, and have rather shown a propensity, in all ages, to profess the contrary opinion."[70] When they are shown the consequences of the doctrine, says Priestley, "they are staggered, and withhold their assent."[71] Harvey Fergusson, writing more recently, says of "the common man": "...I have been naïve enough to try to present him with the idea of determinism, and to him it is inconceivable, as an idea."[72]

Anticipating the prejudice and misunderstanding which would be thrown up against a recognizable determinism, Whitman was constrained by good judgment to offer his readers only the fruits of his philosophy, not the philosophy itself. He knew that his book was to be radical: "I could clearly see that such an enterprise would meet with little favor — at all events at first — that it would be hooted at (as it was) and perhaps hooted down."[73] He dared not include a determinist philosophy explicitly stated.

He told Edward Carpenter, "I think there are truths which it is necessary to envelop or wrap up."

> I charge you forever reject those who would expound me, for I cannot expound myself,
> I charge that there be no theory or school founded out of me,
> I charge you to leave all free, as I have left all free.[74]

Whitman speaks here of his determinism! The last word, "free," means free in the naïve, non-philosophical sense. The message conveyed by Whitman in these lines is that he was wary of leading others into his belief. On different levels, or in various ways, one who accepts the steps leading to a full understanding of determinism faces dangers which in their psychological effect can be profound, even tragic. On a lower level one may accept the negative side of determinism and fail to go beyond that negative concept. This danger was pointed to by C. J. Herrick, a determinist who had mastered the struggle:

> If now one should become convinced that his former belief in freedom is not well founded, that for instance the mystical freedom that he supposed

he possessed is fictitious, then he may decide that there is no such thing as freedom, and thereafter his conduct may be radically different from what it was before. Self–culture, personal and social ideals have lost their controlling power as determining motives of conduct. But the more elementary instincts of self-preservation and selfish gratification persist, released from the inhibitions of higher control. The personality deteriorates.[75]

Whitman cautions:

> The way is suspicious, the result uncertain, perhaps destructive,
> You would have to give up all else, I alone would expect to be your sole and exclusive standard,
> Your novitiate would even then be long and exhausting,
> The whole past theory of your life and all conformity to the lives around you would have to be abandon'd,
> Therefore release me now before troubling yourself any further....
>
> . . . .
>
> But these leaves conning you con at peril,
> For these leaves and me you will not understand,
>
> . . . .
>
> For it is not for what I have put into it that I have written this book,
> Nor is it by reading it you will acquire it,
> Nor do those know me best who admire me and vauntingly praise me,
> Nor will the candidates for my love (unless at most a very few) prove victorious,
> Nor will my poems do good only, they will do just as much evil, perhaps more,
> For all is useless without that which you may guess at many times and not hit, that which I hinted at;
> Therefore release me and depart on your way.[76]

These lines contain an allusion to one of the most forceful arguments against urging the philosophy of determinism upon others. "Your novitiate," says Whitman, if you *should* accept "would even then be long and exhausting." "The conditions," he wrote in a preparatory note, "are long and arduous and require faith, they exist altogether with the taught and not with the teaching or teacher."[77] Whitman's choice of "novitiate" to describe the painful process will later be shown to be appropriate (Ch. III). The conversion to determinism almost inevitably involves mental suffering. The "whole past theory of your life," to use Whitman's phrasing, "would have to be abandon'd." Nietzsche says of he new determinist: "All his valuations, distinctions, disinclinations, are thereby deprived of value and become false."[78] Charles Bray, who had experienced the conversion, says that "every system built upon an opposite principle, by whatever authority supported, cannot be true."[79] After that realization, says Bray, what usually follows is "the most uncomfortable of all states — a state of doubt and unbelief."[80] Compare Whitman's "doubt, despair and unbelief" ("Song of Myself," Sec. 43). Bray, during his inquiry into the problem of religion, was lent by one of his friends Jonathan Edwards' *Freedom of the Will.* "Here," says Bray in his autobiography, "I found Philosophical Necessity clearly and logically proved ... but what was I to do with it? It was fundamentally opposed to all my previously recognized principles of ethics. And here I must pause. The next year was certainly the most miserable year of my life.... I had to begin to build my life over again; my mind was in a complete anarchy, or in a state of blank despair."[81] Compare, again, Whitman's "doubt, despair and unbelief" ("Song of Myself," Sec. 43).

> The whole past theory of your life and all conformity to the lives around you would have to be abandon'd,
> Therefore release me now before troubling yourself any further ....

No twisting of Whitman's words is necessary to equate their meaning with those of Nietzsche and Bray. For Whitman's possible debt to Bray see Ch. IV.

Most readers will be puzzled by the line, "Nor do those know me best who admire me and vauntingly praise me." Obversely, Whitman is saying here that those who know him best would not praise him. This very limited group, you see, are those who are determinists. For clarification, read William James: "If our acts were predetermined, if we merely transmitted the push of the whole past, the free-willists say, how could we be praised or blamed for anything?"[82] Whitman pleads:

> (O admirers, praise not me — compliment not me — you make me wince, I see what you do not — I know what you do not.)[83]

How many, or what, precautionary considerations Whitman may have had in mind when he inserted certain veiled (and some not so veiled) references to determinism into his poems is a question that cannot really be decided. That he did not deny inserting such references is evidenced by his comment on a letter written to him by his friend Ernest Rhys. Traubel read the letter aloud to Whitman. (The bracketed comments are Whitman's.)

> This evening Herbert Gilchrist is coming down here to look through Kennedy's book, and something may suggest itself to us. We are going on afterwards to Costelloe's, as H. G. is anxious to know Mrs. C., who has been away in Surrey over Easter with her husband. I look forward with delight to seeing her again. She is truly a most noble and delightful nature. ["That — and more than that, too!"] She is a little afraid perhaps of your deterministic theories (further elaborated by Doctor Bucke) and non-moral apotheosis of evil; but that is natural enough. ["I shouldn't wonder: yes, it's

natural enough: few can stomach me whole: I don't blame them!"] I, too, often doubt any absolute empire, even the most cosmic, over the human will: that is my feeling only, for I don't pretend to any philosophical complete creed.[84]

I must stress that I have made no mistake in transcribing this passage. The last sentence is *not* a remark by *Whitman*. It was written by Rhys as a modest protest against what he considered to be Whitman's opinion. The bracketed remarks, which *are* Whitman's, are, in view of all that has been set forth in this chapter, illuminating and confirmatory. Whitman agrees that to be "a little afraid" of his "deterministic theories" is "natural enough"—and he adds, "few can stomach me whole." Whitman's "few" here is an echo of "very few" in a line quoted above:

> Nor will the candidates for my love (unless at most a very few) prove victorious....

And there is a "very few" in the teasing quotation near the beginning of this chapter:

> What lies behind "Leaves of Grass" is something that few, very few, only one here and there, perhaps oftenest women, are at all in a position to seize.

But take note of Whitman's curious phrase "perhaps oftenest women." It may be significant that in the letter from Rhys it is a *woman* who was aware of Whitman's "deterministic theories." Can it be that Mrs. Costelloe was one of the "women" who were "perhaps oftenest ... in a position to seize" what "lies behind 'Leaves of Grass'"?

◆ ◆ ◆

Little wonder that the critics have overlooked or ignored the full relationship of determinism to Whitman's thought. Most of them simply have no grasp of what determinism is. Gay Wilson Allen demonstrates this lack of understanding when he writes: "Yet Emerson is not a Determinist."[85] How can Allen have read, as surely he must have, Emerson's essay "Fate" without discovering that Emerson was a full-fledged determinist?! Allen, a victim of his own ignorance, was unable to realize the usefulness of determinism in unveiling Whitman's meanings. And he is typical of Whitman's would-be interpreters, few of whom have even mentioned determinism.

One who has, is Norman Foerster. He saw that Whitman "experienced at times the deterministic feeling that 'The whole matter has gone on, and exists today, probably as it should have been, and should be.'" But Foerster did not *understand* determinism and indeed hated it, as is evident later when he complains that "Determinism has robbed life of purpose and even of adventure." It is clear, he says, that "the exalted expectations that gave such power to Whitman's prophetic criticism seem far less plausible than they were in the romantic epoch before the Civil War. We are not living in a time, and cannot foresee a time, characterized at once by an ardent belief in democracy, a high satisfaction with science, and an all-suffusing religious spirit. Since the late war, disillusionment, skepticism, and cynicism have crowded upon us. Determinism [*sic*] has robbed life of purpose and even of adventure."[86]

Joseph Beaver, in his book on Whitman and science, misinterprets the consolatory determinism of "As I Ebb'd with the Ocean of Life" as "a dull, fatalistic brooding over the meaninglessness of the universe."[87] If Beaver had not confused determinism with fatalism, he might have rescued himself from the swampy inexactitude with which he, following others, classes these lines as "pessimism, futility, meaninglessness at its most intense."[88] But it is obvious that Beaver mistakenly thinks of the two terms determinism and fatalism as synonyms, for a few pages further on he states that "Whitman occasionally gives voice to a kind of fatalism" and after instancing a few lines from "To Think of Time" goes on to say, "The same scientific determinism is present in parts of 'Song of Prudence.'"[89] We shall see in Chapter II that is a mistake to call determinism fatalism. Most people, including most Whitman scholars, do not understand this.

One might expect Whitman critics, most of whom surely share the anti-determinist bias, to emphasize that Whitman *could not have been* a determinist. Few have.

One who has, is, surprisingly, himself a determinist. Newton Arvin, after many pages of good analysis, concludes that Whitman "could not bring himself ... to face the full rigor of the truth that events follow one another in a necessary sequence of causes and effects. Still less could Whitman tolerate the assumption ... that the real freedom of the human will lies not in defiance of physical causation but in a clearer knowledge of it."[90] Arvin understands determinism well enough, and he understands a great deal about Whitman, but he is mistaken if he believes that Whitman's concept of freedom was not fully as philosophically sophisticated as his own.

Arthur E. Briggs, who shows little understanding of Whitman and even less of determinism, has also emphasized, mistakenly, that Whitman was not a determinist. "Against naturalistic determinism with its enslavement of the human spirit," says Briggs, "he asserted man's creative freedom. His humanism projected the self of man into the external world to make it subject to man's will."[91] Again, Briggs exclaims, "How different Whitman's conception than that of a deterministic materialistic scientificism!... Whitman could not believe that science shuts off experiment or freedom of will. That was the very essence of his faith in freedom."[92] Briggs is confused, but there is no need to refute his conclusions here. The bias which he exhibits is precisely the reason this book had to be written.

Henry Seidel Canby confirms Whitman's allegiance to science but finds in him a refusal to accept the logical consequences (as conceived by Canby) of the determinism which science mistakenly (as Canby sees it) supported. By a sort of transference, Canby assigns to Whitman something of his own prejudice against determinism. Whitman, he says:

> did not rebel against the science which made that century famous. He rebelled against the gross and premature materialism which resulted from the supposed discovery that man and nature were both superior mechanisms, subject like dead matter to measurement and complete explanation by physical and chemical laws. We are aware now that this is not true, even of inert matter, but we are still in the downward swing away from religion and faith which has been responsible for so much in the cynical present. Whitman, never a dogmatist, was in rebellion against all this. Science, for him, was the great hope of the future, but it was ultimately a mysticism, as it is to most of the physicists today.[93]

If Whitman rebelled against the belief that man is "subject like dead matter to measurement and compete explanation by physical and chemical laws," why did he write the following line?

(I reckon I behave no prouder than the level I plant my house by, after all.)[94] Without actually using the word, Canby alludes to determinism but dismisses it as the "supposed" discovery of earlier science. In fact, he dismisses it altogether: "We are aware now that this [determinism] is not true, even of inert matter." Looking past the clever phrasing, we discern that he has joined the ranks of the vast crowd of modern indeterminists, those who fervently propagate the belief that the "new" science, with its "principle of indeterminacy," has declared determinism null and void. Not so, not so! as will be seen in my Chapter II. Read, in that chapter, about the "supposed" modern indeterminism which Canby cherishes, and then come back and make an assessment of Canby's joyous disavowal of Whitman's determinism.

Daniel G. Hoffman compares the worlds of Stephen Crane and Walt Whitman: "...while Crane interprets life almost solely in terms of necessity, one is tempted to call Whitman the poet of the absolutely free will." He says, further, Crane's "deterministic world" contrasts with Whitman's "world where necessity is abstract and the will is free."[95] Hoffman can be credited with a certain amount of perspicacity. But when one has grasped the nuances, one will see that though the philosophic tenors of Crane and Whitman *seem* to conflict, Whitman was no less a determinist than Crane.

In 1999, after reading David S. Reynolds's commendable, thorough, and in many instances perceptive *Walt Whitman's America*,[96] I felt that here was a Whitman scholar who might agree with me. Accordingly, I wrote him, with the thought that he could give my book status by writing a Foreword for it.

Alas, he did not consent to this and showed no interest in reading my manuscript. But an important outcome was the revelation, in his reply, that here was one more Whitman critic that I could add to my small anthology of deniers. "I just can't buy," he said, "the argument that Whitman 'studiedly concealed' his determinism." And he continued: "Nor do I see him as strictly a determinist. There are elements of determinist philosophy in him. But also there's a good amount of what I see as very different from determinism: an assertion of free will, total independence, self-reliance."[97]

◆ ◆ ◆

I should be glad if it were possible for me to avoid the task of clarifying determinism. If I am to show what determinism meant to Whitman, I shall have to erase the false image of it which men like Canby and Reynolds, men of scholarly accomplishment, intelligence, and good intentions, have drawn. It would please me if such a procedure could be avoided, for it will appear that I am unforgivably relentless in my search for truth. But I see that I must weed some intellectual gardens, even at the risk of trampling on the flowers.

II

Determinism

Some people will never learn any thing because
they understand every thing too soon.
— Alexander Pope[1]

Long and persistent study of the free will problem has led me to the conviction that determinism, even as a mere hypothesis, has been misunderstood by practically every one of those who have sought to discredit or condemn it. It is true that at first sight determinism is erroneously equated with the notorious (and fallacious) doctrine of (superstitious) fatalism. In this view, determinism is likely to appear to be a very dark philosophy indeed. It is understandable that people who are dedicated to morality and to the support of freedom are quick, too quick, to condemn it.

Determinism is maligned and spit upon and called a great insult to the dignity of man. Benjamin Franklin (some may be surprised to learn that he was a determinist) says in his essay on determinism (known as necessity in Franklin's day): "I am sensible that the Doctrine here advanc'd, if it were to be publish'd, would meet with but an indifferent Reception. Mankind naturally and generally love to be flatter'd: Whatever sooths our Pride, and tends to exalt our Species above the rest of Creation, we are pleas'd with and easily believe, when ungrateful Truths shall be with the utmost Indignation rejected.... But, (to use a Piece of *common* Sense) our *Geese* are but *Geese* tho' we may think 'em *Swans*; and Truth will be Truth tho' it sometimes prove mortifying and distasteful."[2]

I would not, frankly, expect more than a few, after reading what I have written, to be convinced that determinism is true. I am sure my enthusiasm for the doctrine will show through, but it is not my intention to convert others to my (and Whitman's) beliefs. You will not be able to understand Whitman if you do not understand his determinism.

28

So, without proselytizing, I want to provide that understanding — to show that determinism is something less than a bugaboo.

What is it, then, this philosophy which has been called "the nineteenth century nightmare"?[3] Definitions were given in Chapter I from six dictionaries. A seventh, *The American College Encyclopedic Dictionary* (1959), gives a definition which is my favorite:

> **determinism**, n. the doctrine that neither outer events nor human choices are uncaused, but are the results of antecedent conditions, physical or psychological.

"Nothing happens without a cause." Simply, that is what determinism says. Most people readily agree with this statement — and most would be horrified by its philosophic extenuations: Everything is predetermined. All that happens is all that can happen.

Quite bluntly, Albert Einstein (*the* Albert Einstein) stated his philosophy, determinism, as follows:

> Everything is determined, the beginning as well as the end, by forces over which we have no control. It is determined for the insect as well as for the star. Human beings, vegetables, or cosmic dust, we all dance to a mysterious tune, intoned in the distance by an invisible piper.[4]

"...there will be a necessary connexion," says Joseph Priestley, "between all things past, present and to come, in the way of proper *cause and effect*, as much in the intellectual, as in the natural world; so that, how little soever the bulk of mankind may be apprehensive of it, or staggered by it, according to the established laws of nature, no event could have been otherwise than it *has been, is, or is to be....*"[5] Whitman admired Joseph Priestley. At the end of a note in which he *referred to* and *defined* Priestley's determinism, Whitman wrote, "He must have been a *real man*" (below, Ch. IV, Sec. 3).

The determinist believes that his whole life, down to the minutest detail, including every fleeting thought which he will have, will be the result of conditions which existed even before the beginning of the sun, even before the beginning of the farthest galaxies, billions of light-years away.

> With Earth's first Clay They did the Last Man knead,
> And there of the Last Harvest sow'd the Seed:
> And the first Morning of Creation wrote
> What the Last Dawn of Reckoning shall read.[6]

If one is truly a determinist, he must believe this. He must believe that his whole life has, in effect, been planned for him. And even if he should decide, upon reflection, that life is not worth living, this decision itself, as well as his suicide, if it shall follow, has been "planned." If he decides to accept life joyously, this also has been planned. His mate, if he will marry, was selected for him aeons ago. His children were conceived for him in the womb of time. No evil thing that he has done could have been avoided, no good deed that he has done could have but been done, no "accident" was accidental. When faced with a choice of this or that, he may take whichever he pleases, but his pleasure was predetermined. A million years ago the causes were in operation which would eventuate in this particular choice, however insignificant or however momentous the choice may be. When he goes through the cafeteria line, he finds cherry, lemon, and apple pie. He is free to take whichever he wishes. But his choice was predetermined! (His mother fed him apple.)

He is free, but his choice is predetermined. How can this *be*?! Well, here we have the crux of the problem — and its solution. Books have been written giving the explanation. Spinoza explained it; so did Locke, Leibniz, Hume, Schopenhauer, Mill, Russell, and countless others.

For instance, Hobbes:

> Liberty and necessity are consistent: as in the water, that hath not only *liberty*, but a *necessity* of descending by the channel; so likewise in the actions which men voluntarily do: which, because they proceed from their will, proceed from *liberty*; and yet, because every act of man's will, and every desire, and inclination proceedeth from some cause, and that from another cause, in a continual chain, whose first link is in the hand of God the first of all causes, proceed from *necessity*. So that to him who could see the connection of those causes, the *necessity* of all men's voluntary actions, would appear manifest. And therefore God, that seeth and disposeth all things, seeth also that the liberty of man in doing what he will, is accompanied with the necessity of doing that which God will, and no more nor less.[7]

Are you not reminded of Whitman's line in the famous Section 5 of "Song of Myself"? "And I know that the hand of God is the promise of my own." Hobbes: "hand of God"; Whitman: "hand of God." Do you see where we are going with this determinism?!

Spinoza offered the same analysis but with a different analogy: a stone, if it had consciousness, would think that it had perfect freedom when thrown through the air. "This," he said, "is that human freedom, which all boast that they possess, and which consists solely in the fact, that men are conscious of their own desires, but are ignorant of the causes whereby that desire has been determined."[8] Spinoza was not denying human freedom; he was affirming it. His position is made evident by a fragment from a letter he wrote to his friend De Blyenbergh: "…we act freely and are the cause of our action, though all the time we are acting necessarily and according to the decree of God."[9]

John Locke, at about the same time, made the answer to the question supremely clear when he wrote in his *Essay Concerning Human Understanding*:

For how can we think any one freer, than to have the power to do what he will? And so far as any one can, by preferring any action to its not being, or rest to any action, produce that action or rest, so far can he do what he will. For such a preferring of action to its absence, is the willing of it; and we can scarce tell how to imagine any being freer, than to be able to do what he wills.[10]

It should be noted that Locke does not say that one can *will* what he wills: he merely calls attention to the fact, known to everybody, that one can *do* what he wills. We cannot, as Locke points out, *imagine anyone freer* than to be able to *do what he wills.*

"By liberty," says David Hume, "we can only mean *a power of acting or not acting, according to the determinations of the will*; that is, if we choose to remain at rest, we may; if we choose to move, we also may. Now this hypothetical liberty is universally allowed to belong to everyone who is not a prisoner and in chains. Here, then is no subject of dispute."[11]

But surely those who would oppose determinism are looking for a better freedom than that repeatedly described here. They would say — and they must say, if they are to be free from determinism — that to be actually free, they must be free of causation, that to be free the act of will must be uncaused. But this sort of freedom, as Hume correctly pointed out, "is the same thing with chance."[12] This, be it noted, is the *indeterminist* view of freedom — but alas, how few indeterminists would admit, even to themselves, the logical implications of this theory. Sober consideration of this concept would surely show that acts of will which arise through sheer chance are entirely beyond anyone's control. The obvious consequence of the prevalence, or even the sporadic appearance, of such a pure spontaneity in the actions of mankind would be both ludicrous and catastrophic.

John Fiske, contemporary of Whitman, stated the case quite clearly:

> If volitions arise without cause, it necessarily follows that we cannot infer from them the character of the antecedent states of feeling. If, therefore, a murder has been committed, we have *a priori* no better reason for suspecting the worst enemy than the best friend of the murdered man. If we see a man jump from a fourth-story window, we must beware of too hastily inferring his insanity, since he may be merely exercising his free-will; the intense love of life implanted in the human breast being, as it seems, unconnected with attempts at suicide or at self-preservation. We can thus frame no theory of human actions whatever.... nothing which anyone may do ought ever to occasion surprise. The mother may strangle her first-born child, the miser may cast his long treasured gold into the sea, the sculptor may break in pieces his lately finished statue, in the presence of no other feelings than those which before led them to cherish, to hoard, and to create.[13]

We turn now to view another facet of the controversy. Freedom, says Joseph Ratner, "is not opposed to necessity or determinism; it is only opposed to an alien necessity or alien determinism."[14] The erroneous identification of determinism with what Ratner calls "alien necessity or alien determinism," or what is popularly called fatalism, has nurtured almost all of the anti-determinist bias.

"Opponents of determinism," says Gordon H. Clark, "argue that if everything is fated, there is no use in exerting oneself, for the event will happen anyway."[15] "What difference can it make how great the effort," asks the distinguished physicist A. H. Compton, "if our actions are already determined by mechanical laws of cause and effect? Our purposes cannot then be effective."[16] Professor Floyd Stovall, an outstanding Whitman scholar, was discussing with his American literature class the deterministic overtones of Stephen Crane's short story "The Open Boat." "If the survivors believed they were predetermined to drown or be saved," Professor Stovall asked (not merely pedagogically), "why did they not stop swimming?" Numerous instances could be cited in which people who should know better, ask, in all seriousness, this question. A noted critic of Shelley, speaking of the "scientific determinism" of the nineteenth century, remarks: "There is in this denial of free will conjoined with a belief in perfectibility a philosophical inconsistency either unperceived or, when perceived, unsuccessfully solved. If the mind is not free, how can humanity become perfect unless perfectibility itself is predetermined? And in such a case why the necessity of effort? Perfection will, if predetermined, come without effort."[17] These men see denials and inconsistencies where none exist. If the event is predetermined, it is predetermined by the causes which effect it. It is clear that the "why try?" question in all these examples indicates a confusion of determinism with superstitious fatalism.

It is an old error. It was, Leibniz tells us, called by the ancients the "Lazy Sophism." The Lazy Sophism, says Leibniz, "ended in a decision to do nothing: for (people would say) if what I ask is to happen it will happen even though I should do nothing; and if it is not to happen it will never happen, no matter what trouble I take to achieve it." Intelligent men today, as we have seen, sincerely believe determinism entails this chain of reasoning. "But the answer," according to Leibniz, "is quite ready: the effect being certain, the cause that will produce it is certain also; and if the effect comes about it will be by virtue of a proportionate cause. Thus your laziness perchance will bring it about that you will obtain naught of what you desire, and that you will fall into those misfortunes which you would by acting with care have avoided. We see, therefore, that the *connexion of causes with effects*, far from causing an unendurable fatality, provides rather a means of obviating it."[18]

Schopenhauer also noted the error, calling it "Turkish faith."[19] Nietzsche, using similar terminology, referred to "the fatalism of the Turk."[20] Leibniz called it *Fatum Mohametanum.*[21]

There is a question as to whether even the Mohammedans, firm as may be their faith, are true fatalists. We have, in support of this view, the testimony of an Englishman, R. V. C. Bodley, who lived seven years in the company of Arabs on the Sahara. His account gives an interesting example of how the Arabs, when lashed by a fierce sandstorm, made immediate efforts to recover afterwards. He does not paint a picture of people folding their hands and submitting to fate when they had opportunity to meet impending doom with action.[22] The Koran says, "No soul can die unless by the permission of God, according to *what is written* in the book containing the determination of things."[23] But the fanatic sacrifices of suicide bombers and the heedless abandon with which Mohammedans traditionally have thrown themselves into battle prove either that they have been misled by an erroneous and self-contradictory religion or, if the religion is sound, by misinterpretation of its preachments. In any case it would appear that they neglect the Koran's admonition, inconsistent or not: "O true believers, take your necessary precaution against your enemies."[24] Firm in their superstition as they are, they assume the same ridiculous view as some modern misinterpreters of determinism.

The superstitious fatalist believes the future is predetermined altogether in spite of what he does. But as Emerson wisely discerned, "if Fate is so prevailing, man also is part of it, and can confront fate with fate."[25] Our wishes are in the stream of causation, not out of it. That the wishes themselves may be predetermined does not detract from their efficacy. Even dictionaries, in defining determinism, do not always avoid the pitfall of abstracting the human will (simply: our wishes and decisions) from the flow of events. Note the illogic of these two entries. This from *The American Heritage College Dictionary*, 1993:

> **determinism** ... The philosophical doctrine that every event, act, and decision is the inevitable consequence of antecedents that are independent of the human will.

And this, from *Longman Advanced American Dictionary*, 2000:

> **determinism** ... the belief that what you do and what happens to you are caused by things that you cannot control.

The first definition fails to note that the "human will" can be an "antecedent" — a cause — a part of the flow. "...the hammer that smites, and the arrow that flies, and the hand that wields, are not tools of the deity, but are the deity itself at work."[26] The second definition is a good definition — of fatalism, not of determinism. We certainly do "control" many of the events and most of the decisions in our lives. There is no mysterious and extrinsic "fate" that compels us against our will. If determinism is true, we are not subject to determinism, we *are* determinism.

No wonder that, failing to understand this, many modern minds despise determinism and fear it. No wonder that fearing it they have sought to escape from it. And we find them grasping at any straw which may save them.

One of those straws was an important turn of events in physics which caused the earlier determinism of the physics of Sir Isaac Newton to fall into disfavor. Astronomer Sir Arthur Eddington and physicists Sir James Jeans and Arthur H. Compton wrote books intimating — averring, actually — that the "new" physics gives hope for the rescue of free will.

Studies of the subatomic, including Planck's development of the theory of quanta in 1900 and Werner Heisenberg's findings, announced in 1927, cast doubt on the ability of science to demonstrate instances of causation in the physical world. Causation may or may not exist in the subatomic realm, but in any case it is not at present discoverable. The beam of light used to determine the *velocity* of an electron unavoidably disturbs the direction of the electron, making its *location* uncertain. That, simply, is all that Heisenberg meant by his "uncertainty principle." Someone later (Jeans?) changed it to "Principle of Indeterminacy," thereby establishing a confusion of Indetermin*acy* with Indetermin*ism* and opening the way to the erroneous conclusion that subatomic events, or some of them, are indeterministic, uncaused. William H. Halverson brings light to the subject when he states: "The principle of indeterminacy is best understood, I think, as a limitation in *our knowledge* of subatomic events rather than a real hiatus in the network of mutually interesting events of which the universe is composed."[27]

Physics has not disproved determinism. And Eddington admits this. "Writer after writer," he concedes, "proceeds to show that neither Heisenberg's Principle of Indeterminacy nor anything else in modern physics disproves determinism. That, I think, is universally agreed...."[28]

But Eddington becomes so enamored of the idea that physics can do without determinism that he at times appears to forget his concession that it has not been disproved. Other scientists (and, it seems, intelligentsia in general) also forget and, like Eddington, seizing upon the remotest proof for their cherished "free will," treasure the possibility that determinism is no longer valid. The layman, further misinterpreting, thinks that determinism has indeed been disproved — and Whitman critics are not immune to the error (see Ch. I).

If the new science offers any support for indeterminism, one might expect that scientists and philosophers and laymen *other* than those who have misinterpreted determinism would have acknowledged that indeterminism has garnered this support. Professor Albert Einstein dismissed the indeterminist hysteria by saying: "That nonsense is not merely nonsense. It is objectionable nonsense."[29] When Einstein was asked, "In what sense then do you apply determinism to nature?" he indicated that he believed the traditional cause-effect concept was in need of refinement. If the traditional determinism had been felt too strict it was not in his opinion strict enough: "Now I believe that events in nature are controlled by a much stricter and more closely binding law than we suspect to-day, when we speak of one event being the cause of another." "Indeterminism," he said, "is quite an illogical concept."[30] Max Planck, discoverer of the quantum on which modern physics is based, was a determinist of the strictest sort (see Ch. IX).

Ted Honderich has examined the quantum argument which, by positing "microcosmic events of pure chance," attempts to substantiate Free Will. Honderich asks, "Is it true?":

> Well, this interpretation of Quantum Theory has been on the table for about 75 years. In that time, no evidence in a standard sense has been produced for there being any such chance events. *There is no direct and univocal experimental evidence at all.* We have sometimes heard from hopeful science writers in good newspapers that the evidence is on the way from research institutions in Switzerland or California but it never actually comes. That is really a remarkable fact that needs to be paid attention — 75 years is a long time in science.
>
> ... it is possible that the real truth about reality will eventually be given by a different physics, one that is deterministic. That remained the conviction of some of the greatest of modern physicists, including Einstein himself.[31]

But even while waiting for developments which may lessen the confusion, we must guard ourselves against the confusion. We must not be misled by the "free will" interpretations of the "new" physics. As an instance in point, attend to this unfortunate statement by a biographer of Whitman: "Where materialistic scientists have been wont to read determinism and invariant law, Whitman read Freedom and Diversity. 20th century science tends to agree with him."[32] What did I tell you!

The most common argument against determinism, at least by the philosophically unsophisticated, is the "I just feel free" argument. For most people this argument for free will is satisfactory. A somehow kindred argument, if it was not the same argument, was that of Emanuel Kant, who asserted that no event occurs without a cause and yet, retreating to what he called the "noumenal" realm, felt that we are free simply because we *must* be — because morality *demands* freedom: we *ought*, said Kant, therefore we *can*. He confessed that he had not *proved* free will and that ordinary logic could not prove it. Bertrand Russell, in his inimitable manner, provides the following analysis:

> In the *Critique of Pure Reason* Kant taught that *pure* reason cannot prove the future life or the existence of God; it cannot therefore assure us that there is justice in the world. Moreover, there was a difficulty about free will. My

actions, in so far as I can observe them, are phenomena, and therefore have causes. As to what my actions are in themselves, pure reason can tell me nothing, so that I do not know whether they are free or not. However, "pure" reason is not the only kind; there is another — not "impure," as might have been expected, but "practical." This starts from the premise that all the moral rules Kant was taught in childhood are true. (Such a premise, of course, needs a disguise: it is introduced to philosophical society under the name of the "categorical imperative.") It follows that the will is free, for it would be absurd to say "you *ought* to do so-and-so" unless you *can* do it.[33]

As some philosophical wag has put it: "I have to believe in free will: I have no choice!" The "I just feel free" defense is neatly countered by Popkin and Stroll:

> The proponents of free will insist that no determinist arguments can elimi-
> nate or account for the actual experience of freedom that we all sometimes
> have when we make our choices. (Of course, the determinists can point out
> that even if one grants that we have this experience, it in no way denies that
> in spite of how we may feel about it, our volitions are nonetheless deter-
> mined.)[34]

The free willist is not deceived by his *feeling* but by his making too narrow an interpretation of it. Nothing better has been said about this than by Friedrich Paulsen:

> But, it is said, *self-consciousness* knows nothing of such necessity. Every
> one has an immediate feeling of certainty that he is not moulded into what
> he is from without, that everything would have happened otherwise if he
> had willed otherwise. And he is likewise absolutely sure that the future
> shaping of his life depends upon his will: I could give up my business right
> now and start another one; I could emigrate to St. Petersburg or to London
> or to America — all this lies wholly in my power; and such a course would
> evidently completely change my life. I could also, and perhaps ought to,
> says self-consciousness, alter my mode of life, my behavior to others, my
> character. Is all this an illusion?
>
> Certainly not. Self-consciousness does not deceive us. But what does it
> say? Surely this, that to the influences which have determined and will con-
> tinue to determine my life and character, must be added my wishes and
> inclinations, my convictions and resolutions, and particularly these. It tells
> me that I am not moved from without like a cogwheel in a machine, but
> through the mediation of an inner element which I call my will.... That is
> what self-consciousness says; never, however, does it tell us that the particu-
> lar processes arise without cause, that at any moment of life any occurrence
> whatever can take place, utterly regardless of all preceding ones; this would,
> if it really happened, be equivalent to the complete resolution of life into a
> series of disconnected and irrational accidents.[35]

In many minds the problem of the maintenance of responsibility is one of the chief obstacles to the acceptance of determinism. It is felt that without indeterminist "free will" moral imputability would be impossible, that under the determinist system there can be no place whatever for praise and blame. "The determinist is inconsistent," says George H. Palmer, "who thanks his friend for a Christmas gift."[36] Such misconceptions have some basis in fact, the fact being, however, that determinism rejects responsibility, praise, blame, reward, punishment in *some* senses of the words but retains them in others. The misconceptions arise from a failure to recognize ambiguities in the words denoting the ideas in question. (Whitman made clever use of such ambiguities in writing *Leaves of Grass*. He called them "indirections.")

From the consideration that the criminal act could not have been otherwise, the determinist is forced to give up one conception of punishment, but from the consideration that human actions are always the result of causes, the determinist draws a strong argument in favor of the adoption of another concept of punishment. The *retributive* incentive for punishment, the determinist rejects altogether. He may, however, with logical support from his philosophy, still hold to a belief in punishment; for the *corrective* incentive for punishment, or the *deterrent* incentive, is quite consistent with determinism. The determinist's understanding of the problem has been summed up quite nicely:

> ... moral responsibility is not only consistent with determinism but requires it. The assumption on which punishment is based is that human behavior is causally determined. If pain could not be a cause of truthtelling there would be no justification at all for punishing lies. If human actions and volitions were uncaused, it would be useless either to punish or to reward, or indeed to do anything else to correct people's behavior. For nothing that you could do would in any way influence them. Thus moral responsibility would entirely disappear. If there were no determinism of human beings at all, their actions would be completely unpredictable and capricious, and therefore irresponsible. And this is in itself a strong argument against the common view of philosophers that free will means being undetermined by causes.[37]

Perhaps nobody has pointed out that there is a certain amount of tit for tat in these arguments. Determinists list the adverse consequences of indeterminism as discredit for indeterminism. Indeterminists rely heavily on playing up supposed adverse consequences in a determinist world. But neither determinism nor indeterminism can be disproved by emphasizing their supposed consequences. As Benjamin Franklin said, "Truth will be Truth tho' it sometimes prove mortifying and distasteful."[38] Each side has a right, however, to clarify, to fend off misinterpretations — to defend its concept *as a hypothesis*.

Bertrand Russell, wise philosopher that he was, used that word, hypothesis, in introducing the following astute analysis:

> Praise and blame, rewards and punishments, and the whole apparatus of the criminal law, are rational on the deterministic hypothesis, but not on the hypothesis of free will, for they are all mechanisms designed to cause volitions that are in harmony with the interests of the community, or what are believed to be its interests. But the conception of "sin" is only rational on the assumption of free will, for, on the deterministic hypothesis, when a man does something that the community would wish him not to do, that is because the community has not provided adequate motives.... Murder is punished, not because it is a sin and it is good that sinners should suffer, but because the community wishes to prevent it, and fear of punishment causes most people to abstain from it. This is completely compatible with the deterministic hypothesis, and completely incompatible with the hypothesis of free will.
>
> I conclude that free will is not essential to any rational ethic, but only to the vindictive ethic that justifies hell and holds that "sin" should be punished regardless of any good that punishment may do. I conclude also that "sin," except in the sense of conduct towards which the agent, or the community, feels an emotion of disapproval, is a mistaken concept calculated to promote needless cruelty and vindictiveness when it is others that are thought to sin, and a morbid self-abasement when it is ourselves whom we condemn.[39]

Do you understand, now, how Whitman could write, "I am the poet of sin,/ For I do not believe in sin"?[40] He never published those lines, but he published many more which could be quoted appropriately here. For determinism as it relates to Whitman's puzzling view of sin and evil, see my Chapter VI. Do you begin to see why the present chapter was necessary?

Monsignor John A. Ryan argues vehemently against what he considers the catastrophes which (he thinks) would logically abound in a determinist world. He declares that the determinist would logically be barred from condemning violations (like those of Hitler) of civil and political freedom. As a cleric, committed to the promotion and protection of morality, he feels that the problem of morality is the snag on which determinism most certainly founders. If determinism were true, he says, people would be "no more justly liable to moral blame or condemnation than the lion, the tiger, the earthquake, or the cyclone."[41] Oddly, most determinists, on this point, would agree with him. Whitman (see Ch. VI) would have agreed with him. So would Francis S. Haserot. The following is from Haserot's essay "Enlightenment":

> If the behavior of men is seen in the same light as the *motions of the stars, the opening of flowers in the sunlight, the tropisms in butterflies, the responses of animals* [my italics], not only would there be considerable revelation as to

their behavior but considerable tolerance and insight in their mutual dealings. It would be much more clear why the different strata of a community, the subnormal, the standard and the supernormal behave as they do — it would be clearer why individuals pursue the different professions, why they acquire the interests, the idiosyncrasies and the hobbies which they do. In short a recognition of the deterministic behavior of humans is one of the principal avenues to the overcoming of the barriers of particularity which cut off communication between private persons and private worlds and which make men act as if they were autonomous individuals not comprehended in a nexus of relations with other things.[42]

We shall see (in Ch. VI) that Whitman, like Haserot, viewed the actions of men "in the same light as the motions of the stars, the opening of flowers," etc. But it is true that both Haserot and Whitman would have looked upon those actions, in another way, as different. This difference has been made quite clear by John Dewey:

> We may seem then to be in a hopeless dilemma. If the man's nature, original and acquired, makes him do what he does, how does his action differ from that of a stone or tree? Have we not parted with any ground for responsibility? When the question is looked at in the face of facts rather than in a dialectic of concepts it turns out not to have any terrors. Holding men to responsibility may make a decided difference in their *future* behavior; holding a stone or tree to responsibility is a meaningless performance; it has no consequences; it makes no difference. If we locate the ground of liability in future consequences rather than in antecedent causal conditions, we moreover find ourselves in accord with actual practice. Infants, idiots, the insane, those completely upset, are not held to liability; the reason is that it is absurd — meaningless to do so, for it has no effect on their further actions.[43]

The determinist does not reject responsibility, he merely considers it from the point of view of the determinist. Responsibility is not negated by the fact that from this point of view we must look upon men as no more to be despised or hated than stones and trees, stars and butterflies, lions and tigers, earthquakes and cyclones. Men may be held responsible for their actions and yet remain, like everything else, a part of Nature.

The determinist, if he can adhere closely to his own philosophy, looks out upon the world with tranquility and love; his attitude toward the actions of men is unalloyed with the vengeful sentiments and passions which so often are characteristic of the "free will" attitude toward the same actions. For him men are responsible only in so far as they may be expected to respond; they are not responsible in that they merit our anger. "It is common for men impressed with the opinion of free will," says Godwin, "to entertain resentment, indignation, and anger against those who fall into the commission of vice. How much of these feelings is just, and how much erroneous? The difference between virtue and vice, will equally remain upon the opposite hypothesis. Vice therefore must be an object of rejection, and virtue of preference; the one must be approved, and the other disapproved. But our disapprobation of vice, will be of the same nature, as our disapprobation of an infectious distemper."[44]

Diderot referred to determinism as "a philosophy full of pity, strongly attached to the good, nor more angry with the wicked than with the whirlwind which fills one's eyes with dust." "Adopt these principles," he urged, "if you think them good, or show me that they are bad. If you adopt them, they will reconcile *you* too with others and with yourself: you will neither be pleased nor angry with yourself for being what you are. Reproach others for nothing, and repent of nothing; this is the first step to wisdom. Besides this, all is prejudice and false philosophy."[45]

Diderot's statement that "you will neither be pleased nor angry with yourself for being what you are" points to an aspect of determinism that is rarely considered, by either side of the controversy. It is, perhaps, the most important aspect of all, for we live with ourself twenty-four hours a day. Regrets and guilt can gnaw at our psyches, often with horrible or miserable results: suicide, abandonment of effort, tragic damage to one's ego. This philosophy puts that ego in perspective, allowing neither a miserable feeling of inferiority nor an overweening smugness about our self-worth. Determinism should not, of course, be relied on too heavily as an excuse; but it can be the balm that soothes our psychological wounds.

Joseph Priestley, whose determinism caught the attention of Whitman (see Ch. IV, Sec. 3: "Whitman and Priestley"), says of sinners, "I, on my system, cannot help viewing them with a *tenderness* and *compassion*."[46] The determinist looks thus upon wrongdoers not "from any womanish pity," as Spinoza so well phrased it,[47] nor from a consciousness of the possibility of his own reward for obeying moral injunctions, but as a result of reflecting on the consequences of his philosophy. Determinism places compassion under the guidance of reason and thus removes from it the tincture of self-righteous piety so often consequent upon the "free will" view, which makes sympathy and forgiveness more an exercise of sheer goodness and less an endeavor to fulfill the dictates of a rational conclusion.

> One of the most beneficent effects of subjecting human conduct to deterministic explanation has been to beget a more sympathetic and kindly feeling toward one's fellow-men. The understanding of the deeper springs and sources of conduct is the necessary condition alike of all true compassion and of all just restraint. If this compassion embraces even the follies and vices of men, it is not a dangerous or indulgent compassion, since it understands all too clearly that in the social order there must be effective motives

working to restrain evil. While it reaches one hand in pity towards a frail and erring humanity, it extends the other in vigorous control.[48]

One may be reminded of Whitman's words to the prostitute: "Miserable! I do not laugh at your oaths nor jeer you" ("Song of Myself," Sec. 15). The usefulness of determinism in understanding Whitman's views of sin and evil will be made evident in Chapter VI.

Monsignor Ryan's statement that "When men reject freedom of the will, their belief in external freedom is inevitably weakened"[49] broaches an aspect of determinism that, because it has bearing on Whitman's support of freedom, calls for clarification.

A little reasoning will show that the question of free will has no direct bearing on the question of political liberty. And it can be pointed out that some of the most zealous champions of freedom have been determinists. The philosophic question has always been, "Are my *actions free?*" The political question is, "Am I *free to act?*" Yet there are those who fail to keep this distinction in mind when accusing determinism of its imagined evils. They forget that a word is a word is a word, that freedom is not simply freedom but has different meanings in different contexts. And they are led so far astray by this forgetfulness that they become confused, some even maintaining that the determinist, in order to have consistency between his philosophy and his politics, must advocate totalitarianism. Consider Judge Jerome Frank's charge against Einstein:

> If Einstein were consistent and carried his cosmic views over into the field of politics and government, he would believe in the desirability of a totalitarian world order, a globe completely organized under one dictatorial government, with world-wide regimentation of everyone down to the minutest detail of conduct. When it comes to politics he goes to the opposite extreme, for he seems to believe in a multitude of small, independent governments.[50]

As Einstein would say, this nonsense is not merely nonsense; it is objectionable nonsense.[51]

Because it is important to make clear that Walt Whitman's ringing pronouncements of his love of freedom are not inconsistent with a basic philosophy of determinism, I want to present here some examples of determinists who have been among the most ardent and best known supporters of freedom. Let us consider Spinoza, Lincoln, Shelley, Mill, and, near the end of the chapter, Einstein.

Spinoza as a determinist declares: "The mind is a certain and determinate mode of thought, and therefore it cannot be a free cause of its own actions, or have an absolute faculty of willing or not willing, but must be determined to this or that volition by a cause which is also determined by another cause, and this again by another, and so on *ad infinitum*."[52] Yet Spinoza as a determinist can also declare:

> ... a government would be most harsh which deprived the individual of his freedom of saying and teaching what he thought; and would be moderate if such freedom were granted....
>
> No, the object of government is not to change men from rational beings into beasts or puppets, but to enable them to develop their minds and bodies in security, and to employ their reason unshackled; neither showing hatred, anger or deceit, nor watched with the eyes of jealousy and injustice. In fact, the true aim of government is liberty.
>
> ... We cannot doubt that the best government will allow freedom of philosophical speculation no less than of religious belief. I confess that from such freedom inconveniences may sometimes arise, but what question was ever settled so wisely that no abuses could possibly spring therefrom? He who seeks to regulate everything by law is more likely to arouse vices than to reform them.[53]

Spinoza, says Joseph Ratner, "was able to write upon Human Freedom with a truth and clarity and force excelling by far all theological, teleological, 'free-will,' idealistic philosophers from Plato to Josiah Royce. Spinoza was able to write thus *because*, not *in spite of* the fact that he placed at the heart of his philosophy the doctrine of necessity...."[54]

Abraham Lincoln. The name is almost a synonym for liberty. (Oh! how Whitman admired him!) but how many freedom-loving Americans know that Lincoln was a determinist! His friend and law-partner Herndon writes: "Lincoln always, to me in our private conversations, said that there was no freedom of the will...."[55] What?! *Surely*, then, Lincoln was "inconsistent." He has been so charged:

> The conviction that man was the necessary product of the universal forces of nature taught Lincoln forbearance and tolerance toward others so that he felt "malice towards none and charity towards all," in spite of bitter provocation in his domestic and political life. But this fatalistic [*sic!*] attitude was blended in him as in Spinoza with a profound respect for the natural worth and dignity of man and the inalienable right of each person to be his own master. Lincoln's success in emancipating the slaves of America was one of the supreme, creative acts of history and altered what seemed to be the inevitable destiny of millions. In this respect he carried into practical social life the principles on which Spinoza founded his Ethics. *Both were inconsistent— in the grand manner— and allowed practice to take precedence over theory.*[56] [The italics are mine!]

According to Herndon, Lincoln was often heard to say, "I always was a fatalist."[57] But he was not, as the paragraph quoted above makes him out to be, a *superstitious* fatalist. He was a determinist. Herndon says of him that "his fatalism was not of the extreme order like the Mahometan idea of fate, because he believed firmly in the power of human effort to modify the environments which surround us. He made efforts at all times to modify and change public opinion and to climb to the Presidential heights; he toiled and struggled in this line as scarcely any man ever did."[58] Lincoln's democracy was a larger democracy than that of most other democrats. There was a reason for it: he was a determinist. His calm regard for the individuality, the rights, the welfare of all men, far from being antithetical to his determinism, must have owed its origin in great part to that philosophy. If that philosophy denies men the freedom of action, it does not, at least, deny them the freedom to act unfreely. And this latter freedom (which is not really so paradoxical as it sounds) Lincoln did *at least* give the slaves with the Emancipation Proclamation. Even interpreting determinism in this way — as the complete denial of free will — it must be evident that Lincoln's action was not inconsistent with his philosophy.

But perhaps such subtleties will only confuse the anti-determinist, who is usually so intent on the abolition of determinism that his ardor will not permit an unhurried analysis of the finer points of the philosophy he opposes.

One of the interpreters of Shelley's determinism, Gingerich, suggests quite frankly that "we need not be disturbed by the subtleties of the arguments." "We shall," he says, "hold to the antithesis: if a poet be found to accept and express the deterministic outlook on life he may be set down as having a weak hold on will and personality, and if he be an ardent exponent of freewill he will be a weak determinist."[59] But there is a third possibility, and this it is that baffles the critics. What if, like Shelley (and, as we shall see, like Whitman), the poet affirms both freedom *and* determinism? Here the interpreting antitheticist must gather his gear and leave the field.

Gingerich, in spite of his aversion to determinism, or at least his misinterpretation of it, is nevertheless convinced, as other Shelley critics have not been, that Shelley was, first to last a determinist.

Ellsworth Barnard, recognizing that "Shelley is one of the great English poets of liberty" lets the recognition of that fact mislead him into thinking that Shelley was not, as Gingerich maintained, "to the last" a determinist but must have *given up* his determinism.[60] After quoting a few inapplicable lines from "Hellas" (lines 34–45) he proclaims: "This one lyric alone would effectually contradict every pedantic argument that Shelley was a Necessarian."[61] For such critics the argument is simple: Shelley supported freedom; therefore he could not have been a consistent determinist.

Both Gingerich and Barnard fail to catch the finer implications of the determinist philosophy. This is evident in Gingerich's erroneous and persistent identification of necessitarianism with fatalism and of "will" with "free will." It is evident in Barnard's ineffectual criticism of Godwin (who may be remembered as Shelley's father-in-law):

It is true that Godwin is a Necessarian, and one so consistent in holding the doctrine that he lets it [here we go] carry him into the absurdest inconsistencies. He declares, "In the life of every human being there is a chain of events, generated in the lapse of ages which preceded his birth, and going on in regular procession through the whole period of his existence, in consequence of which it is impossible for him to act in any instance otherwise than he has acted." Hence, "in a strict sense, there is no such thing as action. Man is in no case, strictly speaking, the beginner of an event or series of events that takes place in the universe, but only the vehicle through which certain antecedents operate." *And this is the man who hoped by his writings to bring about profound changes in society!*[62] [My italics!]

In their ignorance of determinism Shelley's interpreters feel that they have reached a logical conclusion when the idea occurs to them that a belief in determinism is inconsistent with a belief in the expediency of urging social reform. They say that if Shelley believed all things were predetermined he was inconsistent in trying to reform the Irish. If these critics had attentively read Godwin they would have found him saying that it is precisely because men's actions *are* predetermined that reformatory efforts can have any results.[63] For that matter, one does not have to read Godwin to see — indeed a Shelley critic, even, might see it — that if men's actions are predetermined they are predetermined by *something*, and that this "something" may even be the enthusiastic pamphlets of a young poet. As Professor A. C. Ewing has pointed out, we "need not draw the practical conclusion, which has often confusedly been drawn from determinism, that it does not matter what we do because what happens is determined in any case. For even if the future is always determined, this does not prevent our will being one of the causes which determine it, and thus it does matter what we will do."[64]

I have dwelt too long on the stumbling analyses(?) of Shelley's critics. My excuse is that, because the views of Shelley and Whitman in regard both to determinism and to freedom are practically identical, to clarify Shelley is to clarify Whitman.

Barnard's criticism of Godwin is echoed by Sir James Jeans in a similar remark on John Stuart Mill. "Mill," says Jeans, "believed that all human actions are so completely determinate that sociology could be made into a perfectly exact science, in which the future of a society would be seen to follow from its past with a mechanical certainty and after invarying laws. He then, with the characteristic irrationality of the thoroughgoing determinist, wanted these laws to be studied with a view to improving the future of the race!"[65] It is hardly conceivable that a philosopher-scientist of Jeans's stature could hold an opinion so patently naïve. It is *Jeans* who is "irrational," not Mill! There is nothing irrational in Mill's view! Jeans commits what Mill himself calls "the eternally recurring error of confounding Causation with Fatalism."[66] If a determinist scheme be posited, we cannot abstract man and his desires and actions from that scheme, for they are a part of it. "Because whatever happens will be the effect of causes, human volitions among the rest, it does not follow," says Mill, "that volitions, even those of peculiar individuals are not of great efficacy as causes."[67]

Mill certainly was, as Jeans avers, a *thoroughgoing* determinist, but in remarks like the following, from his essay *On Liberty*, he was not, as Jeans would have it, an *inconsistent* determinist.

> The only freedom which deserves the name, is that of pursuing our own good in our own way, so long as we do not attempt to deprive others of theirs, or impede their efforts to obtain it. Each is the proper guardian of his own health, whether bodily, or mental and spiritual. Mankind are greater gainers by suffering each other to live as seems good to themselves, than by compelling each to live as seems good to the rest.
>
> Though this doctrine is anything but new, and, to some persons, may have the air of a truism, there is no doctrine which stands more directly opposed to the general tendency of existing opinion and practice....
>
> Apart from the peculiar tenets of individual thinkers, there is also in the world at large an increasing inclination to stretch unduly the powers of society over the individual, both by the force of opinion and even by that of legislation; and as the tendency of all the changes taking place in the world is to strengthen society, and diminish the power of the individual, this encroachment is not one of the evils which tend spontaneously to disappear, but, on the contrary, to grow more and more formidable.[68]

At a time when determinism is in political ill-repute in the free world as a result of the espousal of this philosophy by those who tried to use it as an argument for the surrender of the individual to the mass, it is refreshing to review these remarks by a determinist who recognized the importance of individual liberty and who noted, more than a century ago, the dangers of "an increasing inclination to stretch unduly the powers of society over the individual."

Our investigation of the question has placed the answer beyond dispute. It is clear that a determinist's support of freedom by no means involves a contradiction of his basic philosophy. It is clear that his philosophy in no way pledges him to the support of a totalitarian state.

We may pay due regard to Einstein's remark, "In human freedom in the philosophical sense I am definitely a disbeliever,"[69] and yet not be alarmed by what may *seem* his disrespect for logic when he goes on to profess a faith in democracy and individual liberty:

> My political ideal is democratic. Let every man be respected as an individual and no man idolised.... I am quite aware that it is necessary for the achievement of any complex undertaking that one man should do the

thinking and directing and in general bear the responsibility. But the led must not be compelled, they must be able to choose their leader. An autocratic system of coercion, in my opinion, soon degenerates. For force always attracts men of low morality, and I believe it to be an invariable rule that tyrants of genius are succeeded by scoundrels. For this reason I have always been passionately opposed to systems such as we see in Italy and Russia today.... I believe that in this respect the United States of America have found the right way.... The really valuable thing in the pageant of human life seems to me not the political state, but the creative, sentient individual, the personality; it alone creates the noble and the sublime, while the herd as such remains dull in thought and dull in feeling.[70]

This is the not illogical, not inconsistent, not irrational view of a determinist. And how strikingly near it is to the view of Walt Whitman, who found that in the edifice of democracy "perhaps the main, the high façade of all" is the principle of individuality, "the pride and centripetal isolation of a human being in himself— identity — personalism."[71]

◆ ◆ ◆

It is regrettable that the inclusion of this chapter has been necessary, but I have deemed it necessary because I am aware of the general ignorance of the true meaning of determinism and because I know that that ignorance stands in the way of the acceptance of my thesis: that Whitman was a determinist and that the fullest understanding of his poems will come with the understanding of the philosophy of determinism and the perception that Whitman made use of that philosophy in the writing of his poems.

III

The Epiphany

"...a usually sudden manifestation or perception of
the essential nature or meaning of something."
— *Webster's Third New International Dictionary.*

All things excellent, says Spinoza, are as difficult as they are rare. Spinoza preached the "Intellectual Love of God." It was through an understanding of determinism that the Intellectual Love of God was to be realized. "But the very doctrine which Spinoza placed at the heart of his philosophy because of the inestimable advantages man could derive from it, people loudly objected to on the ground that it robbed man's life of all moral and religious value. Determinism, they exclaimed, reduces man to the rank of inanimate Nature; without 'free-will' man is no better than a slave, his life doomed by an inexorable fate."[1] Spinoza realized that it is not easy for one to give up the notion that he possesses an independent ego. He knew from personal experience that accommodating oneself to the idea of determinism involves great difficulties. "If the way which, as I have shown, leads hither seem very difficult, it can nevertheless be found. It must indeed be difficult since it is so seldom discovered; for if salvation lay ready to hand and could be discovered without great labour, how could it be possible that it should be neglected almost by everybody? But all noble things are as difficult as they are rare."[2]

The determinist must accustom himself to the idea that his will is a part of the predetermining process in which everything, physical, mental, spiritual, is inextricably and ineluctably enmeshed. The period of adjustment may last for months, even years, and in some instances involves a state of mental anguish so acute as to be almost unbearable. No other single doctrine can, when accepted, cause such a painful change in one's world-outlook. Its effect upon the mind can be cataclysmic. Cherished beliefs are overthrown, only to be replaced by others which for a time may seem utterly repugnant to their possessor. The neophyte determinist is horrified by what seems an avalanche of soul-crushing truths. He will gaze wistfully down the philosophic road he has traveled and reflect bitterly that he might best never have begun his journey. Fichte, assuming the role of the newly convinced determinist, cries out: "Why must my heart mourn at, and be lacerated by that which so perfectly satisfies my understanding?" And he exclaims sadly: "Had I but been contented to remain amid the pleasant delusions that surrounded me, satisfied with the immediate consciousness of my existence, and never raised those questions concerning its foundation, the answer to which has caused me this misery! But if this answer be true, then *I must* of necessity have raised these questions:— I indeed raised them not, but the thinking nature within me raised them. I was destined to this misery, and I weep in vain the lost innocence of soul which can never return to me again."[3]

The determinist's despair arises from a failure to perceive the real consequences of the determinist doctrine. One is so used to thinking of human actions in a context of unqualified freedom that even when one accepts determinism he is still influenced strongly by former "free will" associations and is therefore misled into irrational interpretations of the new doctrine. Even the clearest philosophic minds have thus fallen into error. "I am well aware" concedes Joseph Priestley, "that, notwithstanding all that ever can be advanced in favour of these conclusions, great and glorious as the really are in themselves, it requires so much strength of mind to comprehend them, that (I wish to say it with the least offense possible) I cannot help considering the doctrine as that which will always distinguish the real moral philosopher from the rest of the world...."[4] Even John Stuart Mill, who undoubtedly possessed a mind capable of dealing with most philosophic subtleties, was for a time unable to grasp the full meaning of the determinist concept. He spent many months in a most painful and abject depression:

> ... during the later returns of my dejection, the doctrine of what is called Philosophical Necessity weighed on my existence like an incubus. I felt as if I was scientifically proved to be the helpless slave of antecedent circumstances; as if my character and that of all others had been formed for us by agencies beyond our control, and was wholly out of our own power.... I pondered painfully on the subject, till gradually I saw light through it.... The theory, which I now for the first time rightly apprehended, ceased altogether to be discouraging, and besides the relief to my spirits, I no longer suffered under the burthen, so heavy to one who aims at being a reformer in opinions, of thinking one doctrine true, and the contrary doctrine morally beneficial. The train of thought which had extricated me from this dilemma, seemed to me, in after years, fitted to render a similar service to others; and it now forms the chapter on Liberty and Necessity in the concluding Book of my "System of Logic."[5]

Commenting on Mill's despondency W. L. Courtney remarks, "When the light of newer thoughts breaks upon cherished opinions, a mental tragedy, which is by no means the less real because it is subdued, makes havoc of a man's peace and self-control."[6] Remember Charles Bray's statement (see Ch. I):

> ...I found Philosophical Necessity clearly and logically proved. ...but what was I to do with it? It was fundamentally opposed to all my previously recognized principles of ethics. And here I must pause. The next year was certainly the most miserable year of my life.... I had to begin to build my life over again; my mind was in a complete anarchy, or in a state of blank despair

There is, says Russell, "a cavern of darkness to be traversed."[7] The new determinist finds himself hopeless at the thought of a machine-like existence in a machine-like world. A dreadful soul-anemia leaves him weak and trembling at the prospect of living a life whose every success and every failure were settled in the blank aeons of the infinite past. Proffered love and friendship he bitterly rejects as valueless offerings of an inhuman force. He despises yet envies the normalities of the deluded manikins about him. He is beset by terrors from which the only escape would be suicide, if this too were not a mockery. His world is the world of the "Everlasting No" of Carlyle's *Sartor*: "To me the Universe was all void of Life, of Purpose, of Volition, even of Hostility: it was one huge, dead, immeasurable Steam-engine, rolling on, in its dead indifference, to grind me limb from limb."[8]

But afterwards came Carlyle's Everlasting Yea: "It is from this hour that I incline to date my Spiritual New-birth, or Baphometric Fire-baptism; perhaps I directly thereupon became a Man."[9] Carlyle says elsewhere: "Manhood begins when we have in any way made truce with Necessity; begins even when we have surrendered to Necessity, as the most part only do; but begins joyfully and hopefully only when we have reconciled ourselves to Necessity; and thus, in reality, triumphed over it, and felt that in Necessity we are free."[10] "The gate of the cavern," says Russell, "is despair, and its floor is paved with the gravestones of abandoned hopes. There Self must die; there the eagerness, the greed of untamed desire must be slain, for only so can the soul be freed from the empire of Fate. But out of the cavern the Gate of Renunciation leads again to the daylight of wisdom, by whose radiance a new insight, a new joy, a new tenderness, shine forth to gladden the pilgrim's heart."[11]

The Consolation — the Consolation, as Nietzsche says, comes after. He has admirably described the transition:

> The complete irresponsibility of man for his actions and his nature is the bitterest drop which he who understands must swallow if he was accustomed to see the patent of nobility of his humanity in responsibility and

duty. All his valuations, distinctions, disinclinations, are thereby deprived of value and become false,—his deepest feeling for the sufferer and the hero was based on an error; he may no longer either praise or blame, for it is absurd to praise and blame nature and necessity. In the same way as he loves a fine work of art, but does not praise it, because it can do nothing for itself; in the same way as he regards plants, so must he regard his own actions and those of mankind. He can admire strength, beauty, abundance, in themselves; but must find no merit therein,—the chemical progress and the strife of the elements, the torments of the sick person who thirsts after recovery, are all equally as little merits as those struggles of the soul and states of distress in which we are torn hither and thither by different impulses until we finally decide for the strongest—as we say (but in reality it is the strongest motive which decides for us).... To recognize all this may be deeply painful, but consolation comes after: such pains are the pangs of birth. The butterfly wants to break through its chrysalis: it rends and tears it, and is then blinded and confused by the unaccustomed light, the kingdom of liberty.[12]

Hegel, in his *Logic*, also speaks of Consolation:

Necessity gives a point of view which is very important in its bearings upon our sentiments and conduct. When we look upon events as necessary, we seem at first sight to stand in a thoroughly slavish and dependent position. In the creed of the ancients, as we know, necessity figured as Destiny. The modern point of view, on the contrary, is that of Consolation. And Consolation means that we give up our aims and interests, only in prospect of being compensated for our renunciation.[13]

Schopenhauer, too, revered the Consolation:

... there is for us no consolation so effective as the complete certainty of unalterable necessity. No evil that befalls us pains us so much as the thought of the circumstances by which it might have been warded off. Therefore nothing comforts us so effectually as the consideration of what has happened from the standpoint of necessity, from which all accidents appear as tools in the hand of an overruling fate, and we therefore recognize the evil that has come to us as inevitably produced by the conflict of inner and outer circumstances; in other words, fatalism.[14]

Albert Einstein, revering Schopenhauer, also found consolation:

I do not at all believe in human freedom in the philosophical sense. Everybody acts not only under external compulsion but also in accordance with inner necessity. Schopenhauer's saying, "A man can do what he wants, but not want what he wants," has been a continual consolation in the face of life's hardships, my own and others', and an unfailing well-spring of tolerance. This realization mercifully mitigates the easily paralyzing sense of responsibility and prevents us from taking ourselves and other people all too seriously; it is conducive to a view of life which, in particular, gives humor its due.[15]

There were among the ancients those who, like Nietzsche, Hegel, Schopenhauer, and Einstein, found consolation in necessity. Epictetus, for instance, whom Whitman honored as one of "the great teachers" (see Ch. IV), calmly tells us: "This is the way that leads to freedom, this the only deliverance from slavery, to be able at length to say from the bottom of one's soul,

> 'Conduct me, Jove, and thou, O Destiny,
> Wherever your decrees have fixed my lot.'"[16]

The crux of the conversion is this: to the mind which had before seen necessity as something entirely external comes the realization that necessity is not wholly extrinsic, that it is also intrinsic. Consoled by this realization, Emerson could ask: "Why should we fear to be crushed by savage elements, we who are made up of the same elements?" Once the determinist recognizes the determinism within himself, he is conscious that he is free. This is implicit in the following remark by Hegel:

> Necessity…, in the ordinary acceptation of the term in popular philosophy, means determination from without only; as in finite mechanics, a body moves in the direction communicated to it by the impact. This however is a merely external necessity, not the real inward necessity which is identical with freedom.[17]

Walt Whitman considered Hegel "the choicest loved physician of my mind and soul" (see Ch. IV). It will be noticed that Hegel uses the word "inward." He thus indicates the importance of avoiding the opinion that man is *subject to* determinism in the sense that determinism is something external, something by which we must suffer ourselves to be compelled. Once the determinist learns to look not outward but inward, he realizes his freedom. As Hegel says,

> Necessity is often called hard, and rightly so, if we look only to necessity as such, *i.e.* to its immediate shape…. But, as we have seen already, the process of necessity is of such a nature that it overcomes the rigid externality which it first had and reveals its inward self…. In this way necessity is transfigured into freedom,—not the freedom that consists in abstract negation, but freedom concrete and positive. From which we may learn what a mistake it is to regard freedom and necessity as mutually excluding one another. Necessity indeed qua necessity is far from being freedom: yet freedom pre-supposes necessity, and contains it as an unsubstantial element in itself…. In short, man is most independent when he knows himself to be determined by the absolute idea throughout. It was the consciousness of this, and this attitude of mind, which Spinoza called the Amor intellectualis Dei.[18]

"The iron chain of cause and effect sounds heavily outside in nature," says Tagore, "but in the human heart its unalloyed delight seems to sound, as it were,

> like the golden strings of a harp. It indeed seems to be wonderful that nature has these two aspects at one and the same time, and so antithetical — one being of thralldom and the other of freedom. In the same form, sound, colour, and taste two contrary notes are heard, one of necessity and the other of joy. Outwardly nature is busy and restless, inwardly she is all silence and peace. She has toil on one side and leisure on the other. You see her bondage only when you see her from without, but within her heart is a limitless beauty.[19]

Significantly, Tagore here uses "inwardly." Hegel used "inward." Emerson also used "inward":

> The revelation of Thought takes man out of servitude into freedom. We rightly say of ourselves, we were born, and afterward we were born again…. The day of days, the great day of the feast of life, is that in which the inward [sic] eye opens to the Unity in things, to the omnipresence of law, — sees that what is must be, and ought to be, or is the best. This beatitude dips from on high down on us, and we see. It is not in us so much as we are in it. If the air come to our lungs, we breathe and live; if not, we die. If the light come to our eyes, we see; else not. And if truth come to our mind, we suddenly expand to its dimensions, as if we grew to worlds. We are as law-givers; we speak for Nature; we prophesy and divine.
>   …'Tis the majesty into which we have suddenly mounted, the impersonality, the scorn of egotisms, the sphere of laws, that engage us. Once we were stepping a little this way, and a little that way; now, we are as men in a balloon, and do not think so much of the point we have left, or the point we would make, as of the liberty and glory of the way.[20]

The following lines from the magnificent "Song of the Open Road" seem to have been inspired by a similar conversion:

> From this hour I ordain myself loos'd of limits and imaginary lines,
> Going where I list, my own master total and absolute,
> Listening to others, considering well what they say,
> Pausing, searching, receiving, contemplating,
> Gently, but with undeniable will, divesting myself of the holds that
>   would hold me.

Like one of Emerson's "men in a balloon," Whitman casts off "imaginary lines" — "divesting myself of the holds that would hold me." He proclaims himself "my own master total and absolute." But is he here rejecting determinism? No more than Hegel, who found that "man is most independent when he knows himself to be determined by the absolute idea throughout."

Nor Sri Ramakrishna, who taught that "a man is verily liberated in life" if he "truly believes that God alone does everything." This will be made clear at the end of Chapter V. Whitman's "from this hour" duplicates Carlyle's "from this hour" in his confession of his "Spiritual New-birth."

In the writings of the determinists there are certain passages which, in their fervor, convey an idea of the religious feeling which determinism can inspire in those who sincerely adopt it as a philosophy of life. Here are examples from Priestley, Emerson, Shelley, and Spinoza.

No greater champion of determinism ever lived than Joseph Priestley. "If I were," he says, "to take my choice of any metaphysical question to defend against all oppugners, it should be the doctrine of Philosophical Necessity. There is no truth of which I have less doubt, and of the ground of which I am more fully satisfied. Indeed, there is no absurdity more glaring to my understanding than the notion of Philosophical Liberty."[21] Priestley's philosophical works are probably rarely read now, but the serious student of determinism would be impressed by the almost mystical atmosphere of Priestley's discourses upon that subject. Here are a few excerpts:

> ...I embraced he doctrine of necessity from the time that I first studied the subject; I have been a firm believer of it ever since, without having ever entertained the least suspicion of there being any fallacy belonging to it; I meditate frequently upon it, and yet every consideration of it, and every view of things suggested by it, appears to me to give an elevation to the sentiments, the most exalted conceptions of the great Author of nature, and of the excellence and perfection of his works and designs, the greatest purity and fervour to our virtue, the most unbounded benevolence to our fellow-creatures, the most ardent zeal to serve them, and the most unreserved and joyful confidence in Divine Providence, with respect to all things past, present, and to come.
>
> In short, I have no conception that the man whose mind is capable of entertaining, and duly contemplating what is called the doctrine of necessity, and its genuine consequences, as unfolded by Dr. Hartley, can be a bad man; nay that he can be other than an extraordinary good one.[22]

> It is, alas! only in occasional seasons of retirement from the world in the happy hours of devout contemplation, that, I believe, the most perfect of our race can fully indulge the enlarged views, and lay himself open to the genuine feelings, of the Necessarian principles; that is, that he can *see every thing in God*, or in its relation to him. Habitually, and constantly, to realize these views, would be always to *live in the house of God*, and within the *gate of heaven*; seeing the plain finger of God in all events, and as if the angels of God were constantly descending to earth, and ascending to heaven before our eyes.[23]
> And when our will and our wishes shall thus perfectly coincide with those

of the Sovereign Disposer of all things, *whose will is always done, in earth, as well as in heaven*, we shall, in fact, attain the summit of perfection and happiness. We shall have a kind of *union with God* himself; his will shall be our will, and even his power our power; being ever employed to execute our wishes and purposes, as well as his: because they will be, in all respects, the same with his.

These heart-reviving and soul-ennobling views we cannot, in this imperfect state, expect to realize and enjoy, except at intervals; but let us make it our business to make these happy seasons of philosophical and devout contemplation more frequent, and of longer continuance. Let them encroach more and more on the time that we must give to the bustle of a transitory world; till our minds shall have received such a lasting impression, as that its effect may be felt even in the midst of the greatest tumult of life, and inspire a serenity and joy, which *the world can neither give nor take away*.[24]

These passages may be a solid source for Whitman's famous Section 5 of "Song of Myself." Priestley's "soul-ennobling views" may have inspired the peculiar activities of Whitman's "soul":

> I believe in you my soul, the other I am must not abase itself to you,
> And you must not be abased to the other.
>
> Loafe with me on the grass, loose the stop from your throat,
> Not words, not music or rhyme I want, not custom or lecture, not even the best,
> Only the lull I like, the hum of your valved voice.
>
> I mind how once we lay such a transparent summer morning,
> How you settled your head athwart my hips and gently turn'd over upon me,
> And parted the shirt from my bosom-bone, and plunged your tongue to my bare-stript heart,
> And reach'd till you felt my beard, and reach'd till you held my feet.
>
> Swiftly arose and spread around me the peace and knowledge that pass all the argument of the earth,
> And I know that the hand of God is the promise of my own,
> And I know that the spirit of God is the brother of my own,
> And that all the men ever born are also my brothers, and the women my sisters and lovers,
> And that a kelson of the creation is love,
> And limitless are leaves stiff or drooping in the fields,
> And brown ants in the little wells beneath them,
> And mossy scabs of the worm fence, heap'd stones, elder, mullein and poke-weed.

Whitman sees "the hand of God" as "the promise of my own." Priestley saw the "finger of God in all events," that "his will shall be our will, and even his power our power."

Whitman's "peace and knowledge that pass all the argument of the earth" recalls Priestley's "serenity and joy, which *the world can neither give nor take away*." (Notice the possible interplay of "earth" and "world" in those two statements.) Priestley's "kind of *union with God*" aptly describes Sec. 5, which many have interpreted as describing a mystical event in Whitman's life. Whitman's "summer morning" is perhaps one of Priestley's "occasional seasons of retirement from the world," when one "can indulge the enlarged views." Whitman's line "I mind how once we lay," etc., may bear a figurative kinship to Priestley's "lay himself open to the genuine feelings, of the Necessarian principles." Priestley's "lay himself open" is suggestive of the activity in Sec. 5 of the "soul" which "...parted the shirt from my bosom-bone, and plunged [its] tongue to my bare-stript heart" (echo: "lay ... open"/ "parted ...bare-stript"). It does seem that Whitman was "lay[ing] himself open" to receive the "enlarged views" mentioned by Priestley. His vision convinced him that "all the men ever born are also my brothers, and the women my sisters and lovers,/ And that a kelson of the creation is love." So he shares Priestley's "most unbounded benevolence to our fellow-creatures."

In 1857, just two years after his Section 5 was published, Whitman wrote a note about Priestley in which he referred to and defined Priestley's "great tenet" of "philosophical necessity" (see Ch. IV). That definition of determinism by Whitman will be prominently featured in several places in this book, for it goes far toward bringing out some of Whitman's deepest meanings.

(For an alternate source for Sec. 5 — from another determinist — see Ch. IV. There I shall suggest a source for the last three lines of Sec. 5.)

Priestley's exalted sentiments find an echo in the concluding paragraphs of Emerson's essay "Fate":

> Let us build altars to the Beautiful Necessity. If we thought men were free in the sense that in a single exception one fantastical will could prevail over the law of things, it were all one as if a child's hand could pull down the sun. If, in the least particular, one could derange the order of nature,— who would accept the gift of life?
>
> Let us build altars to the Beautiful Necessity, which secures that all is made of one piece; that plaintiff and defendant, friend and enemy, animal and planet, food and eater, are of one kind. In astronomy is vast space, but no foreign system; in geology, vast time, but the same laws as to-day. Why should we be afraid of nature, which is no other than "philosophy and theology embodied"? Why should we fear to be crushed by savage elements, we who are made up of the same elements? Let us build to the Beautiful Neces-

sity, which makes man brave in believing that he cannot shun a danger that is appointed, nor incur one that is not; to the Necessity which rudely or softly educates him to the perception that there are no contingencies; that Law rules throughout existence,—not personal nor impersonal,—it disdains words and passes understanding; it dissolves persons; it vivifies nature; yet solicits the pure in heart to draw on all its omnipotence.[25]

For Emerson "it disdains words and passes understanding." Whitman gained "the peace and knowledge that pass all the argument of the earth" (Sec. 5). Priestley found "a serenity and joy which *the world can neither give nor take away.*" The statements of Emerson and Priestley, we know from their contexts, are about the revelations of Necessity (determinism). Can Whitman's line be about anything else?

Contemplation of the determinist sequence of events can lead at last, through philosophy, to religion — to a reverence for an unknowable reality that evolves before us and within us. "We live and move and think," wrote Shelley with his beautiful vehemence,

> but we are not the creators of our own origin and existence. We are not the arbiters of every motion of our own complicated nature; we are not the masters of our own imaginations and moods of mental being. There is a Power by which we are surrounded, like the atmosphere in which some motionless lyre is suspended, which visits with its breath our silent chords at will. Our most imperial and stupendous qualities — those of which the majesty and the power of humanity is erected — are, relatively to the inferior portion of its mechanism, active and imperial; but [even] they are the passive slaves of some higher and more omnipotent Power. This Power is God; and those who have seen God, have in the period of their purer and more perfect nature, been harmonized by their own will to so exquisite consentaneity of power as to give forth divinest melody, when the breath of universal being sweeps over their frame.[26]

For Spinoza determinism was a religion; and his worship was so profound that he has been called a mystic. The following passage is from his *Ethics*:

> It remains for me now to show what service to our own lives a knowledge of this doctrine is. This we shall easily understand from the remarks which follow. Notice —
> 1. It is of service in so far as it teaches us that we do everything by the will of God alone [Whitman, Sec. 5: "the hand of God is the promise of my own"], and that we are partakers of the divine nature in proportion as our actions become more and more perfect and we more and more understand God. This doctrine [determinism], therefore, besides giving repose in every way to the soul, has also this advantage, that it teaches us in what our high-

est happiness or blessedness consists, namely, in the knowledge of God alone, by which we are drawn to do those things only which love and piety persuade. Hence we clearly see how greatly those stray from the true estimation of virtue who expect to be distinguished by God with the highest rewards for virtue and the noblest actions as if for the completest servitude, just as if virtue itself and the service of God were not happiness itself and the highest liberty.

2. It [determinism] is of service to us in so far as it teaches us how we ought to behave with regard to the things of fortune, or those which are not in our power, that is to say, which do not follow from our own nature; for it teaches us with equal mind to wait for and bear each form of fortune, because we know that all things follow from the eternal decree of God, *according to the same necessity by which it follows from the essence of a triangle that its three angles are equal to two right angles* [italics mine].

3. This doctrine contributes to the welfare of our social existence, since it teaches us to hate no one, to despise no one, to mock no one, to be angry with no one, and to envy no one. It teaches every one, moreover, to be content with his own, and to be helpful to his neighbor, not from any womanish pity, from partiality, or superstition, but by the guidance of reason alone, according to the demand of time and circumstance, as I shall show.

4. This doctrine [determinism] contributes not a little to the advantage of common society, in so far as it teaches us by what means citizens are to be governed and led; not in order that they may be slaves, but that they may freely do those things which are best.[27]

Will Durant, interpreting Spinoza's philosophy, comments as follows:

Above all, determinism fortifies us to expect and to bear both faces of fortune with an equal mind; we remember that all things follow by the eternal decrees of God. Perhaps even it will teach us the "intellectual love of God," whereby we shall accept the laws of nature gladly, and find our fulfillment within her limitations. He who sees all things as determined cannot complain, though he may resist; for he "perceives things under a certain species of eternity," and he understands that his mischances are not chances in the total scheme; that they find some justification in the eternal sequence and structure of the world. So minded, he rises from the fitful pleasures of passion to the high serenity of contemplation which sees all things as parts of an eternal order and development; he learns to smile in the face of the inevitable, and *"whether he comes into his own now, or in a thousand years, he sits content"* [my italics]. He learns the old lesson that God is no capricious personality absorbed in the private affairs of his devotees, but the invariable sustaining order of the universe....

Such a philosophy teaches us to say Yea to life, and even to death — "a free man thinks of nothing less than death; and his wisdom is a meditation not on death but on life." It calms our fretted egos with its large perspective; it reconciles us to the limitations within which our purposes must be circumscribed. It may lead to resignation and an Orientally supine passivity; but it is also the indispensable basis of all wisdom and all strength.[28]

"…whether he comes into his own now, or in a thousand years, he sits content"—is it really so odd that in explaining Spinoza's determinism Durant thus paraphrases lines from Section 20 of "Song of Myself"? Along with those lines are others equally determinist in tenor:

> I know I am august,
> I do not trouble my spirit to vindicate itself or be understood,
> I see that the elementary laws never apologize,
> (I reckon I behave no prouder than the level I plant my house by, after all.)
>
> I exist as I am, that is enough,
> If no other in the world be aware I sit content,
> And if each and all be aware I sit content.
>
> One world is aware and by far the largest to me, and that is myself.
> And whether I come to my own to-day or in ten thousand or ten million years,
> I can cheerfully take it now, or with equal cheerfulness I can wait.
>
> My foothold is tenon'd and mortis'd in granite,
> I laugh at what you call dissolution,
> And I know the amplitude of time.

"I reckon I behave no prouder than the level I plant my house by, after all." But in these lines there is no trace of that despair which may be expected to accompany the conviction that our behavior is no whit less a manifestation of the irresistible world force than is the behavior of inanimate matter. "(I reckon I behave no prouder than the level I plant my house by, after all.)" We can almost see Whitman studying the level. He did build houses. The philosophic lesson which he drew from the movement of the bubble would cause modern indeterminists to shrink and shudder. But not Whitman. He felt no revulsion at the concept. His mood was one of tranquility and consolation. There is something in his tone which indicates a peaceful resignation. Whitman had come to terms with determinism. He had known "the sea of torment, doubt, despair and unbelief."[29]

Evidently he had experienced a conversion.

◆ ◆ ◆

T. R. Rajasekharaiah, in his commendable search for *The Roots of Whitman's Grass*, states:

Almost every critic, finding himself called upon to answer the riddle of Whitman's transformation from a "worse than mediocre" writer into the titanic genius of *Leaves of Grass*, has, as the first principle on which to understand his poetry, attempted to discover an event in his life that brought about the "miracle."[30]

Steven A. Black states: "Biographies and interpretations of the poems, psychological or otherwise, leave unanswered two questions that have intrigued readers from the beginning: how can someone who seems as ordinary as Whitman become a great poet? And, how can one account for the magnetism that captivated numerous people, many of them far from credulous?"[31] David S. Reynolds feels that "Something happened to Whitman privately that lay behind his poetic flowering."[32] But the transformation, Reynolds thinks, was more gradual than generally conceived. Floyd Stovall agrees: "There was change, to be sure, but no such revolutionary change as to be called a new birth, and no illumination that cannot be accounted for by a normal, if unusual, intellectual and spiritual growth."[33]

But I believe that there *was* a "new birth": a sudden enlightenment which gave the world, eventually, a new Whitman. That enlightenment solved for Whitman the problem of freedom, as it has for many determinists. The answer came to him and triggered a profound change. Notice that I say the answer "came to him." It was not an achievement of logic but a spontaneous event, an event Whitman alluded to in one of his prose notes:

> One having attained those insights and contents which the universe gives to men capable of comprehending it, would publish the same and persuade other men and women to the same. The conditions are simple, spiritual, physical, close at hand ... they are long and arduous and require faith, they exist altogether with the taught and not with the teaching or teacher.[34]

Note here the similarity of Whitman's phrasing: "capable of comprehending it," to Priestley's: "capable of entertaining ...the doctrine of necessity." This is a clue that Whitman, like Priestley, was stressing the difficulty of coming to terms with determinism.

The attainment of the enlightenment is *passive* and in that sense not an attainment at all: the *universe* "gives" the insights. Necessity, by its own nature and function, makes its nature and function known to the receiver. As Hegel says, "the process of necessity ... reveals its inward self." "The conditions," says Whitman, are "long and arduous." Nietzsche tells us, "To recognize all this may be deeply painful," and he continues in beautiful language:

> but consolation comes after; such pains are the pangs of birth. The butterfly wants to break through its chrysalis: it rends and tears it, and is then blinded and confused by the unaccustomed light, the kingdom of liberty.

The "novitiate," according to Whitman, is "long and exhausting."[35] And "novitiate" would be the right word, for the experience is like that so often described as preceding religious conversions. One awakens from a "dark night of the soul." Emerson, in "Fate," described the epiphany:

> We rightly say of ourselves, we were born, and afterward we were born again.... This beatitude dips from on high down on us, and we see.... And if truth come to our mind, we suddenly [sic] expand to its dimensions, as if we grew to worlds.[36]

Carlyle called it "my Spiritual New-birth."[37] Schopenhauer explained the transition as an involuntary "entrance into freedom," — the philosophical equivalent of what he called a religious "new birth":

> ...the old philosophical doctrine of the freedom of the will, which has constantly been contested and constantly maintained, is not without ground, and the dogma of the Church of the work of grace and the new birth is not without meaning and significance. But we now unexpectedly see both [philosophical and religious] united in one.... For precisely what the Christian mystics call the *work of grace* and *the new birth*, is for us the single direct expression of *the freedom of the will.*
>
> ...that entrance into freedom ... proceeds from the inmost relation of knowing and volition in the man, and therefore comes suddenly [sic], as if spontaneously from without. This is why the Church has called it the work of grace.... And because, in consequence of such a work of grace, the whole nature of man is changed and reversed from its foundation, so that he no longer wills so intensely anything of what he previously willed, so that it is as if a new man actually took the place of the old, the Church [therefore] has called this consequence of the work of grace the new birth.[38]

It was such a philosophical-religious conversion that brought about the undeniably remarkable change in Whitman (the "quantum surge," as one biographer has called it[39]), that made him into the "titanic genius of *Leaves of Grass.*"

IV

Inspirations

Having studied the new and antique, the
Greek and Germanic systems,
Kant having studied and stated, Fichte
and Schelling and Hegel.
— "The Base of All Metaphysics."

1—Whitman and the Stoics

"This is the way," says Epictetus, "that leads to freedom, this the only deliverance from slavery, to be able at length to say from the bottom of one's soul,

'Conduct me, Jove, and thou, O Destiny,
Wherever your decrees have fixed my lot.'"[1]

In June, 1888, when he was recuperating from an almost fatal paralytic stroke, Whitman asked Mrs. Davis, his housekeeper, to bring him his "Epictetus,"[2] a volume which he prized probably above all the others in his possession. During his infirmity Whitman often alluded to the teachings of Epictetus and the other Stoics, and it is probable that their determinist views were at that time his greatest consolation. Traubel considered Whitman "philosophically calm" in his attitude toward his illness.[3] Thomas Donaldson says of Whitman, "He had a long and lingering illness, with frightful pain, but it was borne like a stoic.... Mr. Whitman always seemed to me to be at peace with the world.... His practice was to submit cheerfully to the inevitable."[4] In his entry for July 5, 1888, Traubel describes Whitman as "Very calm. Kindly, quiet, serene, undisturbed." And under that date he records the following remarks by Whitman: "I have made up my mind not to worry — not to let even the worst upset me — not to look with dread upon anything. I like to think it over and over and over again with Epictetus — I have often said it to Doctor Bucke and to you, too — 'What is good for thee, O Nature, is good for me!' That is the foundation on which I build — it is the source of my great peace."[5]

Ten months later this philosophy was put to a severe test as Whitman's dear friend O'Connor lingered in an illness sure to end in death. When Traubel had repeated to Whitman something Bucke had said of O'Connor ("It's a damn shame a man so young with such genius should be sitting there waiting to die!"), Whitman said calmly: "I know how natural it is for a fellow to feel that way: that is always the first emotion: it demands to be uttered: but after that, inevitably after that, comes the philosophic thought, the conviction, the vision, that there is after all no mystery in this or any other trouble — that there is always a new or distant good cause to explain it: a cause often in the man himself: if not there, then in the father and mother before him — or perhaps even back in their fathers and mothers: but whatever, always the best reason, the profoundest necessity, the supremest providence." Then, Traubel tells us, Whitman went on to say he could "never forget" Epictetus where he says, "What is good for thee, O Nature, is good for me!" — "it is so subtle, so finally inevitable." Then, after a pause: "But all this has a long tail — a very long tail!"[6]

Whitman classed Epictetus and Marcus Aurelius among "the great teachers,"[7] and he listed Epictetus as one of the authors whom he considered his "daily food."[8] In 1881 T. W. Rolleston sent Whitman his translation of Epictetus' *Enchiridion*. Seven years later Whitman wrote on the flyleaf: "Have had this little volume at hand or *in* my hand often all these years — have read it over and over and over."[9] Traubel, who saw the book, remarks, "His Epictetus has been all underscored with purple pencillings."[10] Numerous passages were "strongly marked and underlined."[11] "I often surprise him reading it," Traubel wrote. "He quotes it often though never literally — always rather in substance. Rolleston sent the book to W. W. writes his name in the more serious books sent him and treasures them, in spite of what he says about books in general."[12] Whitman told Traubel, "This book has become in a sense sacred, precious to me: I have had it about me so long — have lived with it in terms of such familiarity."[13] In one of his entries Traubel relates that Whitman "picked up the invariable Epictetus from a chair" and, remarking on the durability of its binding, suggested the same format for his own *November Boughs*, then in process of being printed. "See, it is made to last: this has stood wear and tear: I have carried it about: used to stick it in my pocket — take it to the privy with me: it was handy." He had "given it to at least twenty persons to read and, wonderful to relate, it came back unharmed!"[14] He gave the book to Traubel to show the printers as a sample but admonished, "Don't leave it with the printers — show it to them — then bring it back: it's a precious book to me — I don't want to even risk losing it."[15] In March, 1889, Whitman asked Traubel: "Do you read Epictetus much? No? Oh! I must give you a copy then: I must have several here: he is one of my old — as also new — enthusiasms."[16]

A few months previously, discussing the Rolleston translation with Traubel, Whitman remarked: "Epictetus is the one of all my old cronies who has lasted to this day without cutting a diminished figure in my perspective. He belongs with the best of the great teachers — is a universe in himself. He sets me free in a flood of light — of life, of vista. Even the preface of that little book is good — Rolleston's little book." Traubel then asked Whitman whether Epictetus had been "a youthful favorite." And Whitman replied, "Yes, quite so — I think even at sixteen. I do not remember when I first read the book. It was far, far back. I first discovered my bookself in the second hand book stores of Brooklyn and New York: I was familiar with them all — searched them through and through. One day or other I found an Epictetus — I know it was at that period: found an Epictetus. It was like being born again."[17]

I have scanned all of Epictetus carefully, including the fragments, and fail to find anywhere the sentence Whitman so fondly attributed to him: "What is good for thee, O Nature, is good for me!" I do find, in one of the translations of Marcus Aurelius' *Meditations,* a passage which states the same tenet in similar words:

> Everything harmonizes with me, which is harmonious to thee, O Universe. Nothing for me is too early nor too late, which is in due time for thee. Everything is fruit to me which thy seasons bring, O Nature....[18]

Traubel, of course, did say of Whitman's *Enchiridion,* "He quotes it often though never literally." There are several passages in Epictetus which come close to Whitman's "quotation." One of these is Epictetus' remark above urging us to say: "Conduct me, Jove, and thou, O Destiny,/ Wherever your decrees have fixed my lot." Some of the other passages are as follows:

> Dare to look up to God and say, "Make use of me for the future as thou wilt. I am of the same mind; I am equal with thee. I refuse nothing which seems good to thee. Lead me whither thou wilt."[19]

> Your business, man, was to prepare yourself for such an use of the appearances of things as nature demands: not to be frustrated of your desires, or incur your aversions; never to be disappointed or unfortunate, but free, unrestrained, uncompelled; conformed to the administration of Jupiter, obedient to that, finding fault with nothing, but able to say from your whole soul the verses which begin, "Conduct me, Jove; and thou, O Destiny."[20]

Now here, we imagine it to be the work of one who studies philosophy to adapt his will to whatever happens; so that none of the things which happen may happen against our inclination, nor those which do not happen be wished for by us.[21]

No matter about specific references; it is clear that Whitman's fond "quotation" aptly summarizes the Stoic philosophy. "The Stoics were determinists; all is in the hands of God, and our task is to accept."[22] This was the philosophy which consoled Whitman in his old age and which had impressed him profoundly in his youth. ("It was like being born again.") This philosophy shaped his character, became a part of him, and helped him write *Leaves of Grass*. It impressed upon his consciousness the concept of a universe in which all that is is the inevitable consequence of what was and each thing and each event fills for its moment its predestined place, human events and thoughts as much as any.

> All things obey, and are subservient to, the world; the earth, the sea, the sun, and other stars, and the plants and animals of the earth. Our body likewise obeys it, in being sick and well, and young and old, and passing through the other changes, whatever that decrees. It is therefore reasonable that what depends on ourselves, that is, our judgment, should not be the only rebel to it. For the world is powerful, and superior, and consults the best for us, by governing us in conjunction with the whole.[23]

Whitman translated this into poetry:

> Air, soil, water, fire — those are words,
> I myself am a word with them — my qualities interpenetrate with theirs....
>
> Embracing man, embracing all, proceed the three hundred and sixty-five resistlessly round the sun....[24]

"Whatever may happen to thee, it was prepared for thee from all eternity; and the implication of causes was from eternity spinning the thread of thy being, and of that which is incident to it."[25] "Has anything happened to thee? Well; out of the universe from the beginning everything which happens has been apportioned and spun out to thee."[26] Convince a man of the truth of this and he may well find himself using, as Whitman did, such phrases as: "always the best reason, the profoundest necessity, the supremest providence."[27]

Whitman's interest in the Stoics was one of the more important factors in the fashioning of his mind. His own words and the other evidence here presented establish this conclusion. What does this mean to our present study? It means that we have discovered one definite source for the determinism which we are looking for in *Leaves of Grass*. It means that we have found one point of orientation for our investigation of Whitman's determinism. Because the Stoic philosophy is "well known" to have been "wholly deterministic."[28] It has been said of the Stoics: "For them the universe is a result of fixed and unchanging law. Everything in it is determined with an absoluteness that permits no break. Even man's will is determined. In the entire universe there is nothing that can happen by chance. From the first beginning to the last end there is an unbroken chain of causes determined by the nature of the universe."[29] And again: "The famous determinism of the Stoics was perhaps the clearest and most emphatic of all their metaphysical tenets...."[30]

Emory Holloway discovered in one of Whitman's notebooks, one containing the dates 1868–1870, the following interesting note:

EPICTETUS

(Description of a Wise Man)

He reproves nobody —
Praises nobody
Blames nobody
Nor ever speaks of himself
If any one praises him, in his own mind he condemns the flatterer
If any one reproves (? Or insults) him he looks with care that it does not irritate him.
All his desires depend on things within his power.
He transfers all his aversions to those things which nature commends us to avoid.
His appetites are always moderate.
He is indifferent whether he be thought foolish or [ignorant] wise.
He observes himself with the nicety of an enemy or spy, and looks on his own wishes as betrayers.

Holloway suggests that this description "is not a translation but a digest, taken from various parts of the writings of Epictetus."[31] Actually, the description is a fairly close restatement of Section XLVIII of the *Enchiridion*, all of the eleven parts being found there, and in the same order as Whitman, in close paraphrase, presents them. Whitman's note does not, therefore represent the summation of a thorough study of the writings, as Holloway seems to suggest, but the note is, in any case, an interesting indication of Whitman's preoccupation with the Stoic tenets.

The note is interesting, too, in that it sets forth some rules of conduct espoused by one of Whitman's great contemporaries, one whom Whitman admired and loved.

2 — *Whitman and Lincoln*

Lincoln's close friend and law partner William H. Herndon gave in various of his letters, later collected, an account of Lincoln's philosophy. Reminiscent of the Whitman note above is the following comment by Herndon on Lincoln: "No man was censured by him or ought to be by others; he was, by his philosophy, full of charity for his fellow-man. No man was to be eulogized for what he did or censured for what he did not do or did do. Hence Lincoln could well exclaim: 'With malice toward none and charity for all.'" In a preceding sentence Herndon gives the key to Lincoln's attitude: "No man was responsible for what he was, thought, or did, because he was a child of conditions."[32] This is the determinist key. It is the key to much that is puzzling in the poetry of Walt Whitman. "Lincoln," said Whitman, "is particularly my man — particularly belongs to me; yes, and by the same token, I am Lincoln's man: I guess I particularly belong to him; we are afloat on the same stream — we are rooted in the same ground."[33] Could it be that Whitman had somehow learned that he and Lincoln shared the philosophy of determinism?

In his 1846 race for the U. S. Congress, Lincoln found it necessary to rebut the charge that he was "an open scoffer at *Christianity.*" In a hand-bill published August 15, 1846, in the *Illinois Gazette* (in Lacon, Ill.) he asserted that he had "never denied the truth of the Scriptures," but he made this confession:

> It is true that in early life I was inclined to believe in what I understand is called the "Doctrine of Necessity"... and I have sometimes (with one, two or three, but never publicly) tried to maintain this opinion in argument — the habit of arguing thus however, I have, entirely left off for more than five years.[34]

Notice that Lincoln said that he had "never publicly" maintained this opinion. Was this to be his only public mention of his interest in Necessity (Determinism)? It would be worth extensive research to determine if Lincoln's statement was reported in the Eastern newspapers, for Whitman at that time, though only 27, was editing his fourth newspaper, the Brooklyn *Daily Eagle,* and would have had a thorough interest in election news. If that search proved fruitful, we would have solid evidence that Whitman could have known about Lincoln's determinism. Other than this possibility, I have no evidence that Whitman was acquainted with Lincoln's private philosophical views.

Lincoln's statement that he was "inclined to believe" in Necessity "in early life" might make one think that he later gave up this belief. But there is abundant evidence, particularly from the letters of Herndon, that Lincoln held firmly to determinism as a philosophy to live by.

> He believed in predestination, foreordination, that all things were fixed, doomed one way or the other, from which there was no appeal. He has often said to me: "What is to be will be and no efforts nor prayers of ours

can change, alter, modify, or reverse the decree." ... Lincoln always, to me
in our private conversations, said that there was no freedom of the will....
This philosophy of Lincoln I have heard him state many, many times in our
philosophical discussions, private office conversations.[35]

Let me stress here the word "private." Lincoln's disbelief in the efficacy of
"prayers" calls to mind Whitman's line, Sec. 20, "Song of Myself": "Why
should I pray? why should I venerate and be ceremonious?"

Further explaining Lincoln's philosophy, Herndon wrote: "Every event
had its cause. The past to him was the cause of the present and the present
including the past will be the cause of the grand future and all are one, links
in the endless chain, stretching from the infinite to the infinite."[36] Compare
Hamlin Garland's surprisingly perceptive statement about Whitman: "He
caught long ago the deepest principle of evolution, of progress, which is, that
the infinite past portends and prefigures the infinite future; that each age is
the child of the past and the parent of the future; that nothing happens, that
everything is caused; and that no age could conceivably have been other than
it was."[37]

Lincoln sometimes called himself a fatalist, but according to Herndon
it would be a mistake to call him that, for "his fatalism was not of the extreme
order like the Mahometan idea of fate, because he believed firmly in the power
of human effort to modify the environments which surround us. He made
efforts at all times to modify and change public opinion and to climb to the
Presidential heights; he toiled and struggled in this line as scarcely any man
ever did...."[38] It has been made quite clear elsewhere in this book that fatalism and determinism are not the same and that determinism in an important
sense does not negate freedom.

In a letter to Truman H. Bartlett, on July 27, 1887, Herndon wrote:
"You ask me if I know Walt Whitman. I do by reputation, have read his
Leaves of Grass, etc. He is a poet truly and indeed. I know Whittier and other
of your poets by reputations. I like the heart and sympathy of Whittier and
the bold originality of Whitman."[39]

The following story, which has been questioned, would support evidence
that Lincoln approved of Whitman's poems.

H. B. Rankin, a young law clerk in Lincoln's office, tells of a heated discussion of *Leaves of Grass* by Rankin, Herndon, and four others present in
the office. He relates that Lincoln, whom they had supposed not to be listening, arose and took up the book and examined it.

That was the first time he had seen Whitman's "Leaves of Grass," although
its publication had already created a furore of discussion, and in some quar-
ters a violence of disapprobation which it is difficult for the reader of this
day to comprehend. Lincoln read and turned the pages leisurely. Evidently

he was enjoying them. After some time he did an unusual thing. He began to read aloud without having made any comment before doing so. He continued from poem to poem with growing relish.... The emphasis he gave to certain passages in "Leaves of Grass" interpreted many meanings and beauties in the text which the rest of us had not discovered.[40]

This good story has been discredited.

There can be no doubt that Lincoln's broad democracy was a result of his determinism. Determinism had a strong influence on Whitman's democratic attitude (see Ch. VI, Sec. 2, below). Whitman believed that "Even the humblest person is entitled to be ... judged in connection with the environment to which he has had to conform."[41] Similarly, Lincoln believed that "men are made by the conditions that surround them."[42] "Each of us inevitable," says Whitman,

> Each of us here as divinely as any is here.
>
> . . . .
>
> I have look'd for equals and lovers and found them ready for me in all lands,
> I think some divine rapport has equalized me with them.[43]

Whitman explained to Traubel: "But in my philosophy [sic] — in the bottom-meanings of Leaves of Grass — there is plenty of room for all. And I, for my part, not only include anarchists, socialists, whatnot, but Queens, aristocrats." At another time, he said, "...I include emperors, lords, kingdoms, as well as presidents, workmen, republics."[44] In "Song of the Answerer" Whitman describes the ideal poet:

> He says indifferently and alike *How are you friend?* to the President at his levee,
> And he says *Good-day my brother,* to Cudge that hoes in the sugar-field,
> And both understand him and know that his speech is right.

For Whitman and for Lincoln *determinism* was the "divine rapport," the great equalizer.

In his poem "I Sit and Look Out," Whitman lays before us a horrific list of sins and evils. He ends the poem with lines which some critics believe are a reflection of utter despondency:

> All these — all the meanness and agony without end I sitting look out upon,
> See, hear, and am silent.

Go to Chapter VI and be convinced that critics have misinterpreted this poem because they do not see its determinism. To understand the poem, listen to Herndon's description of Abraham Lincoln's determinism:

> Everything, everywhere, is doomed for all time. If a man was good or bad, small or great, and if virtue or vice prevailed, it was so doomed. If bloody war, deathly famine, and cruel pestilence stalked over the land, it was to be and *had come*, and to mourn for this, to regret it, to resist it, would only be flying in the face of the inevitable.[45]

Now read Whitman's poem again.

It would not be stating the case too strongly to say that much in the indisputable greatness of both Whitman and Lincoln depended upon the illumination provided them by the philosophy of determinism. William E. Barton thinks that "each of these men had that adult enlightenment, that time of self-discovery, which has characterized most of the founders of religions and the men who have established notable institutions."[46] There is a question in the minds of the critics as to what brought about Whitman's seemingly sudden transformation into a great writer. Whatever happened to him, Barton believes it happened also to Lincoln: "It came to Whitman after many failures and partial successes; it came to Lincoln and changed him, a man of integrity and ability, from a politician to a statesman."[47] Lincoln had become a determinist, and determinism lifted him to his magnificent heights and assisted him in his majestic accomplishments. See Whitman's statement below: "...only that individual becomes truly great who understands well that, while complete in himself in a certain sense, he is but a part of the divine, eternal scheme...."

3—Whitman and Priestley

My professors at Louisiana State University remembered me, I am sure, as an overzealous young man who would go to great lengths to substantiate a theory. In my research I came across a reference to a note which Whitman had written about Joseph Priestley. The reference gave no clues as to what the note contained, but merely mentioned a note, dated 1857, concerning a conversation about Joseph Priestley. The reference, in the catalogue of the Trent Collection,[48] included the datum that that the note had been published in Whitman's *Complete Writings*; but our library did not contain these volumes. Feeling compelled to see the note, I asked the library to secure the volume through interlibrary loan. I must stress that at that point I had no palpable evidence of what the note might contain, but the outcome of this episode confirmed my faith in intuition. Of course, I knew that Whitman was a determinist. I knew also that Priestley was a determinist. So the possibility that the note would have some reference to Priestley's determinism was naturally on my mind. The possibility had such a strong hold upon me that I made a small wager (a nickel) with Professor Arlin Turner, my American Literature teacher, that when the book came we would find that my intuition was valid. He was as astonished as I was, when, a few days later, we read the following:

> Dr. Priestly or Priestley — conversation with Mr. Arnold 7 March '57. Dr. Priestly was quite a thorough man of science (physical science) as well as of morals and mentals. Mr. Arnold says the Dr. first made the definite discovery of oxygen — can this be so? He was a Unitarian — came from England to the United States — settled on a small farm in Northumberland, Pa. — His great tenet seems to be [italics mine] *"philosophical necessity,"* that *all results, physical, moral, spiritual, everything, every kind, rise out of perpetual flows of endless causes* (to state it so for want of more elaboration). Mr. Arnold went to Pittsburgh to preach in a little Unitarian church owned by Mr. Bakewell, a rich person, a follower, admirer, and personal friend of Dr. Priestley. I infer that Dr. P. died somewhere about 1810 — perhaps '20 — I cannot get it exactly. He must have been a *real man.* He was not followed by the American Unitarians. (How these Unitarians and Universalists want to be respectable and orthodox, just as much as any of the old line people!)[49]

I have since seen this note in the original in the Trent Collection at Duke University. It is written in pencil, very neatly, in the best handwriting of Whitman's I have seen. Whitman saved many of his notes and jottings, of course, many of them apparently of little possible future use to him. But that he kept his note on Priestley for the next thirty or so years may indicate a continued interest in Priestley, who was as we have already seen, and as is evident from Whitman's note above, a determinist.

There is other evidence that Whitman for the rest of his life did remain interested in Priestley. In Traubel's entry for March 14, 1889, we find the following:

> 10:30 A.M. W. reading Press. Sitting up of course. He said: "I have been reading the account of the Priestley affair here: they have unveiled a statue or a tablet or something." It was a tablet placed on the First Unitarian Church, across the river. There were speeches by C. C. Everett, of Harvard, Prof. Leidy, and some others. W. said: "I thought the story would give me a good résumé of Priestley's career — some adequate picture in outline: but there is nothing: whether nothing was said, or the reporter missed it if it was said, there's no way of my knowing: all I read here is of the Gas President kind — emphasis on his Unitarianism: as if the world at large cared a damn whether he was or was not a Unitarian." Didn't he think the Unitarian sect an improvement on other Christian sects? "No: I consider the Unitarian as bad as any other sect — as bad as the Methodist." He had always been interested in Priestley from his "earliest youth." "My father was

booked in all those things — took a great caper at all the progressive fellows. Priestley was a man who lived in a time that tried men's souls: the feeling against him in England was very violent. He came to this country — went off into Pennsylvania — out into the State. He was a man of the big kind: a genuine character — to go with Tom Paine, Franklin, I think even Voltaire: a scientist, but more learned than most scientists. This report, dealing altogether in gas-Presidential stuff as I call it, quite knocks me out." Had his father personally known Priestley? "No — no: not personally: but he watched his career devotedly."[50]

In these remarks there is a subtle distinction to be made: Why did Whitman admire Joseph Priestley? Because of his Unitarianism? The Unitarian was "as bad as any other sect." But in spite of his disdain for Priestley's Unitarianism, Whitman admired Priestley greatly. Why? Because he was a *determinist!* He was "a man of the big kind." In the 1857 note he was "a real man." And in that earlier note Whitman showed an interestingly revealing comprehension of Priestley's philosophy:

His great tenet [*sic*] seems to be "philosophical necessity," that all results, physical, moral, spiritual, everything, every kind, rise out of perpetual flows of endless causes (to state it so for want of more elaboration).

Was it an unphilosophic Whitman who wrote this very original and more than creditable definition of determinism? The way in which Whitman adds "to state it so for want of more elaboration" indicates that even at that early date, 1857, he was well versed in determinism. He seems to be saying, "I could go on and on on this subject if I wanted to." Remember that in discussing Epictetus' determinism Whitman ended by saying, "But all this has a long tail — a very long tail!"

On January 31, 1889, six weeks before the conversation about Priestley, Whitman spoke to Traubel of the "free will and necessity asininities," of "how little" they "contained, amounted to." But this did not mean that Whitman was contemptuously dismissing the problem or proclaiming his disinterest in the controversy. For at the same time, he told Traubel the problem of freedom was "a fruitful subject" and asked him, "Is it clear to you? Perfectly clear?" and added, "Freedom under law: there's no fact deeper, more engrossing, than that."[51] He begins his significant paragraph on "Freedom" (see Ch. V) by saying, "It is not only true that most people entirely misunderstand Freedom, but I sometimes think I have not yet met one person who rightly understands it. The whole Universe is absolute Law. Freedom only opens entire activity and license *under the law*. To the degraded or undevelopt — and even to too many others — the thought of freedom is a thought of escaping from law — which, of course, is impossible." These words were published, inconspicuously, in *Specimen Days and Collect*, 1881–83, a quarter of a century after Whitman wrote his note on Priestley in 1857.

There would have been, in the nineteenth century, many opportunities for a prospective poet to become engrossed in the study of determinism. In that century determinism began to mean more than merely the one side of a metaphysical dispute. With the increased emphasis on a knowledge of scientific law as the solution to the difficulties of mankind, determinism descended into the realm of the practical. And if determinism was, as Miss Stebbing has called it, "the nineteenth century nightmare,"[52] it was also a part of the nineteenth century dream of progress. The world, especially the scientific world, was ready to agree with Charles Bray that we have "only to seek and apply the proper cause, and the effect desired will inevitably follow."[53] The middle and latter part of the century was, indeed, the golden age of determinism. And Whitman, emancipated as he was from traditional sentimentalism, might even have taken determinism for granted, as the Greek poets did their gods. It is more probable, however, that at some time, certainly before he wrote his 1857 note on Priestley, he gave determinism intensive study. At the end of Section 5 below I present parallels which, to me, are convincing evidence that Whitman, early in 1842, had read attentively Charles Bray's *Philosophy of Necessity*, which had just been published in the fall of 1841. But his interest in determinism could have begun much earlier — as early as 1836, when, as a young man of seventeen or so, he attended the lectures of Frances Wright in New York.

4—Whitman and Frances Wright

Whitman's liberal turn of mind came in large part from his father, who, from the little we know about him, may be presumed to have been an independent thinker with philosophic predispositions. Whitman tells us that his father "was booked in all those things — took a great caper at all the progressive fellows" and "watched [Priestley's] career devotedly." Walt, doubtless on this very account, "had always been interested in Priestley from his 'earliest youth.'"[54] While this one interest would have been enough to draw Whitman's attention to determinism, which probably permeated Priestley's thought, Whitman became interested, probably also through his father, in at least one other individual who may have inspired in him a wholehearted respect for the tenets of determinism.

Walt's father, as Whitman himself tells us, was a subscriber to Frances Wright's *Free Inquirer*, a reform periodical which was, like its humanitarian-feminist sponsor and editor, almost too radical for its day.[55] Whitman, perhaps even as a boy of ten or so, read the *Free Inquirer*. From this reading and from his acquaintance with Frances Wright through her speeches in "the anti-slavery halls, in New York,"[56] he developed a profound admiration for Frances Wright, an admiration which was to remain with him for a lifetime. He may even have heard her speak when he was about ten years old, during her first tour: 1828–30. He would have been seventeen in 1836, when her second tour began. In 1888 he reminisced often about "Fanny," as he liked to call her, and related to Traubel the circumstances of his early acquaintance with her writings and speeches.

> In those days I frequented the anti-slavery halls, in New York — heard many of their speakers — people of all qualities, styles — always interesting, always suggestive. It was there I heard Fanny Wright: the noblest Roman of them all, though not of them, except for a time: a woman of the noblest make-up whose orbit was a great deal larger than theirs — too large to be tolerated for long by them: a most maligned, lied-about character — one of the best in history though also one of the least understood.[57]

Frances Wright was twenty-four years older than Walt Whitman, yet Whitman told Traubel, "I never felt so glowingly towards any other woman."[58] "She was," he said, "one of the few characters to excite in me a wholesale respect and love: she was beautiful in bodily shape and gifts of soul." Traubel adds that Whitman "frequently advised" him to read Frances Wright's book, *A Few Days in Athens.*[59]

Speaking of the book Whitman said, "Her book about Epicurus was daily food to me: I kept it about me for years. It is young, flowery, yet has attributes all its own. I always associated that book with Volney's Ruins, which was another of the books on which I may be said to have been raised."[60] Newton Arvin describes the world of Volney and Frances Wright as a world "in which all events have their adequate causes and their inevitable effects; a world in which no mere accidents, no inexplicable miracles, whimsically interfere with the intelligible movement of phenomena; an inherently orderly world of which the principles of order are accessible to the inquiring reason. It is a world, as Volney said, 'governed by *natural laws*, regular in their operation, unerring in their effects, immutable in their essence.' They hold sway, these natural laws, not only in the sidereal heavens, not only in the behavior of gases, not only in the vegetable and animal kingdoms, but in human experience, in the relations between man and man, as well."[61]

A Few Days in Athens is a curious little book, written by a young lady of nineteen in a flowery and elevated style and serious with the seriousness only found in the attitudes of a youthful mind just awakening to philosophy.[62] It is so intensely serious indeed that one could hardly read it today without feeling a certain tenderness toward its young and feminine author and a certain respect for a mind trying valiantly to free itself from contemporary dogma. It is easy enough to see how the young Whitman may have taken the book to heart. And, judging from his own expression of his admiration for the book and its author, it is easy to see that the book may have had something to do with shaping Whitman's thought.

The book is not, as its author feigns it to be, a "Translation of a Greek Manuscript Discovered in Herculaneum." Purportedly a presentation of the philosophy of Epicurus, it is not entirely that, either. In at least one essential respect Fanny's Epicurus differs from the Epicurus who has come fragmentarily down to us through history. Frances Wright's Epicurus is a necessitarian, a determinist. The real Epicurus was not a determinist. He believed in pure chance. His views in this respect anticipated remarkably those of present-day indeterminists. Epicurus, the real Epicurus, says of the Epicurean,

> He thinks that with us lies the chief power of determining events, some of which happen by necessity and some by chance, and some are within our control, for while necessity cannot be called to account, he sees that chance is inconstant, but that which is in our control is subject to no master, and to it are naturally attached praise and blame. For, indeed, it were better to follow the myths about the gods than to become a slave to the destiny of the natural philosophers: for the former suggests a hope of placating the gods by worship, whereas the latter involves a necessity which knows no placation.[63]

Epicurus was no more a determinist than our modern Eddington or our modern Jeans. He figured out the formula, much as they did, for having one's deterministic cake and eating it too. He introduced the possibility, says P. E. More, of having at one and the same time order and variety, "order from the systematic motion of the atoms, variety from the spontaneous motion of each individual atom." Thus, says More, "Epicurus shuns the impasse of absolute determinism."[64]

The real Epicurus said, "Necessity is an evil, but there is no necessity to live under the control of necessity."[65] So Frances Wright's Epicurus is quite out of character when she has him speak of "necessity — the most simple and evident of moral truths, and the most darkened, tortured, and belabored by moral teachers."[66] The real Epicurus was *himself* one of those who "darkened, tortured, and belabored" this doctrine which Fanny Wright's Epicurus so vehemently favors. Perhaps the young Miss Wright was wise enough to see the irony; perhaps she delighted to fashion her Epicurus over a bit so that he more nearly conformed to her own ideal. "We have seen, in the course of our investigation," her Epicurus tells his followers, "that an analogous course of events, or chain of causes and effects, takes place in morals as in physics — that is to say, in examining those qualities of the matter composing our own bodies, which we call mind, we can only trace a train of occurrences, in like manner as we do in the external world; that our sensations, thoughts and emotions are simply effects following causes, a series of consecutive phenomena, mutually producing and produced."[67] Whitman's reading of this passage certainly must have helped him later when he fashioned his definition of "philosophical necessity" in his note on Priestley: "'philosophical necessity,' that all results, physical, moral, spiritual, everything, every kind, rise out of perpetual flows of endless causes."[68] His reading of this passage must have helped him too when, as follows, he attempted to evaluate the philosophy of Hegel: "He has given the same clue to the fitness of reason and the fitness of things and unending progress to the universe of moral purposes that the sciences in their spheres, as astronomy and geology, have established in the material purposes, and the last and crowning proof of each is the same, that they fit the mind, and the idea of the all, and are necessary to be so in the nature of things."[69] It is not the real Epicurus speaking in Frances Wright's book; it is really William Godwin speaking, the William Godwin who said, "In the life of every human being there is a chain of events, generated in the lapse of ages which preceded his birth, and going on in regular procession through the whole period of his existence, in consequence of which it was impossible for him to act in any instance otherwise than he has acted."[70] In making Epicurus a determinist Frances Wright carried out the precepts, not of Epicurus, but of eighteenth- and nineteenth-century British philosophers like Godwin and Hartley and Priestley and John Stuart Mill and Mill's father, James Mill (whom she knew personally)—and Jeremy Bentham, whose close friendship she cherished and to whom her book is "respectfully and affectionately" dedicated.

Thus we see that this little book, though its references to determinism are few, may have served as an important link between Whitman's thought and the strong and outspoken determinism of the influential British philosophers whom I have named. Or, to change the figure, this book may have been the spark which lighted Whitman's interest in the determinist philosophy.

5—*Whitman and the Phrenologists—and Emerson*

Perhaps the best clue to Whitman's early interest in determinism is the well-known fact of his preoccupation at one time with phrenology. It has never occurred to Whitman's interpreters to investigate the determinist implications of that long ago rejected science, but these implications should be explored, for phrenology was for Whitman at one time in his life, and perhaps for a long time afterwards, a profound fact. He kept his infamous "chart of bumps," made out by Lorenzo Fowler on July 15, 1849, until his death, in 1892.

When one thinks of phrenology, with its "scientific" prediction of conduct and character, the concept of determinism does not seem alien. "Phrenology," says Perry Miller, "raised in a totally new form the spectre of determinism."[71] But it is possible that, notwithstanding its disrepute, phrenology conveyed no slight degree of truth. Its effort to bring mental functions under scientific study was a step toward giving them determinist explanation. The close kinship of phrenology and contemporary determinist ideas may have intensified Whitman's interest in determinism.

Based on science, though mistakenly, rather than on *philosophical* deduction, phrenology did not usually stress determinism explicitly as a philosophy. But determinism seems often to have been tacitly assumed as an allied truth by phrenological theorists. At other times, determinism seems to have been taken implicitly by phrenologists as a practical consequence of their theory. The phrenologists did lay great stress on natural law and on the, to them, obvious assumption that man was under its reign. But only two of them, that I have found, made explicit references to determinism.

One of these was J. G. Spurzheim. Spurzheim was first in the line of descent from the founder of phrenology, F. J. Gall. He was a pupil of Gall, and later he was Gall's colleague and collaborator. It was Spurzheim who coined the word phrenology and whose philosophical presentation of the theory laid the foundation of its great, but brief, popularity. In his *Phrenology, or the Doctrine of the Mental Phenomena* (enthusiastically reviewed by Whitman in 1846 as editor of the Brooklyn *Eagle*) Spurzheim declares his belief in "a certain kind of Necessity":

> The doctrine of necessity has also occupied many minds; it has been admitted by some and denied by others. It is necessary to come to a clear understanding about the meaning of the word. I take it as the principle of causation, or in the sense of the relation between cause and effect. This principle is admitted in the physical and intellectual world; but in the moral operations of the mind it is not sufficiently attended to. Yet there is no moral effect without a moral cause, any more than a physical or intellectual event without an adequate cause. the principle of causation in the moral world is expressed by the connexion between motives and actions. It seems to me surprising, that this connexion should have been theoretically questioned, while every human being is daily dependent upon its truth. ...in reality man is subjected to the law of causation like the rest of nature.[72]

Spurzheim's inclusion here of the "moral" in the determinist scheme is echoed by Whitman in an identical application of "moral" in his note on Priestley in Section 3 of this chapter. In his review of Spurzheim's book Whitman wrote: "This large volume of Harpers, well printed, teaches of course from the fountain head — from the most cautious, skeptical and careful of the Phrenologists, Dr. Spurzheim."[73]

Another phrenologist for whom determinism was more than a tacit assumption was Charles Bray. He was not a "practicing" phrenologist but was an enthusiastic phrenological theorist. Unlike the famous Spurzheim and Combe and Fowler, he made no evangelizing tours and was better known for the ribbons produced in his Coventry textile factory than for his philosophical phrenology or for the book in which he presents it: *The Philosophy of Necessity*.[74] Compared to the others, he deserved a greater fame, for in both thought and literary quality his book excels the other books on phrenology that I have seen. (His philosophy and his close friendship were elemental in the intellectual development of young Mary Ann Evans, who later came to be known as the famous novelist George Eliot.)

The second of the two volumes of Bray's book is not of much consequence to our study. It deals almost exclusively with economics and social science. Approximately the first half of the first volume (pp. 1–157) is on phrenology; the remainder of the first volume (pp. 158–299) is on determinism. In this volume I have found numerous suggestive parallels to *Leaves of Grass*.

In an autobiography published in 1885, forty-four years after the 1841 appearance of *The Philosophy of Necessity*, Bray speaks of the earlier work as having a "phrenological basis."[75] And in the autobiography he makes quite clear his opinion that phrenology and determinism are mutually implicated. Speaking of his acceptance of phrenology, he says, "Thus, in Phrenology, I was introduced not to Free Will, but to the Natural Laws of Mind,— the machinery by which the 'Soul of each and God of All' worked such wonderfully varied but invariable effects."[76] And again, "The doctrine of Philosophical Necessity, that every thing necessarily acts in accordance with the laws of its own nature was by no means a barren truth to me, nor was Phrenology or the cerebral machinery by which this takes place in man."[77]

It may be — indeed it is probable — that Whitman at some time during the 1840's came across Bray's *Philosophy of Necessity* and read it, for during those years he was avidly and personally interested in phrenology and probably read almost everything he could find on the subject. He may well have encountered the book at the "Phrenological Cabinet" of Fowler and Wells, which he describes as "One of the choice places of New York to me.... Here were all the busts, examples, curios and books [*sic*] of that study obtainable. I went there often, and once for myself had a very elaborate and leisurely examination and 'chart of bumps' written out (I have it yet)...."[78] *The Philosophy of Necessity* was published in 1841. In Whitman's writings there are a good many close thought-parallels to Bray's pages on determinism, though nothing that I have discovered established Bray's book as one of Whitman's sources.

Independent belief in phrenology by Whitman and Bray, and a shared belief in determinism, could have given rise to similarities, but the strong kinship of their ideas, *together with* the frequency of fleeting duplications of words and phrases in the writings, is enough to arouse the suspicion that the Bray book was a significant formative force in the development of Whitman's thought.

Compare, for instance, Whitman's questions in "Song of Myself," Sec.

20, "Why should I pray? Why should I venerate and be ceremonious?" with Bray's dictum that "he who looks deeper into the ways of Providence ... knows that the laws of God are not changeable ... and that there is no necessity for us to pray to God that He will alter His laws for us to be happy."[79] "Did you guess the celestial laws are yet to be work'd over and rectified?" Whitman asks.[80] Bray asserts that God "works not by partial laws, but by such as pervade the whole sensitive creation, and cannot be resisted...."[81] Whitman agrees: "The law of the past cannot be eluded...."[82] Echoes: "laws ... cannot be resisted"/ "law ... cannot be eluded." Whitman says, "I see tremendous entrances and exits, new combinations, the solidarity of races...."[83] And Bray also saw "new combinations" (can it be coincidence?!): "generation after generation of men ... are organized, vitalized, and again return to their mother Earth to form new combinations."[84] I bequeath myself to the dirt," says Whitman, "to grow from the grass I love...."[85] Echo: "Earth" / "dirt." Whitman refers to "investigation of the depths of qualities and things"[86]; Bray "looks deeper into the ways of Providence."[87] Echo: "depths"/ "deeper." Bray speaks of a mind able to reject "what is inconsistent with the highest principles of its of its own nature."[88] This echoes Whitman's "never inconsistent with what is clear to the senses and to the soul."[89] Note the *exact* echo: "inconsistent with" / "inconsistent with." All of the Bray quotations here come from the final three pages (297, 298, 299) of Bray's Volume I. Three of the five come from one page (298). This remarkable concentration of parallels lowers the possibility of coincidence.

Beyond these, on the final page, comes the following quotation, which, as I shall show, may have a peculiar significance:

> To the man who can divest his mind of the degrading superstitions of his childhood, and exercise it upon the great plan of Providence, every cause that he may discover, is a new illustration of the goodness of God. To see Him in His works; to know what he does, and wherefore He does it, is to feel for ever in His presence: he who thus seeks the Pervading and Creating Spirit of the universe, sees on every side of him wonders going forward which only a God can perform; each atom obeying the laws of order given it; each plant elaborately and systematically assuming the form peculiarly its own; each animal working out the object of its being, and Sensation — Feeling — the great Soul of the world, periodically changing its garment....[90]

I had read many times these glowing words without realizing that in the heart of them lies a possible source for the famous Section 5 of "Song of Myself." The almost mystical, almost rapturous, vision of this passage is indeed reminiscent of Whitman's Sec. 5, which is invariably interpreted by the critics as mystical. Bray's reference to "the great Soul of the world" recalls Whitman's strange affair with his "soul" in Sec. 5. The concluding stanza reads:

Swiftly arose and spread around me the peace and knowledge that pass all
the argument of the earth,
    And I know that the hand of God is the promise of my own,
    And I know that the spirit of God is the brother of my own,
    And that all the men ever born are also my brothers, and the women my
sisters and lovers,
    And that a kelson of the creation is love,
    And limitless are leaves stiff or drooping in the fields,
    And brown ants in the little wells beneath them,
    And mossy scabs of the worm fence, heap'd stones, elder, mullein and
poke-weed.

I had never been able to see why Whitman included the last three lines, but
now I am inclined to believe that Bray's words give us the answer:

> ... each plant elaborately and systematically assuming the form peculiarly
> its own; each animal working out the object of its being....

The reader may recall that in Chapter III I indicated that the inspiration for
Sec. 5 may have come from Joseph Priestley. The evidence presented there is
more compelling than the evidence presented here. It may be that Sec. 5
shows the combined influence of the passages from Priestley and Bray. The
ending certainly did not come from Priestley, but it may well have come, as
shown here, from Bray. Perhaps in both cases I am merely chasing rainbows —
but I have at least not thrown up my hands and, like most critics, called Sec.
5 an example of Whitman's mysticism. I believe that it is actually a reflection
of determinism, the same determinism championed by both Priestley and
Bray.

    Besides the suggestiveness of parallels, there is *concrete evidence* that Whit-
man could have been influenced by Charles Bray — though in an indirect way.
It is a *fact* that Emerson, whose possible influence on Whitman the critics
will never allow us to forget, did *read* Bray's *Philosophy of Necessity*, and it is
interesting, and no less a fact, that the book so impressed Emerson that on
his visit to England (1847–48) he made a special trip to Coventry to visit its
author, on Tuesday, July 11, 1848.

    Moncure Conway mentions Bray in his autobiography as "the author of
a work on the 'Philosophy of Necessity,' which had much interested Emerson."[91] Bray himself, in his *Phases of Opinion and Experience During a Long
Life*, speaks with fond remembrance of Emerson's visit: "A Coventry gentle-
man meeting Emerson in the north soon after his arrival in England invited
him to visit the old city. Emerson replied that if he came to Coventry it would
be to see Charles Bray, the author of the 'Philosophy of Necessity.' Accordingly he came to Rosehill. There was an exceeding simplicity about him and
an utter absence of pretension, so that you felt at home with him at once.. I
have met no man to whom I got so much attached in so short a time."[92]

"Emerson," says Conway, "remembered well that visit to the Brays at Rose-hill, when he sat with them under the beautiful acacia, and talked with Charles Bray on the 'Philosophy of Necessity,' which had reached him in Concord and spoke to his mind."[93] Years later, in 1871, Emerson wrote in a letter to his son, "...at Coventry, Mr Charles Bray, a silk or a ribbon manufacturer, is a steadfast friend of mine for twenty years, & has just sent me his books...."[94]

A second edition of *The Philosophy of Necessity* was published in 1863. This edition gave more emphasis to the Necessity section by placing it before the section on phrenology. "It had taken twenty years," wrote Bray, "to sell the first edition. But its truths were as new and unacknowledged as when it was first published. It had a small but steady sale, and Longmans said it was *the* book upon the subject, which I took to mean the best book because there was no other; like the boy who was top but one in his class of two."[95] But Bray published other books, and several pamphlets. One of his books appeared in 1866 and another in 1871, and these may have been the ones he sent Emerson in 1871.[96]

Emerson, it would seem, owned a copy of *The Philosophy of Necessity* as early as 1843. On May 9 of that year Emerson's good friend Margaret Fuller wrote him a letter in which she asked, "Can you send me the vol[.] on Philo-sophical Necessity giving an acct[.] of the St[.] Simonians &c[?]"[97] Bray includes in the second volume of his first edition a lengthy appendix written by his sister-in-law Sarah Hennell and devoted exclusively to a description of various Utopian socialistic movements and experiments. An account of "St. Simon and His System" is given on pages 548–64. This evidence indicates that Emerson owned Bray's *Philosophy of Necessity* in 1843. It is certain that he had read the book or at least parts of it, before his 1848 visit to its author.

It is probable, in view of all this, that Emerson was influenced, perhaps greatly influenced, by Bray's presentation of the determinist philosophy. It can-not be doubted that this philosophy, whether it came to him from Bray or from some other source, impressed him profoundly. Emerson's "Fate," deliv-ered as a lecture in 1851 and published as one of the nine essays in *Conduct of Life* in 1860, was the product of thinking which included careful consid-eration and serious contemplation of the same principles set down by Bray. There is no positive evidence in the essay, that I can find, of Bray's influence. It can hardly be denied that the essay is a wholehearted affirmation of Bray's determinism. G. W. Allen, betraying the profound ignorance of determinism characteristic of Whitman's critics, states summarily, "Yet Emerson is not a Determinist" (Ch. I). Bray speaks of laws which "pervade the whole sensitive creation, and cannot be resisted by any supposed freedom of will."[98] Emer-son, in "Fate," urges us to "build altars to the Beautiful Necessity" and says, "If we thought men were free in the sense that in a single exception one fantastical will could prevail over the law of things, it were all one as if a child's hand could pull down the sun."[99] One wonders how Allen would *define* determinism!

Traubel relates in his entry for April 2, 1889, the following conversation with Whitman:

> I had with me, under my arm, Emerson's Conduct of Life [*sic*]. It was a first edition — Ticknor's. He asked: "What have you there?" I showed it to him. He handled it fondly. "I know it well — oh! I know it well! How often I have handled these books! And in the old, old, days, too! The print, paper, simple garb — all fine: none better, none so good, even today!" And then: "The wise and gentle Emerson! Greatest of all the men of his time!"[100]

The philosophical relationships of Bray, Emerson, and Whitman are intriguing. It would be impossible to ascertain the weight of Bray's influence on either Emerson or Whitman, but the question of influence lessens in importance when we consider the convincing evidence that the three men were, influence or no influence, very much akin philosophically. It is of little importance that Whitman did or did not read Bray; it is of great consequence that he would have agreed with him. To be sure, it would be interesting to know that Whitman at some time in the early 1840's, perhaps in 1842, as parallels which I will now reveal would indicate, did become acquainted with this newly published book.

On February 26, 1842, the *Brother Jonathan*, a New York weekly, published a letter by Whitman defending Charles Dickens against an attack by the Washington *Globe*.[101] The phrasing, tone, and thought of Whitman's letter point to the Bray book as a source, with parallels being localized mostly in Bray's pages 203–206 and 271–298.

Whitman's suggestion that the tendency of Dickens' stories is "to make us love our fellow-creatures" echoes Bray's preachment (p. 283) that we should "love our neighbour as ourselves" and miss no "opportunity of making a fellow creature happier." (Echoes: "*love our*" / "*love our*"; "*fellow-creatures*" / "*fellow creature*.") Whitman's "brethren of the Great Family" is perhaps akin to Bray's "great body of society" (p. 271) and his "*great body* of mankind ... the whole human family" (p. 51). (Echo: "*Great Family*" / "*great ... family*.") Whitman speaks of "the tyranny of partial laws ... social distinctions," and Bray (p. 273), of "class interests ... selfish and noxious laws" and (p. 298), of "partial laws." (Echoes: "*social distinctions*" / "*class interests*"; "*partial laws*" / "*partial laws*.") Whitman sees "human beings alike, as links of the same chain," and Bray (p. 271) considers man "a mere link in the chain of causation." (Echo: "*links of the same chain*" / "*link in the chain*." Whitman's "the richer classes" recalls Bray's "the indolent in the lap of luxury" (p. 203). And Whitman's "thousands" who "toil on year after year" translates Bray's "a multitude whose incessant toil" (p. 203). (Echoes: *"thousands"*/ *"multitude"*; *"toil"*/ *"toil"*; *"year after year"*/ *"incessant."*) Bray's metaphoric "Some vital organ is diseased…. Robbers and murderers are diseased parts of the body of society" (p. 203) finds a metaphoric counterpart in Whitman's letter, where Dickens "puts the searing iron to wickedness." Bray's opinion (p. 204) that the results of wrongdoing "induce men to look to the causes of crime, and to apply those measures that are calculated to restrain it" is echoed by Whitman's opinion that by Dickens' characterizations "we are always in some way reminded how much need there is that certain systems of law and habit which lead to this poverty and consequent crime should be remedied." And Bray agrees (p. 206) that "the laws and social institutions of mankind are at variance with the laws of nature." Echoes: *"causes of crime"*/ *"consequent crime"*; *"law"*/ *"laws."*)

At this time, February 26, 1842, Whitman was not quite twenty-three years old. Bray's *Philosophy of Necessity* was perhaps less than four months old. It was published late in 1841, probably sometime after October 30. On p. 635 of Vol. II appears a note: "See Spectator, Oct. 2, 1841. London Phalanx, Oct. 30." The Preface is dated September, 1841.

Within a long list of subjects for treatment in his poems, Whitman wrote: "philosophy, look at phrenological list."[102] Perhaps he was referring to the phrenological lists in Charles Bray's *The Philosophy of Necessity*.

6—Whitman and the Orientals

Professor Susan Stebbing states that Sir Arthur Eddington (who will be recalled as having been one of the leading indeterminists discussed in Chapter II) "finds the standard definition of determinism in a well-known stanza of *The Rubáiyát of Omar Khayyám*." She then quotes the stanza which Eddington uses:

> With Earth's first Clay they did the Last Man's knead,
> And there of the last Harvest sowed the Seed:
> And the first Morning of Creation wrote
> What the Last Dawn of Reckoning shall read.[103]

Aside from the fact that to the superficial mind this stanza may seem to stress materialism overmuch, it serves very well as a definition of determinism. Eddington was wise in choosing it. It states, in effect, the Laplacean opinion (see Ch. V), famous in the history of determinism, that from any given state of the universe will come all that will exist in any succeeding state — that *theoretically* it would be possible for a mind, perhaps necessarily an infinite mind, to calculate mathematically from the given data all succeeding events in the universe. John Sterling stated the same hypothesis in a letter to Carlyle: "determinism … could we go back five thousand years, we should only have the prospect of travelling them again, and arriving at last at the same point at which we stand now."[104] And Whitman, too, in "Song of Myself," Sec. 45:

> If I, you, and the worlds, and all beneath or upon their surfaces were this moment reduced back to a pallid float, it would not avail in the long run,
> We should surely bring up again where we now stand....

These lines, like those of Omar Khayyám, give a perfect picture of a determinist universe. (Isn't it odd that Whitman and Sterling echo: "where we now stand"/"at which we stand now"?!) (And there are other echoes: "back"/ "back"; "We should... again"/ "we should... again.")

One might suspect that Whitman, if he ever had come across FitzGerald's translation, would have found much in it of particular interest to him. It is a matter of record that Whitman did own a copy of the *Rubáiyát*. He later presented it to his friend Thomas Donaldson, whose comments on Whitman's markings in the book are, in the context of our present study, worthy of note:

> Sometimes authors mark passages in the works of fellow authors and thus indicate their own opinions. Mr. Whitman occasionally did this, and, generally, by way of approval. One day, in 1890, he gave me a copy of then Rubáiyát of Omar Khayyám, the astronomer-poet of Persia. The book, a plain cloth-covered one, is the edition of Bernard Quaritch; Piccadilly, London, 1872. It was the first translation of Omar he had ever seen. In it he had inserted or pinned many newspaper slips relating to the poet, and marked many passages with a blue pencil.
> Omar's philosophy of the universe and of life finds much similarity in Mr. Whitman's — a coincidence, of course. I presume in the marked passages given Mr. Whitman found congenial ideas and may have recognized in them parallels in his own work.[105]

The *Rubáiyát* is often called deterministic, though something might be said on the point that Omar's philosophy leans toward the side of superstitious, negativistic fatalism and differs in attitude from modern determinism. Indeterminists like Eddington shudder over Omar's verses. Miss Stebbing says,

> Omar Khayyám's statement presents the picture of a universe in which everything is predestined, but his vision recalls the nineteenth century nightmare. All the imagery of FitzGerald's poem suggests that human beings are puppets controlled by Fate. *The Rubáiyát* is, indeed, commonly regarded as an expression of Fatalism and pessimism. Consider for instance,
> But helpless Pieces of the Game He plays
> Upon this Chequer-Board of Nights and Days;
> Hither and thither moves, and checks, and slays,
> And one by one back in the closet lays.[106]

The stanza quoted here by Miss Stebbing is one of the seventeen which Donaldson instances as having been "marked and bracketed" by Whitman. Merely marking a passage does not indicate agreement, but it does indicate interest. And Donaldson says, "I presume in the marked passages given Mr. Whitman found congenial ideas and may have recognized in them parallels in his own work." There is no doubt that the weight of some of those parallels depends upon a shared belief in determinism. Of course, there are other similarities besides these, but concentration on Omar's fatalistic verses and finding their echoes in Whitman brings out meanings in *Leaves of Grass* that could easily have been overlooked. This is startlingly so in the case of the *Rubáiyát* stanza LXVIII, which Whitman marked:

> We are no other than a moving row
> Of Magic Shadow-shapes that come and go
> Round with the Sun-illumin'd Lantern held
> In Midnight by the Master of the Show.[107]

Whitman, in his own "Sparkles from the Wheel":

> Myself effusing and fluid, a phantom curiously floating, now here
> absorb'd and arrested,
>> The group, (an unminded point set in a vast surrounding,)
>> The attentive, quiet children, the loud, proud, restive base of the streets,
>> The low hoarse purr of the whirling stone, the light-press'd blade,
>> Diffusing, dropping, sideways darting, in tiny showers of gold,
>> Sparkles from the wheel.

With Omar's verse in mind, one discovers the secret analogy of this poem: the children, too, are "sparkles from the wheel." Like Omar's shadow-shapes and Whitman's sparks, they "come and go." It is astonishing how meaningful Whitman's lines become when compared with the *Rubáiyát's* verses. Comparison of the following lines from "Song of the Broad-Axe" (Sec. 10) with the same stanza (LXVIII) brings to the surface their hidden determinism:

> The shapes arise!
> The shape of the prisoner's place in the court-room, and of him or her
> seated in the place,
> The shape of the liquor-bar lean'd against by the young rum-drinker and
> the old rum-drinker,
> The shape of the shamed and angry stairs trod by sneaking foot-steps...
> The shape of the step-ladder for the convicted and sentenced murderer,
> the murderer with haggard face and pinion'd arms,
> The sheriff at hand with his deputies, the silent and white-lipp'd crowd,
> the dangling of the rope.

Whitman concludes the poem, beginning with the previous section, 9, and continuing through 10, 11, and 12, with a veritable swirl of "shapes"—32 in all!

Whitman's "shapes" are no less predetermined than Omar's "Shadow-shapes" (LXVIII). The line in "Song of Myself," Sec. 37, "See myself in prison shaped [*sic*] like another man," now reaches a hitherto undetected level, fulfilling the fatalistic demands of high drama (as defined by Aristotle in the *Poetics*).

If you read Whitman's "Eidólons" with the FitzGerald-Whitman "shapes" as a reminding reference, you may begin to comprehend the significance (and genius) of the poem. In line 48 Whitman speaks of "tendencies to shape and shape and shape." The "eidólons" stand as eternal substantial co-correspondences of the transitory events and persons of the world. The events and persons are, as in FitzGerald's stanza LXVIII, "shadow-shapes"—of their corresponding substantial, pre-determining "eidólons." (David Reynolds, in his *Walt Whitman*, 2005, furnishes evidence that "Eidólons" was influenced by "Swedenborg's doctrine of 'correspondences.'"[108])

Whitman marked FitzGerald's stanza LXXXI:

> Oh Thou, who Man of baser Earth didst make
> And ev'n with Paradise devise the Snake:
> For all the Sin wherewith the Face of Man
> Is blacken'd — Man's Forgiveness give — and take!

The preceding stanza, LXXX, perhaps not marked by Whitman, brings out the meaning more vividly:

> Oh Thou, who didst with pitfall and with gin
> Beset the Road I was to wander in,
> Thou wilt not with Predestined Evil round
> Enmesh, and then impute my Fall to Sin!

Probably from the same inescapable premise, Whitman wrote in his notebook:

> I am the poet of sin,
> For I do not believe in sin[.][109]

Other Whitman parallels to the two verses, LXXX and LXXXI, will be found below in Chapter VI, on sin and evil.

The two poets share, in the parallels which follow, an understanding of the inexorable, if not so clearly deterministic, processes of the all-controlling Nature of which both poets consider human beings to be a part. Whitman marked the following two stanzas. Omar's verses and his share a unique and remarkable beauty.

XIX

> I sometimes think that never blows so red
> The Rose as where some buried Caesar bled;
> That every Hyacinth the Garden wears
> Dropt in her Lap from some once lovely Head.

XX

And this reviving Herb whose tender Green
Fledges the River-Lip on which we lean —
Ah, lean upon it lightly! for who knows
From what once lovely Lip it springs unseen!

Whitman, "Song of Myself," Sec. 6:

Tenderly will I use you curling grass,
It may be you transpire from the breasts of young men,
It may be if I had known them I would have loved them,
It may be you are from old people, or from offspring taken soon out of
their mothers' laps,
And here you are the mothers' laps.

This grass is very dark to be from the white heads of old mothers,
Darker than the colorless beards of old men,
Dark to come from under the faint red roofs of mouths.

O I perceive after all so many uttering tongues,
And I perceive they do not come from the roofs of mouths for nothing.

As Donaldson says, "Omar's philosophy of the universe and of life finds much similarity in Mr. Whitman's." We would be too hasty to suppose that there are not significant differences in the attitudes of the two poets. Omar's verse is tinged with a pessimism and futility originating from a somewhat warped view of determinism. Whitman's more hopeful and optimistic view springs from an interpretation of the same philosophy.

On January 22, 1891, Whitman asked Traubel, "Have you seen 'Poet-Lore' this month? Yes? Well, there is a fine bit of writing, of its kind, there — 'Some Characteristics of Persian Poetry' by a fellow named Buckham — James Buckham. It is a trifle *recherché* but of its kind a good piece of work. It interested me. I read it all."[110]

Thoreau considered *Leaves of Grass* "wonderfully like the Orientals." But when he asked Whitman if he had read them he answered, "No: Tell me about them."[111] The critics are confused about Whitman's similarities to the writers of the East. Whitman's determinism, even if no other influences were present, would have been enough to give certain Oriental qualities to his thought and poetry. Gay Wilson Allen says that "almost from the first edition students of Oriental thought have recognized in *Leaves of Grass* such striking parallels to the *Bhagavad Gita* and other Hindu poems that they have speculated on Whitman's use of translations as primary sources for his poems."[112] An excellent account of the determinism of the *Bhagavad Gita* is S. K. Maitra's essay "The Gita's Conception of Freedom as Compared with That of Kant." The type of free will revered by Kant, Maitra says, is one which the Gita "will not touch with a pair of tongs."[113] Maitra, interpreting the philosophy of the very same *Bhagavad Gita* in which "students of Oriental thought" have found such "striking" parallels to *Leaves of Grass*, comments: "Man's spiritual ascent consists in his renouncing this [Kantian] freedom of the will for the sake of enjoying his true freedom, which consists in union with God."[114] We are reminded, of course, again, of the famous Section 5 of "Song of Myself":

> Swiftly arose and spread around me the peace and knowledge that pass all the argument of the earth,
> And I know that the hand of God is the promise of my own....

In "A Backward Glance O'er Travel'd Roads" Whitman mentions as one of the "embryonic facts of 'Leaves of Grass'" his having read "the ancient Hindoo poems."[115] If Whitman's "garrulity of advancing age,"[116] to use his own phrase, is reliable testimony he did, then, read at least some of the Hindu poems before the first edition of *Leaves of Grass*. T. R. Rajasekharaiah has shown rather convincingly in his book *The Roots of Whitman's Grass* (1970) that Whitman drew inspiration from — indeed almost plagiarized — the Hindu scriptures.[117] If Whitman did deny to Thoreau any acquaintance with the Orientals, he probably was exhibiting a reluctance to have his indebtedness discovered. Indebted or not, he was attracted to the writings of the East, perhaps at first by Thoreau's remark that *Leaves of Grass* resembled them. In 1888, the year "A Backward Glance" first appeared, he is reported by Traubel as having one day mentioned the *Bhagavad Gita* among other "formal classics" with which Traubel presumed him "very familiar." Here is Traubel's entry:

> W. is very familiar with the formal classics in a general way. In our talk today he referred at different times to Aristophanes, Plato, Socrates, Marcus Aurelius, the Bagavad Gita, Euripides, Seneca. Once he quoted the Bible. He also advised me to read all I could "in Buddhist and Confucian books," saying: "Tackle them anyhow, anyhow: they will reward you."[118]

The endless repetitions of some of the Buddhist scriptures would drive an Occidental reader mad in the course of an hour or two. I have searched these writings for similarities to Whitman's writings and also for some clue to the extent of their determinism, but I could not persist in the task long enough to find what I was looking for, though my intuition, which I rely on heavily in investigations of this kind, tells me that a prolonged search would be rewarding. Mrs. Lily Adams Beck in her *Story of Oriental Philosophy* devotes about twenty pages to a discussion of Buddhism, and in elucidating the Buddhist philosophy she gives us what may be the deterministic clue to Whitman's interest:

The Buddha saw the world as a process of incessant change and becoming. Nothing ever is. All is becoming....

That is to say everything is at every moment passing into fresh forms of being, as a flowing river is ever and never the same.

The teaching follows that whatever arises is inevitably the effect of a previous cause, and therefore Law is the universe and the universe is Law. Does this apply to the body of man? Absolutely. To the mind? Again, absolutely. To what we call the soul? Absolutely. All these are forces, sequences, processes, as is everything in the universe. Nothing is unrelated.[119]

Scratch out "The Buddha" and write in "Whitman" and you will have a wonderful description of the world of *Leaves of Grass*. This description of Buddha's philosophy certainly reminds us of Whitman's definition of determinism in his note on Priestley:

"...'philosophical necessity,' that all results, physical, moral, spiritual, everything, every kind, rise out of perpetual flows of endless causes (to state it so for want of more elaboration)."[120]

At one point in her discussion of *Taoism* Mrs. Beck *quotes* Whitman.[121] There are indeed parallels between Whitman and the *Tao Teh King*, some of which were pointed out by Edward Carpenter in 1906.[122] Lin Yutang mentions Whitman twice in the introduction to his translation of the *Tao Teh King* and compares its author to Whitman: "Laotse was like Whitman, with the large and generous humanity of Whitman."[123]

The *Tao Teh King*. The book is filled with subtleties and paradoxes. But one cannot blame the author, for his subject is a subtle subject. Tao is subtle, so subtle that translators stumble for words to describe it. Tao is usually translated as the Way, but some translators avoid substituting a word and, perhaps wisely, merely leave it Tao. For "Tao" I would substitute "Determinism" — that is, if I were trying to explain what Tao is. In that event I should be faced with the task of explaining the finer implications of determinism, and I should not get very far from where I started. Perhaps it should be left "Tao" after all.

> When the highest type of men hear the Tao (truth)
> They try hard to live in accordance with it,
> When the mediocre type hear the Tao,
> They seem to be aware and yet unaware of it.
> When the lowest type hear the Tao,
> They break into loud laughter —
> If it were not laughed at, it would not be Tao.[124]

(Cf. Whitman: "ironical smiles and mockings" — Ch. I)

For the early Chinese, "Tao was the force that controlled the universe." One "could see its workings by observing nature."[125] Simply, was it not determinism? Sometimes, as in the foregoing quotation, the word Tao refers to the doctrine; at other times it refers to what the doctrine talks about, as in the line "The Great Tao flows everywhere."[126] Similarly we speak of determinism as a doctrine and as a universal force. The Great Tao which "flows everywhere" is like the "perpetual flows of endless causes" in Whitman's definition of determinism.

A great Hindu contemporary of Whitman's, one of the greatest mystics of all the ages, was Sri Ramakrishna. Ramakrishna was a strict determinist, though he probably never pursued the question of determinism in a formal way, gaining most of his knowledge — other than that he may have received from mystical insight — from reading Hindu scriptures and hearing about them from others. He was to some extent familiar with the scriptures of other religions. He taught that "there are many paths to the one God."[127] Again and again he would compare himself to "the machine" and God to "the Operator" or speak of himself as "the chariot" and God as the Charioteer.[128] He was adamant in his refusal to admit "what the 'Englishman' calls free will."[129] (This was the way he phrased it.) He had a singular grasp of the free will problem, a fact which is established by various of his conversations, which were taken down by one of his intimate disciples over a period extending from 1882 to his death in 1886 (just two years before Traubel was to begin his very similar account of conversations with Whitman).

Ramakrishna, like Whitman, had his visiting devotees. One of the doctors who attended Ramakrishna in his long illness was a free-willist of the "I just feel" variety. He was asked by one of the visiting devotees, "How do you know that free will exists?" He replied, "Not by reasoning; I feel it." "In that case," rejoined the devotee, "I may say that I and others feel the reverse. We feel that we are controlled by another." Whereupon all of the several devotees present burst into laughter.[130] A long exchange had preceded, with devotees, and particularly Ramakrishna himself, defending determinism. Finally Ramakrishna summed up, saying to the doctor:

> Look here. If a man truly believes that God alone does everything, that He is the Operator and man the machine, then such a man is verily liberated in life. "Thou workest Thine own work; men only call it theirs." Do you know what it is like? Vedanta philosophy gives an illustration. Suppose you are cooking rice in a pot, with potato, egg-plant, and other vegetables. After a while the potatoes, egg-plant, rice, and the rest begin to jump about in the pot. They seem to say with pride: "We are moving! We are jumping!" The children see it and think the potatoes, egg-plant and rice are alive and so they jump that way. But the elders, who know, explain to the children that the vegetables and the rice are not alive; they jump not of themselves, but because of the fire under the pot; if you remove the burning wood from the hearth, then they will move no more. Likewise the pride of man, that he is the doer, springs from ignorance. Men are powerful because of the power

of God. All becomes quiet when that burning wood is taken away. The puppets dance well on the stage when pulled by a wire, but they cannot move when the wire snaps.

A man will cherish the illusion that he is the doer as long as he has not seen God, as long as he has not touched the Philosopher's Stone. So long will he know the distinction between his good and bad actions. This awareness of the distinction is due to God's maya; and it is necessary for the purpose of running His illusory world. But a man can realize God if he takes shelter under His vidyamaya and follows the path of righteousness. He who knows God and realizes Him is able to go beyond maya. He who firmly believes that God alone is the doer and he himself a mere instrument is a jivanmukta, a free soul though living in a body. I said this to Keshab Chandra Sen.[131]

Determinism can have great meaning for the religious mind. It would seem that in Sri Ramakrishna's case determinism was an indispensable stepping-stone to his vision of God. His concept of determinism is far different from that usually put forward by its opponents. His realization that man is "a machine" had upon him none of the horrifying effect so often evident in the arguments of indeterminists like Compton and Eddington. The mere contemplation of the "machine" image was enough to send him into the rapt ecstasy of a mystic trance. Whitman in his religious attitude was not very unlike Sri Ramakrishna. Whitman's frequently being classed as a mystic is due to the fact that his determinism led him up into then regions, or near the regions, attained by true mystics like Ramakrishna. Whitman was a mystic only in so far as his determinism made him one, just as Spinoza was led, by his determinism, into the borderlands of mysticism.

It would not be easy to demonstrate that Whitman's seeming mysticism was a result of his determinism. But there are certain clues and hints in his poetry that reveal mystical nuances of his determinism. Sometimes the hints are strong, as in "A Voice from Death":

> Thou ever-darting Globe! through Space and Air!
> Thou waters that encompass us!
> Thou that in all the life and death of us, in action or in sleep!
> Thou laws invisible that permeate them and all,
> Thou that in all, and over all, and through and under all, incessant!
> Thou! Thou! The vital, universal, giant force resistless, sleepless calm,
> Holding Humanity as in thy open hand, as some ephemeral toy,
> How ill to e'er forget thee!

The following lines are from a song which Sri Ramakrishna often sang:

> Eternal One! Thou great First Cause, clothed in the form of the Void…!
> Thou art the Mover of all that move, and we are but Thy helpless toys;
> We move alone as Thou movest us and speak as through us Thou speakest.[132]

The employment in the respective cases of the word "toy" (or "toys") may not be coincidental.

Whitman's "A Persian Lesson," quoted here in part, provides another clue to Whitman's interest in the determinism of the East:

> Finally my children, to envelop each word, each part of the rest,
> Allah is all, all, all — is immanent in every life and object,
> May-be at many and many-a-more removes — yet Allah, Allah, Allah is there.

Chapters VIII and IX will make further references to the religions of the Orient. We may be able there to learn more about the common denominator of the philosophies of Whitman and the Orientals.

It is time now to hurry the present chapter to a close. But a chapter on Whitman's "inspirations" would not be complete without consideration of Whitman's kinship to Hegel.

7—Whitman and Hegel

It is in the Introduction to his *Philosophy of History* that the voice of Hegel's determinism is loudest, and it is, significantly, this part of Hegel's message on which Walt Whitman seems to have concentrated his attention. Here human beings are viewed by Hegel as puppet-like creatures unconsciously carrying out the irresistible edicts of the absolute Idea. Here every form of corruption, malice, deceit, cruelty — even war — is justified as an indispensable and inevitable element in the working out of the divine plan.

Keep the following excerpts from Hegel in mind. They will be echoed by similar statements by Whitman.

> ... the Idea is, in truth, the leader of peoples and of the World; and Spirit, the rational and necessitated will of that conductor, is and has been the director of the events of the World's History.[133]

> ... those manifestations of vitality on the part of individuals and peoples, in which they seek and satisfy their own purposes, are, at the same time, the means and instruments of a higher and broader purpose of which they know nothing....[134]

> Without rhetorical exaggeration, a simply truthful combination of the miseries that have overwhelmed the noblest of nations and polities, and the finest exemplars of private virtue, — forms a picture of most fearful aspect, and excites emotions of the profoundest and most hopeless sadness, counterbalanced by no consolatory result. We endure in beholding it a mental torture, allowing no defence or escape but the consideration that what has happened could not be otherwise; that it is a fatality which no intervention could alter.[135]

One of Whitman's notes reads, "I do not condemn either the Past or the Present. Shall I denounce my own ancestry — the very ground under my feet? that has been so long building. I know they are and were what they could not but be."[136] Echo: Hegel, "could not be otherwise"; Whitman, "could not but be." Whitman's words are from notes which "probably belong to the early fifties."[137]

There is ample evidence that Hegel's ideas could have been available to Whitman before *Leaves of Grass*, possibly eight years before, in 1847. In that year was published Frederick Hedge's *Prose Writers of Germany*. Whitman on at least three occasions spoke to Traubel about his high regard for this book. After Hedge's death in 1890, Whitman mused: "I am personally greatly indebted to Hedge — have been for 40 years. He was the man opened German literature to me." In Traubel's account, Whitman "turned in his chair — shoved about several books, etc., on floor — and drew out 'Prose Writers of Germany,' edition 1848." Whitman went on, "It was a great book for me — I shall not forget its influence. It was a necessity, nobly answered."[138] A month later Whitman again mentioned Hedge: "His 'Prose Writers of Germany' has been one of my longest treasures. I can never be shaken from my love of it. I can hardly tell how many years it has been inspiration, aid, sunlight."[139] Eight months before that, Traubel on one of his daily visits to the ailing Whitman, found him reading the book. "Do you know anything about this book? It seems to me a great, a teeming book. I have had it about me for a full thirty years, and from time to time gone through it again." Traubel adds, "His copy is an edition of 1848 [*sic*]." "I guess I've had it nearly from that date."[140] Hedge's book contains an anonymous translation of about a third of Hegel's hundred-page-plus Introduction to his *Philosophy of History*. There are many omissions, all unnoted; but here were presented in clear language the essential Hegelian ideas, those which most attracted Whitman.

Another book. Published a year before *Leaves of Grass*, in 1854, definitely supplied ideas which Whitman made use of. This was Joseph Gostwick's *German Literature*. The author's name was misspelled on the title page, providing a curious clue to the legitimacy of the book as a Whitman source. In the following note Whitman uses the same misspelling:

> The varieties, contradictions and paradoxes of the world and of life, and even good and evil, so baffling to the superficial observer, and so often leading to despair, sullenness or infidelity, become a series of infinite radiations and waves of the one sea-like universe of divine action and progress, never stopping, never hasting. "The heavens and the earth" to use the summing up of Joseph Gostic [*sic*] whose brief I endorse: "The heavens and the earth and all things within their compass — all the events of history — the facts of the present and the development of the future (such is the doctrine of Hegel) all form a complication, a succession of steps in the one eternal process of creative thought."[141]

"...a series of infinite radiations and waves of the one sea-like universe of divine action and progress, never stopping, never hasting" — this almost duplicates part of Whitman's definition of determinism in his note on Priestley: "...perpetual flows of endless causes...." The ending of this statement was repeated almost word-for-word by Whitman years later (my italics):

> Great as they are, and greater far to be, the United States, too, are but *a series of steps in the eternal process of creative thought.*[142]

This is in a footnote to one of the essays in *Specimen Days and Collect*, published in 1882. In the same footnote Whitman asks — and the phrasing of the question betrays its Hegelian inspiration: "Is there not such a thing as the philosophy of American history and politics? And if so, what is it?" Whitman then suggests the answer, which is also, of course, Hegelian:

> Wise men say there are two sets of wills to nations and to persons — one set that acts and works from explainable motives — from teaching, intelligence, judgment, circumstance, caprice, emulation, greed &c. — and then another set, perhaps deep, hidden, unsuspected, yet often more potent than the first, refusing to be argued with, rising as it were out of abysses, resistlessly urging on speakers, doers, communities, *unwitting to themselves* [my italics] — the poet to his fieriest words — the race to pursue its loftiest ideal....[143]

Interrupting, I want to give attention to an important point. As Whitman puts it here, "there are two sets of wills": one, evidenced in the conscious activities and strivings of people and nations, and another, "deep, hidden, unsuspected," of which, as Hegel says, "they know noting," which *predestines* the conscious strivers, as Whitman says, "unwitting to themselves." Obviously Whitman and Hegel share this concept of a duality of wills. Aware of this concept, we can grasp certain easily overlooked concepts in Whitman's poems. In "Thou Mother with Thy Equal Brood," Sec. 3, Whitman salutes the New World as an inevitable outgrowth of the past, of the Old World,

> Its poems, churches, arts, *unwitting to themselves*, destined with reference to [the New World]....

The italics are mine. The Hegelian "two sets of wills" might easily be passed over in lines from "Song of the Redwood-Tree" (Whitman changes "wills" to "volitions"):

> You occult deep volitions...
> You that, sometimes known, oftener unknown, really shape and mould the New World, adjusting it to Time and Space,
> You hidden national will lying in our abysms, conceal'd but ever alert,

> You past and present purposes tenaciously pursued, may-be *unconscious of yourselves* [my italics]....

Hang on to that phrase, "unconscious of yourselves"; let it remind you of "unwitting to themselves" in Whitman's note and the identical "unwitting to themselves" in the quotation above from "Thou Mother with Thy Equal Brood." If, in that poem, Whitman saw the old poems as inevitable, "unwitting to themselves," so did he look upon his *own* poems: as part of the same determinist process. This is brought to light in "To Thee Old Cause," where we find "this book *unwitting to itself*" (my italics):

> Thou seething principle! thou well-kept, latent germ! thou centre!
> Around the idea of thee the war revolving,
> With all its angry and vehement play of causes,
> (With vast results to come for thrice a thousand years,)
> These recitatives for thee,— my book and the war are one,
> Merged in its spirit I and mine, as the contest hinged on thee,
> As a wheel on its axis turns, this book *unwitting to itself* [my italics],
> Around the idea of thee.

The poem begins:

> To thee old cause!
> Thou Peerless, passionate, good cause,
> Thou stern, remorseless, sweet idea,
> Deathless throughout the ages, races, lands,
> After a strange sad war, great war for thee,
> (I think all war through time was really fought, and ever will be really
> fought, for thee,)
> These chants for thee, the eternal march of thee.

This poem will be given fuller consideration in Chapter VI, Sec. 3, where Whitman's concept of evil is given treatment. But here it is relationships of Whitman and Hegel that concern us. The poem is actually, along with whatever other meanings it may have, Whitman's excuse for the Civil War. Yes, Whitman's *excuse for the Civil War!* In constructing this excuse he poetically restates Hegel's pronouncement, at the end of the third quotation above:

> We endure in beholding it a mental torture, allowing no defence or escape but the consideration that what has happened could not be otherwise; that it is a fatality which no intervention could alter.

The "old cause," in its essential meaning, is the cause of cause-and-effect — it is the Hegelian "Spirit," working out the destiny of the world! Some critics have said the "old cause" is "the cause of freedom." Well, it is that; but it is much more than that, as one will see when he looks on it in its full kinship to the ideas of Hegel.

Resuming the quotation interrupted above:

The glory of the republic of the United States, in my opinion, is to be that, emerging in the light of the modern and the splendor of science, and solidly based on the past, it is to cheerfully range itself, and its politics are henceforth to come, under those universal laws, and embody them, and carry them out, to serve them. And as only that individual becomes truly great who understands well that, while complete in himself in a certain sense, he is but a part of the divine, eternal scheme ... so the United States may only become the greatest and the most continuous, by understanding well their harmonious relations with entire humanity and history, and all their laws and progress, sublimed with the creative thought of Deity, through all time, past, present, and future. Thus will they expand to the amplitude of their destiny, and become illustrations and culminating parts of the kosmos, and of civilization.

No more considering the States as an incident, or series of incidents, however vast, coming accidentally along the path of time, and shaped by casual emergencies as they happen to arise, and the mere result of modern improvements, vulgar and lucky, ahead of other nations and times, I would finally plant, as seeds, these thoughts or speculations in the growth of our republic — that it is the deliberate culmination and result of all the past — that here, too, as in all the departments of the universe, regular laws (slow and sure in planting, slow and sure in ripening) have controll'd and govern'd and will yet control and govern; and that those laws can no more be baffled or steer'd clear of, or vitiated, by chance, or any fortune or opposition, than the laws of winter and summer, or darkness and light.[144]

Whitman's statement, "And as only that individual becomes truly great who understands well that, while complete in himself in a certain sense, he is but a part of the divine, eternal scheme," bears out Hegel's contention (see Ch. III) that "man is most independent when he knows himself to be determined by the absolute idea throughout." By analogy (and with Hegel's help?) Whitman extends that concept to the *nation*: Just as individuals are in one sense free but in another determined, we must consider that the United States, though free, are ultimately a part of the determinist unfolding of history and time.

Evidence of Whitman's recognition of and regard for Hegel's determinism is to be found in the concluding sentence of his notes on Hegel:

He has given the same clue to the fitness of reason and fitness of things and unending progress, to the universe of moral purposes that the sciences in their spheres, as astronomy and geology, have established in the material purposes, and the last and crowning proof of each is the same, that they fit the mind, and the idea of the all, and are necessary to be so in the nature of things.[145]

Whitman's reference here to "geology" is singularly interesting when compared to his employment of the word in other contexts. Let us hark back, as we have so often done, to Whitman's definition of determinism in his note on Priestley. It will be remembered that Whitman there is careful to include "all results, physical, moral, spiritual, everything every kind." All these, he says, "rise out of perpetual flows of endless causes."[146] In the note on Hegel just quoted Whitman gives very similar emphasis to the *two* realms: the physical and the non-physical or spiritual. He says that Hegel has given the same assurance of the "fitness" of moral events that the sciences — and he mentions geology — have given of the fitness of material events. And Whitman ends by saying that both the moral and the physical are "necessary to be so in the nature of things." He thus draws attention to the physical-moral determinism of the Priestley note. The determinist significance of his co-mentioning of the physical and moral becomes clear in another note in which he uses the term "geology" to represent the physical correlative of the spiritual aspect of determinism:

> One religion wonders at another. A nation wonders *how* another nation can be what it is, wonders how it can like what it likes and dislike what it dislikes; a man wonders at another man's folly and so on. But what a nation likes, is part of that nation; and what it dislikes is part of the same nation; its politics and religion, whatever they are, are inevitable results of the days and events that have preceded the nation, just as much as the condition of the geology of that part of the earth is the result of former conditions.[147]

There can be no mistaking Whitman's meaning here. He is asserting an absolute and universal determinism. And here again the inspiration may have come from Hegel's "Introduction." Here is part of the 1849 (significant date!) translation:

> This spirit of a people is a definite spirit; its character is determined by the historical stage of their development. This spirit is the basis out of which proceed all the forms of national culture. It is an individuality, which in religion is represented, reverenced, and loved in its essential character, in art, it is exhibited in visible images and forms; in philosophy, it is known and apprehended as thought. The forms which these things take are in inseparable union with the spirit of the people; the substance of which they are formed and their objects are originally the same; hence, only with such a religion can we have such a state; in such a state only such a philosophy and art.[148]

The two statements echo, augment, and explain one another. Whitman's statement amplifies the implicit determinism of Hegel's.

Another endorsement of Hegel's determinism by Whitman is found in the following remarks, which he made to Traubel:

"When I hit I want to hit hard, but I don't want to hit any man, the worst man, even the scoundrel, one single blow that belongs to the system from which we all suffer alike." Could this suffering have been avoided? "No more than the weather: it is as useless to quarrel with history as with the weather; we can prepare for the weather and prepare for history." Then was history automatic? "Not at all: it is free in all its basic dynamics: that is, the free human spirit has its part to perform in giving direction to history." Was this statement not self-contradictory? "I shouldn't wonder: in trying to represent both sides we always run some risk of finishing on the vague line between the two."[149]

The paradox, as Whitman must have remembered, had been explained away by Hegel:

> While these limited sentiments are still unconscious of the purpose they are fulfilling, the universal principle is implicit in them, and is realizing itself through them. the question also assumes the form of the union of *Freedom* and *Necessity*; the latent abstract process of Spirit being regarded as *Necessity*, while that which exhibits itself in the conscious will of men, as their interest, belongs to the domain of *Freedom*.[150]

"Spirit" here and in the other quotations from Hegel, is the spirit of necessity; for "spirit," translate "determinism." If one keeps in mind this connotation of "spirit," some of Whitman's poetry suddenly becomes alive with a meaning it never has had for us before. Here is his "Spirit That Form'd This Scene":

> Spirit that form'd this scene,
> These tumbled rock-piles grim and red,
> These reckless heaven-ambitious peaks,
> These gorges, turbulent-clear streams, this naked freshness,
> These formless wild arrays, for reasons of their own,
> I know thee, savage spirit — we have communed together,
> Mine too such wild arrays, for reasons of their own;
> Was't charged against my chants they had forgotten art?
> To fuse within themselves its rules precise and delicatesse?
> The lyrist's measur'd beat, the wrought-out temple's grace — column and
> polish'd arch forgot?
> But thou that revelest here — spirit that form'd this scene,
> They have remember'd thee.

In the statement quoted above Whitman uses "geology" as a symbol for determinism. There, he points to "astronomy and geology" as "established" determinist processes and indicates that "the universe of moral purposes" is no less a determinist function. This concept is brought into focus several times in Whitman's poems and notes — and even as early as 1855 he made an implicit statement of it, in the Preface to the first *Leaves of Grass*:

... whatever is less than the laws of light and of astronomical motion... or less than vast stretches of time or the slow formation of density or the patient upheaving of strata — is of no account.[151]

And here in "Spirit That Form'd This Scene" (1881) we have evidence of the "patient upheaving of strata" of the 1855 Preface: "tumbled rock-piles," "reckless heaven-ambitious peaks," "gorges," "formless wild arrays." So in this poem we have again, in the subtlest way, a use by Whitman of this, one of his favorite figures, to illustrate the concept of physical-spiritual determinism. The geology of Platte Canyon represents the physical, but to one who understands as Whitman did, it reflects the spiritual. The spirit that formed the canyon is the same spirit the formed *Leaves of Grass*. The (seemingly) chaotic disarray of the canyon is analogous to the often criticized (seeming) lawlessness of the poems.

The powerful influence of Hegel on Whitman has been unquestionably indicated by the evidence presented in this section. Reference to the philosophy of Hegel has been particularly helpful in clarifying Whitman's idea of freedom. The constraining thought in the minds of nearly all Whitman critics is that since Whitman so obviously is the champion of freedom he could not possibly have been a convinced determinist. At the end of the next chapter will be presented further clarification of this question and, again, compelling evidence that some of Whitman's most important ideas came from, or at least were corroborated by, Hegel.

There is hardly any chance that more than a few Whitman critics will be enlightened by what I have discovered. But maybe we shall have *new* Whitman critics! Among the old ones is Arthur E. Briggs, who claims to have found in Whitman a firm denial of determinism. He says of Whitman:

> As for history he said to Traubel it is not automatic. "The free human spirit has a part to perform in giving direction to history." Numerous expressions in *Leaves of Grass* show that he gave a unique significance to the spirit of man as a creative and effective power by virtue of its own will and desires which is quite alien to Hegel's and German philosophy in the general trend.[152]

But go back to note 149 above and see what Whitman *really* said to Traubel! Whitman's view was far from being what Briggs reports as "alien to Hegel's." Whitman could write, "To you, O Freedom, purport of all!"[153] and yet be a determinist, no less a determinist than Hegel, who viewed history as "the development of that principle whose substantial *purport* is the consciousness of Freedom."[154] Note the echoes. Whitman: "Freedom," "purport." Hegel: "*purport*," "Freedom."

◆ ◆ ◆

Inspiring Determinists:

  Epictetus—"with the best of the great teachers."

  Lincoln—"particularly my man."

  Priestley—"a *real man*," "a man of the big kind."

  Frances Wright—"one of the few characters to excite in me a wholesale respect and love."

  Spurzheim—"the most cautious, skeptical and careful of the Phrenologists."

  Emerson—"Greatest of all the men of his time."

  Hegel—"humanity's chiefest teacher and the choicest loved physician of my mind and soul."[155]

V

A Few Faint Clews

Only a few hints, a few diffused faint clews and indirections....
— "When I Read the Book"

Whitman was a determinist, but unlike most determinists he did not merely assent to the concept: he made practical use of it, in writing *Leaves of Grass*. A sense of its pervading presence makes the whole book astonish with a new interest, impress with a new profundity, satisfy (for the first time) with a discernible unity.

With the preliminary chapters of this book in mind the reader should have no difficulty in identifying some determinism in the poems; but there are many passages in which the determinism is far from obvious, even to the initiated, and in some cases too elusive even to be effectively suggested.

After much experimentation, including two or three laborious writings and rewritings over a period of months (years?), I have found it most expedient to present Whitman's determinism under four divisions, the boundaries of which are somewhat roughly defined by his use of four important determinist metaphors. It should be noted that the language in which determinism is expressed is, even in prose, often figurative. This made Whitman's poetic presentation of the ideas of determinism easier for him; but it also served to obscure Whitman's determinism from the gaze of those who are unmindful of the metaphors customarily used by determinists. At the same time, this use of traditional figures facilitates interpretation by those who are not strangers to the philosophy.

Four metaphors are frequently used to express the idea of determinism: 1) the "push" metaphor, 2) the "chain" metaphor, 3) the "thread" metaphor, and 4) the "flow" metaphor. Each of these metaphors is used by Whitman over and over. It will be my task to indicate that Whitman's use of them is not just coincidence, that in his use of them they bear the same determinist connotations which they bear in prose writings on determinism. This I intend to accomplish by showing that Whitman's lines fit nicely in a determinist context supplied by a study of that philosophy and by closely analyzing Whitman's ideas as they are revealed in his poems and in his notes and prose writings and in his remarks as quoted by his friends.

1—The Determinist "Push"

"America does not repel the past or what it has produced under its forms or amid other politics or the idea of castes or the old religions...." Thus begins the 1855 Preface to *Leaves of Grass*.[1] When the significance of this opening statement becomes clear, we shall see that Whitman, in the first utterance in his book, proclaimed his allegiance to determinism. One of his notes gives us the clue: "I do not condemn either the Past or the Present. Shall I denounce my own ancestry — the very ground under my feet? that has been so long building. I know that they are and were what they could not but be."[2] America does not repel the past, because the past could not have been otherwise than it was, and without the past the present would not be what it is. Whitman considered America "the deliberate culmination and result of all the past."[3] The past grew out of *its* past, and out of the past grew America. "As America fully and fairly construed is the legitimate result and evolutionary outcome of the past, so I would dare to claim for my verse."[4] Nothing can be other than it is. *All that happens is all that can happen.* These are basic presuppositions of Whitman's poetry.

> I assert that all past days were what they must have been,
> And that they could no-how have been better than they were,
> And that to-day is what it must be....
>
> ["With Antecedents," Sec. 2.]

Joseph Priestley in defining "philosophical necessity" states:

> ...there will be a necessary connexion between all things past, present and to come, in the way of proper *cause and effect*, as much in the intellectual, as in the natural world; so that, how little soever the bulk of mankind may be apprehensive of it, or staggered by it, according to the established laws of nature, no event could have been otherwise than it *has been, is, or is to be*, and therefore all things past, present and to come, are precisely what the Author of nature really intended them to be, and has made provision for.[5]

"I do not doubt," says Whitman in one of his poems, "that whatever can possibly happen anywhere at any time, is provided for in the inherences of things...."[6] Note the echo!: "provision for"/ "provided for." There is no need to stress the compatibility of Whitman and Priestley: it was made clear in the previous chapter.

The most famous statement of the determinist "push" was made by Laplace:

> We ought then to regard the present state of the universe as the effect of
> its antecedent state and the cause of the state that is to follow. An intelli-
> gence knowing, at a given instant of time, all forces acting in nature, as well
> as the momentary positions of all things of which the universe consists,
> would be able to comprehend the motions of the largest bodies of the world
> and those of the lightest atoms in one single formula, provided his intellect
> were sufficiently powerful to subject all data to analysis; to him nothing
> would be uncertain, both past and future would be present to his eyes.[7]

"None has begun to think," says Whitman, "...how certain the future is";[8]
and again, "...the future is no more uncertain than the present...."[9] Whitman's "uncertain" duplicates Laplace's "uncertain." For Whitman, just as for
Laplace, the future was contained in the present. The Laplacean view is
expressed in Whitman's "Germs":

Germs

Forms, qualities, lives, humanity, language, thoughts,
The ones known, and the ones unknown, the ones on the stars,
The stars themselves, some shaped, others unshaped,
Wonders as of those countries, the soil, trees, cities, inhabitants, whatever
they may be,
Splendid suns, the moons and rings, the countless combinations and
effects,
Such-like, and as good as such-like, visible here or anywhere, stand pro-
vided for in a handful of space, which I extend my arm and half enclose
with my hand,
That containing the start of each and all, the virtue, the germs of all.

Here again, "provided for," another echo of "provision for" in Priestley's
definition of determinism. Firm evidence that Whitman would have agreed
with Laplace's assertion that we can "regard the present state of the universe
as the effect of its antecedent state and the cause of the state that is to follow" is found in the 1855 Preface. There Whitman asserts that "no result
exists now without being from its long antecedent result, and that from its
antecedent, and so backward without the farthest mentionable spot coming
a bit nearer the beginning than any other spot."[10] Boatright, in a brilliant
flash of insight, saw that "throughout the poetry of Walt Whitman, the
present is implicit in the past, and the future is implicit in the present."[11]
Strangely, Boatright does not seem to have understood the logical impact of
his words; if he had, he would have written a book like this one explaining
Whitman!

"Determinists," William James tells us, "...say that individual men originate nothing...."[12] Whitman wrote of his own "philosophy" that it was one

of his "peculiarities" but not one of his "originalities." The author of *Leaves of Grass*, Whitman continued, "disclaims originality — at least in the superficial sense. His notion explicitly is that there is nothing actually new only an accumulation or fruitage or carrying out of the old...."[13] According to James, determinists say that individual men "merely transmit to the future the whole push of the past cosmos...."[14] "The past," says Whitman, "is the push of you, me, all, precisely the same...."[15]

> For what is the present after all but a growth out of the past?
> (As a projectile form'd, impell'd, passing a certain line, still keeps on,
> So the present, utterly form'd, impell'd by the past.)[16]

"Why," asks Fichte, "had Nature, amid the infinite variety of possible forms, assumed in this moment precisely these and no others? For this reason, that they were preceded by those precisely which did precede them and no others; and because the present could arise out of those and out of no other possible conditions."[17] Whitman describes the same determinist process in his "the curious years each emerging from that which preceded it."[18] (Echo: "preceded"/ "preceded.") In "A Song of the Rolling Earth" he expresses the same idea:

> Embracing man, embracing all, proceed the three hundred and sixty-five
> resistlessly round the sun;
> Embracing all, soothing, supporting, follow close three hundred and
> sixty-five offsets of the first, sure and necessary as they.[19]

Throughout this poem are unmistakable clues that the earth symbolism is being used in a poetic statement of the nuances of the determinist philosophy. That the earth was thus symbolic becomes manifest in Whitman's 1872 preface, where he quite obviously uses the earth to declare determinism. He states that in writing *Leaves of Grass* he fulfilled "an imperious conviction, and the commands of my nature as total and irresistible as those which make the sea flow, or the globe revolve."[20] Here the revolving globe equates the rolling earth — both determinist symbols. Whitman's insistence in including man ("Embracing man" in the lines above) makes clear his determinism, as does his phrase "enclosing me the same" when he catches the "mystic human meaning" of the tides. The careful inclusion of man in the determinist scheme is evident also in Whitman's definition of necessity in his note on Priestley, with the listing of "all" results, "physical, moral, spiritual, everything, every kind."[21] Here "all" is echoed by "all ...all" in the lines above. The inclusion is evident also in Whitman's statement that Hegel had "given the same clue" to the operation of the "universe of moral purposes" that "astronomy and geology" (note "geology") had given to the operation of the material realm.[22] "Geology" is, like the earth, a determinist metaphor. This is obvious in

Whitman's assertion that a nation's politics and religion, "whatever they are, are inevitable results of the days and events that have preceded the nation [again, "preceded"], just as much as the condition of the geology [sic] of that part of the earth is the result of former conditions."[23] So we have identified two of Whitman's most important determinist symbols: the *geology* of the earth and the *earth* itself, the "rolling" earth.

Whitman associates the two in a fragmentary note in which he contemplates a "Poem of Geology — not a good word? — the processes of the earth."[24] Both "geology" and the "earth" served Whitman in his effort to make clear that the inevitable processes of the physical universe were correlative of the equally inevitable spiritual or moral processes. "Embracing *man*, embracing all, proceed the three hundred and sixty-five *resistlessly* round the sun." The italics are mine. "Resistlessly" is a key word which unlocks the meaning of this line, as will be readily apparent when we look at Whitman's other uses of the word or of its cognates (my italics): "…we are from birth to death the subjects of *irresistible* law'; "the vital, universal, giant force *resistless*"; "commands … as total and *irresistible* as those which make the sea flow, or the globe [note globe] revolve." Emerson, using "inflexible law" and "the ball," provides evidence of the appropriateness of Whitman's use of the earth as a symbol for determinism:

> … the next lesson taught is, the continuation of the inflexible law of matter into the subtle kingdom of will, and of thought; that if, in sidereal ages, gravity and projection keep their craft, and the ball never loses its way in its wild path through space, — a secreter gravitation, a secreter projection, rule not less tyrannically in human history….[25]

If from the "inflexible law of matter" and "the ball" (earth) Emerson had learned a "lesson," so had Whitman: "This is the Earth's Word — the pervading sentiment or lesson [note "lesson"] is to be that the only good of learning the theory of the fluency and generosity and impartiality, largeness and exactitude of the earth is to use all those toward the theory of character — human character."[26] Note the precise Whitman/Emerson echo: "human"/"human." Careful consideration of the symbolic clues reveals that Whitman is here affirming a determinist theory of human character:

> Allons! Whoever you are come travel with me!
> Traveling with me you find what never tires.
>
> The earth never tires,
> The earth is rude, silent, incomprehensible at first,
> Nature is rude and incomprehensible at first,
> Be not discouraged, keep on, there are divine things well envelop'd,
> I swear to you there are divine things more beautiful than words can tell.[27]

Can the last line be equivalent to "the peace and knowledge that pass all the argument of the earth" in Section 5 of "Song of Myself"? Can it be that there, and here, Whitman is recounting a conversion like that outlined in our Chapter III? In Sec. 5, he sees that "the hand of God is the promise of [his] own." That, in essence, is what the converted determinist concludes after the conversion. The lines above may describe the hardships the determinist goes through on his way to the conversion. The following prose note by Whitman is a fairly obvious restatement of those lines: "One having attained those insights and contents which the universe gives to men capable of comprehending it, would publish the same and persuade other men and women to the same. The conditions are simple, spiritual, physical, close at hand ... they are long and arduous and require faith, they exist altogether with the taught and not with the teaching or teacher."[28] Here Whitman's use of "comprehending" and, in the poem, "incomprehensible" are a clue that both the poetic and prose statements have the same referent. And in this prose note the co-mention of "spiritual, physical," echoes the "physical, moral, spiritual" of Whitman's Priestley note[29]—an indication that Whitman here had in mind the same determinism which he used those words to define in the note on Priestley. There are other clues to Whitman's meaning. Charles Bray says that he as a determinist was firmly convinced that "every system built upon an opposite principle, by *whatever authority supported*, cannot be true."[30] It appears that Whitman expressed the same conviction when he wrote:

> There can be no theory of any account unless it corroborate the theory of the earth,
> No politics, song, religion, behavior, or what not, is of account, unless it compare with the amplitude of the earth...

Unless it face the exactness, vitality, impartiality, rectitude of the earth.[31] In these lines the "exactness ... impartiality ... of the earth" repeats the "impartiality ... and exactitude of the earth" in the prose quotation above. Also "theory of the earth" echoes "theory ... of the earth." There, "largeness," here, "amplitude." And "rectitude" is akin to "exactitude" of the prose. And culminating this whole analysis is the conclusion that the earth in three of these quotations symbolizes determinism. Hold firmly to the evidence that this is so: that Whitman's "earth" can be literally translated "determinism." Look back and re-read the quotation from "A Song of the Rolling Earth." Then turn to the poem and read some of the other lines. This one:

> The best of the earth cannot be told anyhow....

and these:

> I swear I see what is better than to tell the best,
> It is always to leave the best untold.[32]

You see, I have said all along that Whitman chose to keep his determinism secret. Do you not now believe me?

2—The Determinist "Chain"

The second of the four aspects under which we shall view Whitman's determinism is the "chain" metaphor. The "chain" idea bears a close resemblance to, and is in fact inseparable from the idea of the "push," already discussed. It is closely related, also, to the "thread" idea, which will be taken up in the next section.

The chain metaphor is the most common metaphor applied to determinism. One will not read far in anti-determinist writings without coming across some reference to "the iron chain of cause and effect," and determinists themselves are fond of the chain figure, though they rarely make use of an "iron" chain, since that modifier gives anti-freedom connotations to the figure. Determinists sometimes refer to the "links" of the chain. Seneca, for instance: "Cause is linked with cause, and all public and private issues are directed by a long sequence of events."[33] In our crude attempts to comprehend reality we break up what may in fact be an eternal One into "a long sequence of events." We speak of cause and effect and can think of all causes as effects and all effects as causes. The idea of a regress of causes (perhaps necessarily an infinite regress, though the idea is inconceivable) is really the basis of the "chain" metaphor, the chain idea implying the inescapability of the result from its cause or the cause from its result.

The determinist's mind, as he contemplates the amplitude of time, plays up and down the chain. And he is sometimes vividly conscious of what appears to him the fact that his very thoughts are a part of the chain. "The mind," says Spinoza, "is determined to wish this or that by a cause, which has also been determined by another cause, and this last by another cause, and so on to infinity."[34] We remember that Herndon said of Lincoln: "The past to him was the cause of the present and the present including the past will be the cause of the grand future and all are one, links in the endless chain, stretching from the infinite to the infinite."[35] To the determinist, all that now exists, every event of the present time, is causally related to all that was, all that is, and all that will be. "Everything that exists," says Oersted, "depends upon the past, prepares the future, and is related to the whole."[36] "Every condition," says Whitman, "promulges not only itself, it promulges what grows after and out of itself...."[37] And again: "Past and present and future are not disjoined but joined."[38]

The simplest kind of determinism-consciousness is the conviction that what now is is the result of what was. This idea naturally leads the mind back along the chain of causes, toward the infinite past. We find in Whitman's writings striking examples of this kind of thought. Whitman's preoccupation with things past supplies impressive evidence of his preoccupation with determinism. "Indeed, when we pursue it," he added in a footnote, "what growth or advent is there that does not date back back, until lost — perhaps its most tantalizing clues lost — in the receded horizons of the past?"[39] Whitman is here going back along the determinist "chain." His words are actually an implicit pledge of allegiance to determinism, as will be seen by comparing his remark to that of another writer who states the same idea more explicitly: "The deterministic view maintains that all events in man's mental life equally with events in the physical world, must be conceived as antecedently conditioned, as having their origin in preceding events of which they are the necessary consequence.... One's character and environment are regarded, by the determinist, as the product of conditioning forces which reach back in an unending chain of succession."[40] This comes close to duplicating Whitman's statement in the 1855 Preface (already quoted several times) that

> no result exists now without being from its long antecedent result, and that from its antecedent, and so backward without the farthest mentionable spot coming a bit nearer the beginning than any other spot.[41]

This statement by Whitman is so obviously a statement of determinism that one wonders how his critics can so long have ignored it. The answer must be that it is *not recognizable* as determinism by Whitman's critics, that they are ignorant of determinism, so much so that they can look right at it and not see it. It is hardly conceivable that this could be the case, but it must be. I may quote the following as a perfect parallel to Whitman's remark: "A man's actions form part of the present state of the universe, and like everything else in it, are determined by the previous state; this again, is determined by its predecessor, and so on backward until we reach a state of things which existed before the human race itself came into being."[42] Notice the duplication of phrasing in the "and so on backward" and Whitman's "and so backward." A more amazing duplication of Whitman's words is to be found in Lord Kames's remark in his essay "Of Liberty and Necessity" that "What is a cause with respect to its proper effect, is considered as an effect with respect to some prior cause, and so backward without end."[43] Kames's "and so backward without" anticipated Whitman's "and so backward without" by a hundred and four years.

When Whitman later translated parts of the 1855 Preface into poetry, he re-stated the "no result exists" assertion in "Song of Prudence," and the lines we find there, besides offering proof that the idea was no passing fancy with Whitman, illustrate, when compared with the prose version, Whitman's care and calculation in covering up determinist ideas in his poetry. The new phrasing carries the old thought, but in his poetic version Whitman drops the precise and revealing philosophic terminology "result ... antecedent" and substitutes words less technical, less philosophic, less revealing:

> No consummation exists without being from some long previous con-
> summation, and that from some other,
>   Without the farthest conceivable one coming a bit nearer the beginning
> than any.

One of the purposes of *Leaves of Grass* was to make the reader conscious of determinism without letting him know that it was determinism of which he was conscious. Perhaps this is why even the critics do not see the determin-ism as determinism. It is as if Whitman wanted the reader to absorb the idea of determinism intuitively or even subconsciously. Whitman was not inter-ested in conveying the philosophy, in its technical form, to the reader. "*Leaves of Grass*, anyhow," he said, "does not teach anything absolutely: teaches more by edging up, hinting, coming near, than by definite statement, appeal. ."[44] Whitman wanted to present to the reader not the philosophy but the *effects* of the philosophy, these effects being stated poetically. The trick was to accom-plish this without revealing the philosophy itself. His success in doing just that was masterful.

I do not doubt that the determinism in *Leaves of Grass* achieves the effect that Whitman intended, but I think Whitman recognized that on most readers the effect would be a rather vague and unpointed one and that very few read-ers, specifically only those who were themselves determinists who understood the philosophy as Whitman did, would in the greatest degree be receptive of the effect intended. However this may be, it is certainly true that a consciousness of determinism heightens the effect of many passages in Whitman's poetry immea-surably and gives to *Leaves of Grass* as a whole a remarkable unity which the reader without this consciousness would not be able to perceive.

The foregoing discussion of the determinist "chain," for instance, if it is understood, will make one more receptive to the effect which Whitman tried to convey in the following lines from "Song of Myself":

> I am an acme of things accomplish'd, and I an encloser of things to be....

> Rise after rise bow the phantoms behind me,
> Afar down I see the huge first Nothing, I know I was even there,
> I waited unseen and always, and slept through the lethargic mist,
> And took my time, and took no hurt from the fetid carbon.

> Long I was hugg'd close — long and long.

> Immense have been the preparations for me,

Faithful and friendly the arms that have help'd me.

Cycles ferried my cradle, rowing and rowing like cheerful boatmen,
For room to me the stars kept aside in their own rings,
They sent influences to look after what was to hold me.

Before I was born out of my mother generations guided me,
My embryo has never been torpid, nothing could overlay it.

For it the nebula cohered to an orb,
The long slow strata piled to rest it on,
Vast vegetables gave it sustenance,
Monstrous sauroids transported it in their mouths with care.

All forces have been steadily employ'd to complete and delight me,
Now on this spot I stand with my robust soul.[45]

How truly great this passage becomes when read with an understanding of its determinism! It would be easy to overlook one of the clues to the "chain" in these lines. That clue, in the second quoted line, is the word "rise," which becomes unsuspectedly meaningful when it is seen as associated with the chain idea. It will be recalled that in his definition of determinism in his note on Priestley, Whitman explains that "all results ... *rise* [my italics] out of perpetual flows of endless causes" (above, Ch. IV). The "rise-endless" combination is expressed elsewhere, confirming the determinist import of "rise" in the passage quoted here. The entire "flows-rise-endless" combination is found in "Passage to India": "As a *rivulet* running,... / A *ceaseless* thought, a varied train ... they *rise*" (Sec. 4, my italics). In the title "Rise O Days from Your Fathomless Deeps," "Rise" and "Fathomless" again express the "rise-endless" idea of Whitman's definition of determinism. In "Song of the Broad-Axe" Whitman repeatedly exclaims, "The shapes arise!"; and the "shapes" which "arise" are (for one who understands) *predetermined*— so that "arise" is the equivalent of "rise" in the determinist context suggested here. All of these examples reinforce the evidence that Whitman was aware of, and made use of, the determinist chain in his poems.

And nowhere is that more evident than in the lines quoted, lines which, no doubt, are often interpreted as being preoccupied with evolution, but that interpretation would be erroneous. It is not man, *homo sapiens*, who has evolved: it is *a* man, Walt Whitman, brought into being by the determinist process of which evolution is itself a product. Tracing back along the chain, Whitman discovers, just as did the poet Omar, that "the first Morning of Creation wrote/ What the Last Dawn of Reckoning shall read" (see Ch. II). Whitman goes back in thought to the "huge first Nothing" (a terrific figure!— cf. Omar's "first Morning") and returns along the chain to the present, finding as he goes the causal links which fill the gap between what was and what is. In doing so he sees clearly the inevitability of his own birth and being.

The democratic import of the lines quoted from Sec. 44 of "Song of Myself" is made evident by comparing them with lines in Sec. 7 of "I Sing the Body Electric." Whitman looks on a slave being auctioned:

> Gentlemen look on this wonder,
> Whatever the bids of the bidders they cannot be high enough for it,
> For it the globe lay preparing quintillions of years without one animal or plant,
> For it the revolving cycles truly and steadily roll'd.

The "cycles" here are doubtless the same "cycles" which Whitman says "ferried my cradle" in Sec. 44. He and the slave are on equal footing, have been predetermined by the same "influences" (Sec. 44). The "cycles" which "truly and steadily roll'd" reinforce the idea expressed above that the earth, the "rolling" earth (echoing "roll'd" here), symbolizes determinism. The phrasing "For it the globe lay preparing" is surely akin to "For it the nebula cohered to an orb" in Sec. 44.

The lines from Sec. 44 are presaged by a passage in Sec. 31 beginning:

> I find I incorporate gneiss, coal, long-threaded moss, fruits, grains, esculent roots,
> And am stucco'd with quadrupeds and birds all over....

How bizarre these lines must seem to one unacquainted with Whitman's determinism! Reynolds completely misinterprets them, calling them — unbelievably! — "wacky."[46]

No description of the world of determinism can ever be adequate, but a very good description was written down by Fichte. What Fichte says here of determinism will be seen upon analysis to be an apt description of the universe of *Leaves of Grass*.

> In every moment of her duration Nature is one connected whole; in every moment each individual part must be what it is, because all the others are what they are; and you could not remove a single grain of sand from its place, without thereby, although perhaps imperceptibly to you, altering something throughout all parts of the immeasurable whole. But every moment of this duration is determined by all past moments, and will determine all future moments; and you cannot conceive even the position of a grain of sand other than it is in the Present, without being compelled to conceive the whole indefinite Past to have been other than what it has been, and the whole indefinite Future other than what it will be. Make the experiment, for instance, with this grain of quicksand. Suppose it to lie some few paces further inland than it does:— then must the storm-wind that drove it in from the sea have been stronger than it actually was;— then must the pre-

ceding state of the weather, by which this wind was occasioned, and its degree of strength determined, have been different from what it actually was; and the previous state by which this particular weather was determined,—and so on; and thus you have, without stay or limit, a wholly different temperature of the air from that which really existed, and a different constitution of the bodies which possess an influence over this temperature, and over which, on the other hand, it exercises such an influence. On the fruitfulness or unfruitfulness of countries, and through that, or even directly, on the duration of human life,—this temperature exercises a most decided influence. How can you know,—since it is not permitted us to penetrate the arcana of Nature, and it is therefore allowable to speak of possibilities,—how can you know, that in such a state of weather as may have been necessary to carry this grain of sand a few paces further inland, some one of your forefathers might not have perished from hunger, or cold, or heat, before begetting that son from whom you are descended; and that thus you might never have been at all, and all that you have ever done, and all that you ever hope to do in this world, must have been obstructed, in order that a grain of sand might lie in a different place?

I myself, with all that I call mine, am a link in this chain of the rigid necessity of Nature.[47]

I suspect a distinct and direct influence of this passage upon Whitman. Selections from *The Vocation of Man*, including this very passage, appeared in Hedge's *Prose Writers of Germany*, a copy of which Whitman owned (see Ch. IV). Especially reminiscent of this passage is Whitman's poem "As I Ebb'd with the Ocean of Life," in the section called "Sea-Drift." Fichte's "experiment" with the grain of sand driven in from the sea by the storm-wind may have enabled Whitman to confess,

> I too but signify at the utmost a little wash'd-up drift,
> A few sands and dead leaves to gather,
> Gather, and merge myself as part of the sands and drift.

But the tenor of Fichte's analysis helps us to see the meaning of many lines in *Leaves of Grass*. For instance: "For room to me the stars kept aside in their own rings,/ They sent influences to look after what was to hold me." Now, do you grasp the determinism of those lines? Or these?:

> And am not stuck up, and am in my place.

> (The moth and the fish-eggs are in their place,
> The bright suns I see and the dark suns I cannot see are in their place,
> The palpable is in is place and the impalpable is in its place.)
> ["Song of Myself," Sec. 16.]

Note, respectively, from Fichte and Whitman, the echoes: "place ... place"/"place ... place ... place." The "place" echo is heard also ("place ...

place") in a definition of determinism by Shelley — and note, also, the "chain" metaphor:

> He who asserts the doctrine of Necessity means that, contemplating the events which compose the moral and material universe, he beholds only an immense and uninterrupted chain of causes and effects, no one of which could occupy any other place than it does occupy, or act in any other place than it does act.[48]

Whitman confirms this definition in "The Sleepers," with, again, "place ... place ... place":

> The universe is duly in order, every thing is in its place,
> What has arrived is in its place and what waits shall be in its place....

I am sure you see the implicit determinism in these lines. And of these, in "Starting from Paumanok," Sec. 12:

> I will not make poems with reference to parts,
> But I will make poems, songs, thoughts, with reference to ensemble,
> And I will not sing with reference to a day, but with reference to all days....

Whitman's "parts" echoes Fichte's "part": "...Nature is one connected whole; in every moment each individual part must be what it is, because all the others are what they are; ... every moment of this duration is determined by all past moments, and will determine all future moments."
     "I am an acme of things accomplish'd, and I an encloser of things to be." "I myself, with all that I call mine, am a link in this chain of the rigid necessity of Nature." Which words are Whitman's and which are Fichte's?!
     Gay Wilson Allen, in his *Whitman Handbook*, denies that we could take literally Whitman's claim to "having studied and stated Fichte and Schelling and Hegel."[49] But we see here that, in part Whitman does state Fichte, poetically.
     If you contemplate causation and lose yourself in the thought, if you think of the determinist chain and think of yourself as a part of the chain, then you will begin to understand Whitman. This thought that comes to you now, without Walt Whitman it would never have been, and without America, without Columbus, without Cheops and the pyramids and the workers who built the pyramids, Walt Whitman would never have been. Think! If you think in this way, if you think poetically, think religiously, you will begin to "feel" Whitman's determinism. Think thus, feel thus, and then read the following poem.

With Antecedents

1

With antecedents,
With my fathers and mothers and the accumulations of past ages,
With all of which, had it not been, I would not now be here, as I am,
With Egypt, India, Phenicia, Greece and Rome,
With the Kelt, the Scandinavian, the Alb and the Saxon,
With antique maritime ventures, laws, artisanship, wars and journeys,
With the poet, the skald, the sage, the myth, and the oracle,
With the sale of slaves, with enthusiasts, with the troubadour, the crusader, and the monk,
With those old continents whence we have come to this new continent,
With the fading kingdoms and kings over there,
With the fading religions and priests,
With the small shores we look back to from our own large and present shores,
With countless years drawing themselves onward and arrived at these years,
You and me arrived — America arrived and making this year,
This year! sending itself ahead countless years to come.

2

O but it is not the years — it is I, it is You,
We touch all laws and tally all antecedents,
We are the skald, the oracle, the monk and the knight, we easily include them and more,
We stand amid time beginningless and endless, we stand amid evil and good,
All swings around us, there is as much darkness as light,
The very sun swings itself and its system of planets around us,
Its sun, and its again, all swing around us.

As for me, (torn, stormy, amid these vehement days,)
I have the idea of all, and am all and believe in all,
I believe materialism is true and spiritualism is true, I reject no part.

(Have I forgotten any part? Any thing in the past?
Come to me whoever and whatever, till I give you recognition.)

I respect Assyria, China, Teutonia, and the Hebrews,
I adopt each theory, myth, god, and demi-god,
I see that the old accounts, bibles, genealogies, are true without exception,
I assert that all past days were what they must have been,
And that they could no-how have been better than they were,

And that to-day is what it must be, and that America is,
And that to-day and America could no-how be better than they are.

3

In the name of these States and in your and my name, the Past,
And in the name of these States and in your and my name, the Present time.

I know that the past was great and the future will be great,
And I know that both curiously conjoint in the present time,
(For the sake of him I typify, for the common average man's sake, your
sake if you are he,)
And that where I am or you are this present day, there is the centre of all
days, all races,
And there is the meaning to us of all that has ever come of races and
days, or ever will come.

The concept of determinism illuminates lines heretofore obscure (Sec. 2):

We touch all laws and tally all antecedents,
We are the skald, the oracle, the monk and the knight, we easily include
them and more....

The skald, the oracle, the monk, the knight were a part of what determined us;
and, in a sense not just poetic, they are a part of us. This illuminating sequitur
is found elsewhere in *Leaves of Grass*: in "Thou Mother with Thy Equal Brood,"
Whitman, viewing the nation as the determinist outgrowth of the past, devotes
Sec. 4 to a reminder that the "ship of Democracy" bears a responsibility to assure
that the "antecedent nations" shall not have endured their contributions in vain:

Sail, sail thy best, ship of Democracy,
Of value is thy freight, 'tis not the Present only,
The Past is also stored in thee,
Thou holdest not the venture of thyself alone, not of the Western conti-
nent alone,
Earth's *résumé* entire floats on thy keel O ship, is steadied by thy spars,
With thee Time voyages in trust, the antecedent nations sink or swim
with thee,
With all their ancient struggles, martyrs, heroes, epics, wars, thou bear'st
the other continents,
Theirs, theirs as much as thine, the destination-port triumphant;
Steer then with good strong hand and wary eye O helmsman, thou carri-
est great companions,
Venerable priestly Asia sails this day with thee,
And royal feudal Europe sails with thee.

"The Past is also stored in thee"—determinism makes it so. What a refreshing view of our country is given here! We must realize a dignity in us that we
did not realize before. In the ultimate sense, we did not really gain our Inde-

pendence, cherished as independence may be: what we fought to be free from is still a part of us. Our very language attests to that. We can never be free from the past which predetermined us, and to that past we owe the debt of our heritage.

What predetermines us is a part of us. In "A Song for Occupations" Whitman gives a bizarre twist to the same idea, turning determinism upside down:

> The gist of histories as far back as the records reach is in you this hour,
> and myths and tales the same,
> If you were not breathing and walking here, where would they be?
> The most renown'd poems would be ashes, orations and plays would be
> vacuums.

We exist because of what predetermined us, but because we do exist, what predetermined us had to exist. *But if we did not exist, what predetermined us would not have existed.* This is an astounding concept. To have thought of it is genius. I know of no philosopher, no historian, no other poet who has stated it. Whitman is emphasizing the importance of each of us by explaining that without the existence of any one of us the whole past history of the world would have had to be different. Who can say what magnificent works might never have been created? "The most renown'd poems would be ashes"! This illuminating thought fits nicely into — may even have given rise to — Whitman's belief in the dignity of the individual, or "one's-self." The determinism involved is made clearer by Fichte in the long quotation above:

> ... you cannot conceive even the position of a grain of sand other than it is
> in the Present, without being compelled to conceive the whole indefinite
> Past to have been other than what it has been....

So you see, I am sure, how Whitman's concept of "antecedents" fits in in places other than "With Antecedents."

I have made it clear that "antecedents," as Whitman uses it, is a determinist word. Dictionaries that I have checked almost invariably use "antecedents" in defining determinism (see Ch. I, for six examples). The word is naturally often used in writings on determinism. In John Stuart Mill's chapter on "Liberty and Necessity," for example, we find in the opening remarks:

> The question whether the law of causality applies in the same strict sense
> to human actions as to other phenomena, is the celebrated controversy con-
> cerning the freedom of the will, which, from at least as far back as the time
> of Pelagius, has divided both the philosophical and religious world. The
> affirmative opinion is commonly called the doctrine of Necessity, as assert-
> ing human volitions and actions to be necessary and inevitable. The nega-
> tive maintains that the will is not determined, like other phenomena, by

antecedents [my italics], but determines itself; that our volitions are not, properly speaking, the effects of causes, or at least have no causes which they uniformly and implicitly obey.[50]

Mill goes on to say that the affirmative opinion is the one he considers true, and Whitman makes clear his own stand when he asserts in his Preface that *no result* exists "without being from its long antecedent result," etc.[51] Whitman's use of "With Antecedents" as a title is an obvious endorsement of determinism.[52]

When Whitman says (Sec. 2), "I assert that all past days were what they must have been," there is no mistaking his meaning. Other lines in "With Antecedents" are more subtle than this but nevertheless deterministic. It would be easy to overlook the determinism of "This year! sending itself ahead countless years to come." But a consciousness of the "chain" metaphor helps one to divine Whitman's meaning. Just as the past sent itself ahead, link by link, to "this year," so does this year send itself ahead to other years. In "Song of the Open Road," Sec. 12, we find "the curious years each emerging from that which preceded it."

"Determinism," says A. C. Garnette, "is the theory which maintains that the chain of causation between events is such that the events of the present (including human actions) are absolutely determined by the events of the past, and those of the future by those of the present."[53] Whitman says exactly that in "Passage to India":

> The past — the infinite greatness of the past!
> For what is the present after all but a growth out of the past?
> (As a projectile form'd, impell'd, passing a certain line, still keeps on,
> So the present, utterly form'd, impell'd by the past.)[54]

Whitman would have agreed with J. W. Draper's conviction "that the civilization of Europe has not taken place fortuitously, but in a definite manner, and under the control of natural law; that the procession of nations does not move forward like a dream, without reason or order, but that there is a predetermined, a solemn march, in which all must join, ever moving, ever resistlessly advancing, encountering and enduring an inevitable succession of events...."[55] "Pioneers! O Pioneers!" is obviously a poetic restatement of this Draperian view. "We must march my darlings," says Whitman in the second verse. Is this not Draper's "solemn march, in which all must join"? Throughout his poem Whitman portrays the pioneers, just as Draper had predicted, as "resistlessly advancing, encountering and enduring an inevitable succession of events."

In "Salut au Monde!" Whitman marvels at "Such join'd unended links, each hook'd to the next."[56] As early as the 1855 Preface, he declared, "Past and present and future are not disjoined but joined," and in the next sentence, he added, as if in corroboration of the implicit determinism of that statement, "The greatest poet forms the consistence of what is to be from what has been and is."[57] And in "Passage to India" he prophesies:

> All these separations and gaps shall be taken up and hook'd and link'd together....[58]

He believed, as did Priestley, that "there will be a necessary connexion between all things past, present and to come, in a way of proper cause and effect."[59] It was to be the work of poets of the future to make this "connexion" manifest.[60] But he contributed, as much as he dared, to make the importance of this causal linkage clear. An example of his work in this regard is the following short poem:

To-day and Thee

The appointed winners in a long-stretch'd game;
The course of Time and nations — Egypt, India, Greece and Rome;
The past entire, with all its heroes, histories, arts, experiments,
Its store of songs, inventions, voyages, teachers, books,
Garner'd for now and thee — To think of it!
The heirdom all converged in thee!

3—The Determinist "Thread"

> I know that the past was great and the future will be great,
> And I know that both curiously conjoint in the present time....[61]

Why does Whitman use the word "curiously"? From what we have learned, we can understand that past and future are in his philosophy joined by the chain of causes and effects, but what is "curious" about this conjunction? When you receive from me the answer to this question, you will rise to a higher level of understanding in Whitman's thought — and perhaps in your own thought as well.

Whitman's use of the word "curiously" indicates that he had studied the determinist philosophers enough to develop a sophisticated understanding of the mystery of cause and effect. The Scottish philosopher David Hume focused attention on a fact that was to have a great effect on subsequent philosophy: that *though we perceive in every part of nature (and in the human mind) a sequence of causes and effects, we can never perceive, or even imagine the nature of, that which so closely and invariably ties the cause to its effect.* We see, said Hume, "how one event constantly follows another," but experience gives us no conception of "the secret connection, which binds them together, and renders them inseparable."[62] That which, upon the occurrence of one event, necessitates a second and always identical event, is, Hume emphasized, "unknown and inconceivable."[63]

The importance of Hume's analysis, in bringing to the fore the concept that the causal nexus is mysterious, can hardly, for our present study, be over-emphasized. An entire chapter, Chapter VIII, titled "The Indefinable It," will show how extensive the concept of this unsolvable puzzle is in the philosophies and religions. The great Einstein, whose idea of a new religion coincided with that of Whitman (see Chapter IX), may have been cognizant of the problem, for he said, in rebuttal of indeterminism: "Now I believe that events in nature are controlled by a much stricter and more closely binding law than we suspect to-day, when we speak of one event being the *cause* of another" (see Ch. II). No person who ever lived has delved more deeply into the mysteries of the universe than Einstein. His feeling that there exists a "much stricter and more closely binding law" may mean that he was intrigued by the curious "secret connection" posited by Hume.

It was because he was conscious of this problem that Whitman used the word "curiously" to describe how past and future "conjoint in the present time." His awareness of the mysteriousness and importance of this connector is evident in several places in *Leaves of Grass*.

In one of his poems he pledges that if he were given the chance of becoming as great as the greatest poets, he would gladly surrender this chance in exchange for an understanding of the "trick" of "the undulation of one wave" in the ocean.[64] To one who remembers Hume's analysis Whitman is here expressing his awareness of the elusiveness of what Hume calls "the secret connection" which binds events together. In "Crossing Brooklyn Ferry" Whitman refers to "The simple, compact, well-join'd scheme, myself disintegrated, every one disintegrated yet part of the scheme...."[65] "Well-join'd" echoes "curiously conjoint." Whitman continues (Sec. 8):

> What is more subtle than this which ties me to the woman or man that looks in my face?
> Which fuses me into you now, and pours my meaning into you?[66]

Whitman's understanding of the mysterious connection could have come from Hume or from other philosophers — or from Emerson. "At the conjuror's," says Emerson, "we detect the hair by which he moves his puppet, but we have not eyes sharp enough to descry the thread that ties cause and effect."[67] (Emerson's "ties" echoes Whitman's "ties" in the quotation above.) Here is the explanation, but it only explains Whitman's meaning, not that subtle something, that "indefinable it," as I shall call it later, which is the subject of his lines, which is indeed the hidden subject of *Leaves of Grass*. Contemplating the "unseen force" of the ocean tides, Whitman muses:

> What subtle indirection and significance in you? what clue to all in you" what fluid vast identity,
> Holding the universe with all its parts as one — as sailing in a ship?[68]

And again, in prose, in more obviously determinist form, he speaks of "a soul-sight of that divine clue and unseen thread which holds the whole congeries of things, all history and time, and all events, however trivial, however momentous, like a leash'd dog in the hand of the hunter." This "soul-sight," Whitman tells us, is "the only solace and solvent to be had."[69] Surely Whitman's "unseen thread" is identical to Emerson's "thread" which "we have not eyes sharp enough to descry." In another place Whitman ventures to express the same idea more explicitly. There he speaks enthusiastically of "the potent Law of Laws, namely, the fusion and combination of the conscious will, or partial individual law, with those universal, eternal, unconscious ones, which run through all Time, pervade history, prove immortality, give moral purpose to the entire objective world, and the last dignity to human life."[70] These laws "which run through all Time, pervade history," etc., are identical to the "unseen thread which holds ... all history and time," etc. And surely these laws are nothing more than the eternal prescriptions of determinism — surely Whitman's paradoxical "soul-sight" of the "unseen" thread is really a perception of the higher or deeper truth that, unseen and in its essence unknowable, there exists an all-pervading and all-powerful determinism holding each cause to its effect, guaranteeing the orderly operation of the universe of matter and mind — and, in Whitman's philosophy (as in Hegel's), directing all toward the good.

> O the blest eyes, the happy hearts,
> That see, that know the guiding thread so fine,
> Along the mighty labyrinth.[71]

Whitman is here alluding to the same "thread" which he earlier, in prose, had declared "the only solace and solvent to be had."

The determinist significance of Whitman's "thread" may not be evident in the 1860 line in "Starting from Paumanok":

> And I will thread a thread through my poems that no one thing in the universe is inferior to another thing....

Seven years later this line became:

> And I will thread a thread through my poems that time and events are compact....

The determinism of the later version would not have been obvious without the analysis given above of the "thread" idea, but it is easier to see than the determinism of the earlier version where it is better hidden by the same metaphor but is, nevertheless, still there.

Whitman's choice of the word "thread" to convey in poetic mysteriousness the idea of determinism would not have been whimsical, for the word has frequently been used as a determinist metaphor. In Greek and Roman mythology are to be found, of course, the Moirae or Parcae, the three Fates (Clotho, Lachesis, and Atropos) who respectively spun, measured out, and clipped the thread of human destiny. Epictetus, who was presented in the previous chapter (IV) as one of Whitman's favorite authors, asks, "And will you be angry and discontented with the decrees of Jupiter, which he, with the Fates who spun in his presence the thread of your birth, ordained and appointed?"[72] Marcus Aurelius, another Stoic whom Whitman classed among the "great teachers,"[73] avers: "Whatever may happen to thee, it was prepared for thee from all eternity; and the implication of causes was from eternity spinning the thread of thy being, and of that which is incident to it."[74] Compare Whitman:

> It is not to diffuse you that your were born of your mother and father, it
> is to identify you,
> It is not that you should be undecided, but that you should be decided,
> Something long preparing and formless is arrived and form'd in you,
> You are henceforth secure, whatever comes or goes.

> The threads that were spun are gather'd, the weft crosses the warp, the
> pattern is systematic.[75]

(Echo: Whitman, "long preparing"/ Marcus Aurelius, "prepared ... from all eternity.") It is not surprising, in view of its mythological heritage, that the word "thread" is sometimes used by modern writers to express various aspects of determinism. Holbach, for instance, in his chapter "Of Fatalism," speaks of "those insensible threads that give impulse to the thoughts, decision to the will, direction to the passions."[76] His "insensible threads" may be the same as Whitman's "unseen thread." Further, compare Holbach's reminder on his next page: "Feeble, and vain mortal, thou pretendest to be a free agent; alas, dost not thou see all the threads [sic] which enchain thee." Compare, also, Emerson: "But to see how fate slides into freedom, and freedom into fate, observe how far the roots of every creature run, or find, if you can, a point where there is no thread [sic] of connection."[77] In poetic prose, William James conjectures that a determinist might lament: "The chaplet of my days tumbles into a cast of disconnected beads as soon as the thread [sic] of inner necessity is drawn out by the preposterous indeterminist doctrine."[78] Whitman used almost this identical figure when he wrote of the Bible: "All its history, biography, narratives, etc., are as beads, strung on and indicating the eternal thread [sic] of the Deific purpose and power."[79] A remarkable image, this, "the eternal thread"—and all the more striking when we realize its determinist meaning. Frances Wright, in A Few Days in Athens, which Whitman read and cherished, has her Epicurus remark: "I have traced, through all their lengthened train of consequents and causes, human practice and human theory; I have threaded the labyrinth to its dark beginning...."[80] Here, perhaps, was the inspiration of Whitman's "guiding thread so fine,/ Along the mighty labyrinth." The labyrinthine thread (or thread of Ariadne), of mythological origin apart from that of the Moirae, need not have determinist associations. But it is significant that the labyrinth-thread figure falls naturally into determinist contexts, as instanced above in the quotation from Wright and in the following from W. G. Everett: "The principle of necessary connection has been the guiding thread by which man has slowly escaped from many a fearsome labyrinth of error and superstition."[81] "The causal relation, as ordinarily conceived," says C. E. M. Joad, "may be likened to a thread, which, stretching out from the first event, tacks it on to the second."[82]

And I will thread a thread through my poems that time and events are compact....[83]

4—The Determinist "Flow"

It is a vivid consciousness of determinism, and this consciousness alone, which can bring the reader of Whitman to an understanding of some of the most puzzling passages of his poetry. It is because this consciousness is so rare, that Whitman's innermost meaning and profoundest message have for so long lain hidden in the unexplored depths of his thought. His interpreters have made many attempts to fathom his meaning, but they have not often been able to present more than what can be considered, after all, a superficial view of his poems. Their interpretations have been true enough, but not profound enough — a fact which even the critics themselves, some of them, undoubtedly have realized. If these critics may in a certain sense be considered to have failed, it is not because they lacked the intelligence necessary for proper insight, but simply because they were unfortunately lacking in the thought-patterns requisite to their task. By this I mean that their thought-patterns somehow excluded or denied determinism.

If H. B. Reed and G. W. Allen had concentrated upon the determinist idea of "an unending chain of succession," instead of merely, as Reed did, upon the "concept of endless progression and succession,"[84] or as Allen did, upon the idea of "endless 'procession,'"[85] they might have given us explanations less superficial and more enlightening. Reed was impressed by what he calls Whitman's "Heraclitan Obsession"; Allen discovered in *Leaves of Grass* a "Long Journey Motif." Both titles are appropriate, but it is too bad that Allen did not realize that his "long journey" was actually the determinist "chain." Reed almost hit the mark when he adopted the "flow" metaphor; but, alas, he was not aware that this metaphor, too, can have determinist significance.

Reed makes use of the "flow" metaphor in several places in his article. He adopted it from Heraclitus. Reed suggests that Whitman, like Heraclitus, saw "reality flowing by like an endless river."[86] But, overlooking the genuine metaphysical implications of the "flow" idea, he uses the figure to support his thesis that Whitman's imagery, with its incongruous whirl of colors and forms, its "ceaseless flux," conveys "a poetic or psychological effect of disintegration"[87] rather than the concept of unity, of "the oneness of the phenomenal world."[88] The metaphor as Reed uses it is ill-chosen: it is not easy to see how the idea of a flow of things can be equated with the idea of diversity, particularity, disintegration (terms used by Reed). The image conveys, in fact, just the opposite: if, as Heraclitus asserted, all things flow, then all things are a part of the same stream, and thus in a real sense all are one, a repetition of the idea of the determinist chain (or thread) which binds all events into a unity — and it is in precisely this sense that the "flow" idea applies in Whitman's poetry. "Our ordinary inaccurate observation," says Nietzsche, "takes a group of phenomena as one and calls them a fact. Between this fact and another we imagine a vacuum, we isolate each fact. In reality, however, the sum of our actions and cognitions is no series of facts and intervening vacua, but a continuous stream. Now the belief in free will is incompatible with the idea of a continuous, uniform, undivided, indivisible flow."[89] If Whitman had, as Reed puts it, a "Heraclitan obsession," then he was obsessed, as Heraclitus was, with the idea that "the sum of things flows like a stream."[90] This concept is, as Nietzsche suggests, consonant with the idea of determinism. The metaphor passed on from Heraclitus to the Stoics, who were in some degree influenced by Heraclitus, and who, in turn, had a profound influence on Whitman (above, Ch. IV, Sec. 1). We find Marcus Aurelius expressing the opinion that "substance is like a river in continual flow, and the activities of things are in constant change, and the causes work in infinite varieties; and there is hardly anything which stands still."[91] And Seneca asserting: "Both Gods and men are bound by the same chain of necessity. Divine and human affairs are alike borne along in an irresistible current; cause depends upon cause; effects arise in a long succession; nothing happens by accident but every thing comes to pass in the established order of nature."[92]

When one recalls that Whitman in his own definition of determinism speaks of "perpetual flows of *endless* causes,"[93] Reed's suggestion that the "concept of *endless* progression and succession" was "almost an obsession with Whitman"[94] and Allen's declaration that the idea of "*endless* 'procession'" is "always an underlying motif"[95] (all italics mine) lead one to believe that Whitman in defining determinism was describing his own philosophy, which if we may judge from the unwitting researches of Reed and Allen, was "almost an obsession" with him and is "always an underlying motif." We have had many indications that the determinism defined by Whitman as Priestley's was Whitman's as well, and we shall see that the "perpetual flow" idea so prominently a part of that definition and so obviously equivalent to the ideas discovered by Reed and Allen pervades *Leaves of Grass.*

One who has studied Whitman for a long time gains certain insights into the workings of his mind, and these insights cannot be forgotten when we begin to analyze his symbolism. One of the outstanding characteristics of Whitman's mind is the remarkable constancy of his thought: he remained loyal to the same ideas throughout the thirty-seven years from the publication of *Leaves of Grass* in 1855 to his death in 1892. It is this loyalty, actually, which constitutes the unity of the motley procession of poems which makes up *Leaves of Grass*; and this loyalty must be taken into consideration when we examine a particular metaphor in its various uses throughout the poems. There is a sort of *unity* in *Leaves of Grass* (I repeat myself) which almost precludes the possibility that Whitman's symbolism is indiscriminate or fickle.

Now with regard to the flow metaphor, we should notice that there are certain indications that the significance of the "flow" idea remains constant throughout the poems. Among these indications is the important fact that the flow idea recurs in a *context* which remains fairly constant. And, more importantly, this context is the same as that of the Priestley note, in which Whitman used the flow idea in his definition of determinism. In that definition, Whitman used, *along with* the flow idea the "perpetual" idea and the "endless" idea: "perpetual flows of endless causes."[96] Now it is interesting to note how many times we find him using in his poems these same ideas in conjunction. Note how often the conjunction occurs in the following examples:

I. "Song of Myself," Sec. 20, 1855[97]:

To me the converging objects of the universe perpetually flow....

II. "Song of Myself," Sec. 24, 1855:

Through me the afflatus surging and surging, through me the current and index.

III. "To You," 1856:

From my hand from the brain of every man and woman it streams, effulgently flowing forever.

IV. "Crossing Brooklyn Ferry," Secs. 2, 3, 8, 9, 1856:

The current rushing so swiftly and swimming with me far away,
The others that are to follow me, the ties between me and them....

. . . .

Just as you stand and lean on the rail, yet hurry with the swift current,
I stood yet was hurried....

. . . .

What is more subtle than this which ties me to the woman or man that
looks in my face?
Which fuses me into you now, and pours my meaning into you?

. . . .

Flow on, river! flow with the flood-tide, and ebb with the ebb-tide!
Frolic on, crested and scallop-edg'd waves!

V. "Starting from Paumanok," 1860:

Strains musical flowing through ages, now reaching hither....

VI. "Song at Sunset," 1860:

O strain musical flowing through ages and continents, now reaching me
and America!
I take your strong chords, intersperse them, and cheerfully pass them forward.

VII. "As I Ebb'd with the Ocean of Life," 1860:

I too Paumanok, I too have bubbled up, floated the measureless float and
been wash'd on your shores,
I too am but a trail of drift and debris, I too leave little wrecks upon you,
you fish-shaped island.

VIII. "Rise O Days from Your Fathomless Deeps," 1865:

Something for us is pouring now more than Niagara pouring,
Torrents of men, (sources and rills of the Northwest are you indeed inexhaustible?)

IX. "Whispers of Heavenly Death," 1868:

Ripples of unseen rivers, tides of a current flowing, forever flowing. . . .

X. "Passage to India," Secs. 4, 6, 1868:

Along all history, down the slopes,
As a rivulet running, sinking now, and now again to the surface rising,
A ceaseless thought, a varied train....

. . . .

Cooling airs from Caucasus far, soothing cradle of man,
The river Euphrates flowing, the past lit up again.

XI. "In Cabin'd Ships at Sea," 1871:

We feel the long pulsation, ebb and flow of endless motion,

The tones of unseen mystery, the vague and vast suggestions of the briny world, the liquid-flowing syllables....

XII. "After the Sea-Ship," 1874:

Tending in ceaseless flow toward the track of the ship....

XIII. "As Consequent, Etc.," 1881:

Some threading Ohio's farm-fields or the woods,
Some down Colorado's cañons from sources of perpetual snow,

. . . .

In you who'er you are my book perusing,
In I myself, in all the world, these currents flowing....

XIV. "You Tides with Ceaseless Swell," 1885:

You tides with Ceaseless Swell! you power that does this work!
You unseen force, centripetal, centrifugal, through space's spread,
Rapport of sun, moon, earth, and all the constellations,
What are the messages by you from distant stars to us? what Sirius'? what Capella's?
What central heart — and you the pulse — vivifies all? what boundless aggregate of all?
What subtle indirection and significance in you? what clue to all in you? what fluid, vast identity,
Holding the universe with all its parts as one — as sailing in a ship?

In this last passage the "fluid, vast identity,/ Holding the universe with all its parts as one," must be the same as Whitman's "unseen thread which holds [note "holds"] the whole congeries of things," etc., earlier considered.[98] And the word "unseen" of that quotation appears again here in XIV and also in IX and XI. In all three appearances it bears determinist connotations, as will be evident on reconsidering my earlier analysis in Sec. 3 of the hidden causal nexus. Remembering this and recalling also the "perpetual flows of endless causes," we may skeletonize various of the passages as follows:

I. "*perpetually* flow."
III. "flowing *forever.*"
VII. "floated the *measureless* float."
VIII. "pouring ... *inexhaustible.*"
IX. "*unseen* rivers ... flowing, *forever* flowing."
X. "a rivulet running ... *ceaseless.*"
XI. "flow of *endless* motion ... *unseen.*"
XII. "*ceaseless* flow."
XIII. "*perpetual*"; "flowing."
XIV. "tides with *Ceaseless* Swell; "*unseen* force."

Even in the passages in which the descriptive words do not occur the perpetual/ceaseless/endless/unseen idea may be present, though in some lines subtly.

But as Whitman says (IV), what *is* more subtle than this: "What is more subtle than this which ties me to the woman or man that looks in my face?/ Which fuses me into you now, and pours [note *pours*] my meaning into you?" What is it if not "perpetual flows of endless causes"—or, to use Emerson's metaphor, "the thread that ties cause and effect," the thread "we have not eyes sharp enough to descry"? (No, David Reynolds, it is *not* "magnetic attraction"![99]) It is "that divine clue and unseen thread which holds the whole congeries of things, all history and time, and all events, however trivial, however momentous, like a leash'd dog in the hand of the hunter."

Whitman in XIV salutes an "unseen force," and this force is saluted also in "A Voice from Death"—as a "giant force," which works by "laws invisible":

Thou waters that encompass us!
Thou that in all the life and death of us, in action or in sleep!
Thou laws invisible that permeate them and all,
Thou that in all, and over all, and through and under all, incessant!
Thou! thou! the vital, universal, giant force resistless, sleepless, calm,
Holding Humanity as in thy open hand, as some ephemeral toy,
How ill to e'er forget thee!

For I too have forgotten,
(Wrapt in these little potencies of progress, politics, culture, wealth, inventions, civilization,)
Have lost my recognition of your silent ever-swaying power, ye mighty, elemental throes,
In which and upon which we float, and every one of us is buoy'd.

This passage has obvious echoes in the various quotations (I–XIV) given above. In Whitman's "invisible" we have here again the "unseen" idea; in his "incessant" we have the perpetual-endless idea; in his "float" and "buoy'd" we have again the flow idea. The giant force "resistless" reminds us of Seneca's "irresistible current."[100] Later we shall find Whitman using the phrase "irresistible law": "...we are from birth to death the subjects of irresistible law, enclosing every movement and minute...."[101] Here, "enclosing" echoes "encompass" in the first of the lines from "A Voice from Death."

In the passage (XIV) from "You Tides with Ceaseless Swell," which is the third poem in the group called "Fancies at Navesink," Whitman recognizes the *physical* work of the unseen, giant force, its movement of the tides, its holding the heavenly bodies in their places, and asks, "What subtle indirection and significance in you? what clue to all in you?" In the eighth Navesink poem Whitman reveals the answer to his question:

Then last of all, caught from these shores, this hill
Of you O tides, the mystic human meaning:
Only by law of you, your swell and ebb, enclosing me the same,
The brain that shapes, the voice that chants this song.[102]

The "mystic human meaning" of the tides is the profound and pervading lesson of *Leaves of Grass*: that the omnipotent forces of determinism do not stop with the physical but reign supreme over the non-physical as well.

Whitman never forgot this lesson. Whitman *lived* this philosophy! Shortly after his 70th birthday, when he was beset by ills that were threatening his life, he disclosed to Traubel his method of consoling himself in "periods of trouble — when I am sleepless — lie awake thinking, thinking, of things I ought not to think about at all — am flustrated [*sic*] — worried:

> Then I recover by centering all my attention on the starry system — the orbs, globes — the vast spaces — the perpetual, perpetual, perpetual flux and flow — method, inevitability, dependability of the cosmos. It excites wonder, reverence, composure — I am always rendered back to myself.

Traubel comments: "How sweet his voice! And [his] gesture, look, were full of grace and expression."[103] Did he see Whitman in a near-mystic state of mind? Embedded in Whitman's confession are distinct clues to its determinism: "perpetual, perpetual, perpetual ... flow ... inevitability." Similar clues occurred on another of Traubel's visits to the aging Whitman, kept at home by his illnesses. Traubel relates that Whitman "Spoke of the world at large, its doings, etc." "I suppose nothing startling is going on — yet the countless rills run on, the rivers, the seas flow — incessantly the stir, incessantly the growth, developments!"[104] The phrasing gives evidence that Whitman was looking at a determinist world: "countless rills," "rivers," "flow," "incessantly," "incessantly." Because, as I have too many times pointed out, Whitman incorporated these same ideas in his definition of determinism:

> "philosophical necessity," that all results, physical, moral, spiritual, everything, every kind, rise out of perpetual flows of endless causes.[105]

◆ ◆ ◆

It may be contended that Whitman's determinism represents only *one side* of his thought and that its discovery serves only too well to show what has been believed all along: that Whitman was self-contradictory and made no attempt to resolve his inconsistencies. And inevitably will be quoted Whitman's famous lines,

> Do I contradict myself?
> Very well then I contradict myself,
> (I am large, I contain multitudes.)[106]

"In Philosophy," says Sir Thomas Browne, "where Truth seems double-fac'd, there is no man more Paradoxical than my self."[107] And, I would add, contradictions ofttimes when analyzed do disappear. So especially is this true of the "problem of freedom," of determinism versus "free will," that we cannot dismiss Whitman's determinism as an inconsequential "contradiction" of his "greater" message of freedom.

In "Song of the Open Road" Whitman declares himself his "own master total and absolute."[108] Richard Chase is of the opinion that this poem "is a celebration of free will." "Whitman," he says, "asserted free will with the utmost exuberance, and indeed he entertained no strong idea of necessity at all."[109] On the face of it, Whitman's assertion that he is his "own master total and absolute" may seem an assertion of indeterminist free will, but surely only Chase's misunderstanding of Whitman, not his misunderstanding of determinism — he is not so naïve philosophically as most Whitman critics — can have led Chase to believe that Whitman is here renouncing determinism. In another place Whitman uses the phrasing "master or mistress of all, under the law"; and the words "under the law" should certainly not be passed over as meaningless. In the same place Whitman says he meant Leaves of Grass to be "the Poem of average Identity"; but he is careful to modify this concept also: "To sing the Song of that law of average Identity, and of Yourself, consistently with the divine law of the universal, is a main intention of those 'Leaves.'"[110] He reasserts this intention, with the same careful modification, in the first poem in Leaves of Grass:

> One's-Self I sing, a simple separate person, ...
> Cheerful, for freest action form'd under the laws divine....[111]

"Freedom under law," he mused one day in Traubel's presence: "there's no fact deeper, more engrossing than that."[112]

Whitman's understanding of that synthesis lies at the roots of Leaves of Grass. I confess that in thinking of him as a poet I have not given him proper credit as a philosopher, so that only now am I able to grasp the subtlety of the most memorable line in his famous Section 5 of "Song of Myself":

> And I know that the hand of God is the promise of my own....

Whitman provided a clue to the determinism of this line when he stated (see Ch. IV): "...only that individual becomes truly great who understands well that, while complete in himself in a certain sense, he is but a part of the divine, eternal scheme...." This "divine, eternal scheme" becomes, in "Crossing Brooklyn Ferry," Sec. 2, "The simple, compact, well-join'd scheme." There Whitman declares himself, and everyone, "disintegrated yet part of the scheme." So here we have again Whitman's close attention to the important duality: 1) one's self and 2) that all-encompassing and absolutely governing essence of which we are a part. He saw the hand of God as the promise of his own — with the two wills, his own will and God's will, working congruently and inseparably. We are, he felt, at the same time and without contradiction, free and not free.

A paragraph headed "FREEDOM," tucked away in the section of his prose called "Notes Left Over," seems to have been an energetic, almost desperate attempt by Whitman to make clear the fact that his view of freedom was quite distinct from the view commonly accepted. Certainly Whitman must have recognized the great importance of this paragraph as a key to his thought. His seemingly evident intention not to emphasize this paragraph, either by more conspicuous location or more informative titling, may signify that he was reluctant to be more specific about his philosophy. The very phrasing indicates that he was attempting to make his view of freedom clear without risking the ordinary reader's recognition of the fact that he was actually presenting the *determinist* view of freedom. This is evidenced by his apparently careful avoidance of the traditional philosophic terminology "Free Will and Necessity." He does speak of "free will," but for "Necessity" he substitutes a less technical and not quite equally telling "irresistible law." Perhaps he wished to avoid arousing the hostilities which the mention of the term Necessity would have inspired. The paragraph, with part omitted, is as follows:

FREEDOM

It is not only true that most people entirely misunderstand Freedom, but I sometimes think I have not yet met one person who rightly understands it. The whole Universe is absolute Law. Freedom only opens entire activity and license *under the law.* To the degraded or undevelopt — and even to too many others — the thought of freedom is a thought of escaping from law — which, of course, is impossible.... While we are from birth to death the subjects of irresistible law, enclosing every movement and minute, we escape, by a paradox, into true free will. Strange as it may seem, we only attain to freedom by a knowledge of, and implicit obedience to, Law. Great — unspeakably great — is the Will! the free Soul of man! At its greatest, understanding and obeying the laws, it can then, and then only, maintain true liberty. For there is to the highest, that law as absolute as any — more absolute than any — the Law of Liberty. The shallow, as intimated, consider liberty a release from all law, from every constraint. The wise see in it, on the contrary, the potent Law of Laws, namely, the fusion and combination of the conscious will, or partial individual law, with those universal, eternal, unconscious ones, which run through all Time, pervade history, prove immortality, give moral purpose to the entire objective world, and the last dignity to human life.[113]

It was after Traubel had made reference to this paragraph, that Whitman mused: "Freedom under law: there's no fact deeper, more engrossing than that." Clearly Whitman had resolved for himself the so-called "problem of freedom." And his statements in the paragraph on freedom indicate that his solution of the problem was surely not far different from the *determinist* solution outlined in Chapter II of this book.

Whitman's solution is the same as Hegel's, which, as we have seen, was a determinist solution. The "Freedom" paragraph was, beyond much doubt, inspired by ideas contained in the Introduction to Hegel's *Philosophy of History* and, I would say, was probably written by Whitman with this Introduction before him or at least with a reading of it fresh in his mind. We have already found evidence that Hegel's Introduction influenced Whitman,[114] and here is evidence even more striking and to the point. Reread, if you will, the "Freedom" paragraph and then read these sentences from Hegel:

> Only that will which obeys law, is free; for it obeys itself— it is independent and so free.... [W]hen the subjective will of man submits to laws,— the contradiction between Liberty and Necessity vanishes.[115]

> While these limited sentiments are still unconscious of the purpose they are fulfilling, the universal principle is implicit in them and is realizing itself through them. the question also assumes the form of the union of *Freedom* and *Necessity*; the latent abstract processes of Spirit being regarded as *Necessity*, while that which exhibits itself in the conscious will of men, as their interest, belongs to the domain of *Freedom*.[116]

Aside from the precise duplication of ideas, there are revealing echoes:

> Hegel: "obeys law," "universal," "unconscious."
> Whitman: "obedience to Law," "universal," "unconscious."
> Hegel: "conscious will." Whitman: "conscious will."

Do you see, now, why I say Whitman may have had Hegel's words before him, or at least in his mind, when he clarified the idea of freedom?

The sentences quoted from Hegel make clearer Whitman's meaning, and, importantly, they supply the missing term "Necessity," which Whitman evidently intentionally left out and which orientates for us philosophically Whitman's "irresistible law," or as he variously puts it here and elsewhere, "absolute Law," "the law," "the laws divine," "the divine law of the universal."[117] We may, without twisting Whitman's meaning, replace each of these phrases with the word "Necessity." His statement that a "main intention" of *Leaves of Grass* was to sing the song of one's-self "consistently with the divine law of the universal"[118] cannot but mean that *Leaves of Grass* was composed with the synthesis of freedom and determinism as a central idea.

Quite likely this important philosophic synthesis is the very "principle," the "first essential," which Whitman berated his critics for not grasping. He said to Traubel of his critics,

> Yet not one of them comprehends — not one of them — not one of them

all —(the whole batch who have written, criticized, annulled)— has grasped the truth, the principle: has come into contact with, and prized, what is the first essential. Oh! it is a shallow, shallow brood![119]

"The shallow," he wrote in the paragraph on freedom, "...consider liberty a release from all law, from every constraint." He says of freedom, "...I have not yet met one person who rightly understands"; and here, of his critics, "Yet not one of them comprehends...." "[F]ew, very few," he had said, "only one here and there, are at all in a position to seize" what "lies behind *Leaves of Grass*."[120] The echoes in phrasing are fascinating. To one who is acquainted with the subtlety of the freedom-necessity synthesis and who has perceived the pervasiveness of the concept of determinism in *Leaves of Grass*, these echoes appear to be not necessarily accidental similarities, but more likely, quite logical similarities in the expression of the same idea in various instances — the idea, that is, that "behind" *Leaves of Grass*, "concealed, studiedly concealed,"[121] lies a concept of freedom which is rarely understood.

It is the subtlety or elusiveness, the unobtrusive eccentricity, of Whitman's concept of freedom that has baffled his would-be interpreters and given rise among the critics to the idea that he must remain an enigma. The important nuances of the freedom vs. determinism problem were considered thoroughly in Chapter II.

But further study of the problem has led me to believe that it needs to be reconsidered here.

Some believers in free will posit an entity or faculty called "the will." This "will," they call "free." And they mean that, their will being free, they are able to choose and to act in complete independence of any other causes. Belief in these (indeterministic) *originations* constitutes belief in freedom in the "philosophical sense"— the sense rejected by Einstein (see Ch. III).

Einstein did, nonetheless, believe in freedom. In the same place, he quotes Schopenhauer's saying, "A man can do what he wants, but not want what he wants." In Chapter II, I quoted Locke: "For how can we think anyone freer than to have the power to do what he will?" It does seem paradoxical (as Whitman says in "Freedom") that our wishes are predetermined but are freely carried into effect. But in the only sense that freedom *makes* sense, they are nevertheless free. This position opposes "philosophical" freedom and is called, sometimes derogatorily, "soft determinism." It is the position firmly adhered to by Einstein and quite obviously the position arrived at by Whitman, who would have rejected freedom "in the philosophical sense, "i.e. *indeterministic* freedom.But as a "soft determinist," Whitman did uphold "true free will."

He states exactly that in his paragraph on "Freedom." But in that paragraph he clarifies his position by stressing that "Freedom only opens entire activity and license *under the law*" (his italics) and "we are from birth to death

the subjects of irresistible law." Elsewhere he is also careful to modify "freedom": "Freedom under law," "consistently with the divine law," "under the
laws divine." Freedom in this sense is perfectly compatible with determinism.

All this is confusing. This confusion led Richard Chase to assert that
Whitman was lacking in "philosophical subtlety" and that "Whitman's idea
of free will is naïve." But I think Whitman's understanding of determinism
was as sophisticated as that of Chase, who himself has a good grasp of the philosophy. Chase, still confused, went on to ask a question which relegates him
to the host of mistaken critics who have pushed Whitman's determinism aside:
"But can one after all, imagine Whitman with an idea of necessity?"[122]

"Freedom," says Hegel, "is the truth of necessity."[123] Unfortunately, full
comprehension of this logical synthesis requires what amounts to a religious
conversion (see Chapter III), a conversion, needless to say, which most critics have not experienced; and this leaves them disadvantaged in their search
for Whitman's meanings.

I am free, says Whitman, but: "(I reckon I behave no prouder than the
level I plant my house by, after all.)"[124] When he proclaims himself his "own
master total and absolute,"[125] he is not contradicting determinism, though he
may have enjoyed the flavor of the seeming paradox enough to want to appear
to be.

He illustrates his thesis in the ingenious symbolism of "To a Locomotive in Winter." He calls out to the train:

> Roll through my chant with all thy lawless music...
> Law of thyself complete, thine own track firmly holding....

The locomotive makes "lawless" music yet is bound by the necessity of its
"own track." Who would have thought this was a poem about *determinism*?!
Surely now you understand the symbolism. An elucidation of the Stoic philosophy of Chrysippus yields an eerie parallel (italics mine):

> The external stimulus to human action binds man to the fatalistic chain,
> but from his own nature he has the power of decision for his own virtue
> and vice. Yet even so he can do no more than *run willingly between the shafts
> along the road appointed by fate....* A man's nature is subject to Nature's
> direction, but it is in his power to work hand in glove with Nature itself.[126]

The shafts are symbolic equivalents of Whitman's rails!

Nietzsche joyously shouts to the waves, "Do as ye will, ye wanton creatures! ... You and I are indeed of one race! You and I have indeed one secret!"[127]
Whitman calls himself "a kindred soul" of the sea[128] — and he also knew the
secret:

> Then last of all, caught from these shores, this hill,

Of you O tides, the mystic human meaning:
Only by law of you, your swell and ebb, enclosing me the same,
The brain that shapes, the voice that chants this song.[129]

These lines, written in 1885, are a poetic restatement of Whitman's assertion in 1872 that his poems were written at "the commands of my nature as total and irresistible as those which make the sea flow, or the globe revolve."[130] They actually restate anthropologist Edward Burnett Tylor's determinist declaration, at about the same time, that "our thoughts, wills and actions accord with laws as definite as those which govern the motion of waves."[131] Tylor's statement is a verification of Whitman's lines and also brings to mind these lines from "Song of Myself," Sec. 47:

If you would understand me go to the heights or water-shore,
The nearest gnat is an explanation, and a drop or motion of waves a
key....

Interesting echo: Whitman, "motion of waves"; Tylor, "motion of waves." [Whitman's "heights," here, corresponds to his "hill."] Almost literally, Whitman's lines translate Baron d'Holbach's assertion that "The necessity that governs the physical, governs also the moral world, where everything is also subject to the same law."[132] Echo: "subject to the same law"/ "law ... enclosing me the same." And Whitman's lines uncannily duplicate Holbach's determinist statement that "It is nature who combines, after certain and necessary laws, a head organized in a manner to make a poem, it is nature who gives a man a brain suitable to give birth to such a work."[133] Echoes: "laws"/ "law"; "poem"/ "song"; "brain"/ "brain."

As if ratifying all these findings, a great modern scientist made the following statement:

The principle of causality must be held to extend even to the highest
achievements of the human soul. We must admit that the mind of each one
of our greatest geniuses — Aristotle, Kant or Leonardo, Goethe or
Beethoven, Dante or Shakespeare — even at the moment of its highest flights
of thought or in the most profound inner workings of the soul, was subject
to the causal fiat and was an instrument in the hands of an almighty law
which governs the world.[134]

Thus saith Max Planck, finder of the quantum — determinist. Whitman would have been gratified.

VI

The Meanness and Agony

I make the poem of evil also, I commemorate that part also,
I am myself just as much evil as good, and my nation is —
And I say there is in fact no evil.[1]

Probably few men have lived lives which one could call more moral, yet Whitman chose for himself, and adhered to it with a remarkable consistency, an ethic which was profoundly contemned by the orthodox moralists of his time and which will forever keep him in disrespect among well-meaning moralists who fail to fathom his philosophy.

I shall not say that Whitman was perfectly honest. There was a mischievous deceptiveness in him that puzzles one who tries to evaluate his character. There was, by his own confession, something in his nature "*furtive* like an old hen!" (see Ch. I). Still, no one can study Whitman's life without gaining the conviction that he was above all a *good* man and represented far better the ideal moral type of man than did most of the people who were shocked by what he wrote. True, he deviated somewhat from perfect honesty in seeking acceptance by publishing his own anonymous reviews of his own poems, but in one of those reviews he succeeds in describing the Walt Whitman who he really was and whom many may consider morally superior to themselves: "He is the largest lover and sympathizer that has appeared in literature. He loves the earth and sun and the animals. He does not separate the learned from the unlearned, the northerner from the southerner, the white from the black, or the native just landed at the wharf. Every one, he seems to say, appears excellent to me; every employment is adorned, and every male and female glorious."[2]

That this was an honest appraisal of his own attitude, and not merely a trick of praise to gain publicity, is borne out by the generous testimony of those who became his friends in his later life. John Burroughs said: "So kind, sympathetic, charitable, humane, tolerant a man I did not suppose was possible. He loves everything and everybody."[3]

Whitman's friend Dr. R. M. Bucke was convinced that only by the benefit of a mystic inspiration — or as he terms it, a Cosmic Consciousness — could any man have become so far superior morally to ordinary persons: "He never spoke deprecatingly of any nationality or class of men, or time in the world's history, or feudalism, or against any trades or occupations — not even against any animals, insects, plants, or inanimate things — nor any of the laws of Nature, or any of the results of those laws, such as illness, deformity, or death. He never complains or grumbles either at the weather, pain, illness, or at anything else."[4] Whitman often visited the home of lawyer Thomas Donaldson in Philadelphia. In his book on Whitman, Donaldson says: "He was never a scoffer at the efforts of others or at their views. His mental largeness covered the errors of ignorance, cultivated or otherwise, with a mantle of kindly inattention.... he had an excuse for all of the fallen."[5] "I knew him," wrote C. W. Eldridge, "about 30 years, and during ten of those years as intimately, probably, as one ever knows another. I know and believe that he was a great man, also a good man, and the most truly pious person I have ever personally known. He never would admit, nor even allow any person in his presence to suggest, without rebuke, that the Divine Order of the Universe could ever have been changed or improved, or that there was any ultimate imperfection anywhere."[6] At the end of the preface of his own carefully edited edition of *Leaves of Grass*, David McKay said this:

> Walt Whitman was a unique character. As his most successful publisher I saw much of him, and learned to love his sweet and kindly nature. No one could enter the charmed circle of his friendship without feeling the mastery of his personality. This book, the work of my own hands, I give as a token of those never-to-be-forgotten days. To have met Whitman was a privilege, to have been his friend was an honor. The latter was mine; and among the many reminiscences of my life, none are to me more pleasing than those which gather about the name of "The Good Grey Poet."[7]

Alma Calder Johnston went far toward fathoming the determinist meanings of Whitman's poems. She deeply loved those poems and highly revered and loved their author. Beginning in 1877, she and her husband, New York jeweler John H. Johnston, frequently had Whitman as a guest, sometimes for weeks. Her son and daughter loved Whitman, called him Uncle Walt. As she took leave of Whitman after the last of her many visits to his home in Camden, she was almost overcome by emotion:

> We knew our hands clasped and our lips touched for the last time. When I left home, I had resolved that there be no tears.
> ...Pausing on the opposite sidewalk, I returned the salute of his hand,

uplifted in the open window. The horse-car came. It was empty, and the woman of me broke down! Struggling with handkerchief and purse, I yet glanced at the conductor's face. He brushed the back of his hand across his eyes.

"You've been a-sayin'good-bye toWalt Whitman? I know him," he said.[8]

No one who has read Traubel's almost stenographic reports of Whitman's conversations can fail to catch glimpses of the nearly Christlike character of the old Walt Whitman. To Traubel's, "You always forgive the unforgivable fellows," Whitman answered gently, "I always remember that I am to be forgiven."[9]

The "unforgivable fellows" were Whitman's critics, toward whom, for the greater part of a lifetime, Whitman had displayed an equanimity which was, in view of the insults hurled against him, remarkable. Bucke says:

He always justified, sometimes playfully, sometimes quite seriously, those who spoke harshly of himself or his writings, and I often thought he even took pleasure in those sharp criticisms, slanders, and the opposition of enemies. He said that his critics were quite right, that behind what his friends saw he was not at all what he seemed, and that from the point of view of its foes, his book deserved all the hard things they could say of it — and that he himself undoubtedly deserved them and plenty more.[10]

It is ironic that a man who found so little objectionable in the world was branded by that same world so very objectionable. Perhaps the world objected only because it understood neither the poet nor itself. It objected first of all, and perhaps mainly, to Whitman's unconventional references to sex. Much less shocking, however, would Whitman's celebration of sex have been if this celebration had not represented, in the eyes of his prudish public, merely one more perverted moral attitude among certain others almost equally shocking. Here was a man who professed to be "not the poet of goodness only" but "the poet of wickedness also."[11] Here was a man who "walked with delinquents with passionate love,"[12] who composed a poem "To a Common Prostitute" and was pleased to make public therein his offer of an appointment with such a one. Here was a man so utterly lacking in moral discrimination that he could proclaim, "Of criminals — To me, any judge, or any juror, is equally criminal — and any reputable person is also — and the President is also."[13] Here was a man who, in "You Fellons on Trial in Courts," confessed that he was himself guilty of some terrible secret sin:

You prostitutes flaunting over the trottoirs or obscene in your rooms,
Who am I that I should call you more obscene than myself?

O culpable! I acknowledge — I exposé!

(O admirers, praise not me — compliment not me — you make me wince,
I see what you do not — I know what you do not.)

Who would take the trouble to try to understand such a man? Who *could*
understand him? "He is morally insane," said Max Nordau, "and incapable
of distinguishing between good and evil, virtue and crime."[14] Judged by the
common moral standard he *was* insane. But we must judge him by a different
standard.

1— Sin

Bucke says of Whitman, "He had no sense of sin."[15] And Whitman
would not have denied that. He "gave up" Tolstoy's *A Confession* after reading about a third of it. "I find little pleasure in it," he said to Traubel: "it's
poor reading for me: I was never there. Tolstoy's questionings: how shall we
save men? Sin, worry, self-examination — all that: I have never had them....
There are undeniable and undoubted marks in all that Tolstoy writes, but the
introspective, sin-seeking nature makes no appeal to my constitutional peculiarities."[16]

Whitman's expression of compassion for the sinner and the criminal and
his refusal to rank himself above them in a moral scale are one of the more
puzzling characteristics of *Leaves of Grass*. He was fully aware of the damage
this attitude did to his popularity as a poet: "All moralism, metaphysicalism,
theologicality — pulpits, teachers, all of them — seem to go down on that snag:
that seems the fatal point in the course."[17] Yet he told Traubel: "If I were to
write my 'Leaves' over again, I should put in more toleration and receptivity
for those we call bad, or the criminal."[18] "...I do not think I should in any
way touch or abate the sexual portions, as you call them: but in the other
matter, in the good and evil business, I should be more definite, more
emphatic, than ever."[19]

Whitman's refusal, or failure, to reveal the explanation of his peculiar
attitude toward evil placed his friends and his friendly critics at an embar-
rassing disadvantage. How were they to make plain to the public the
justification of their faith in the essential goodness of a poet who professed
to be a consort of sinners and avowedly celebrated evil?

The standard solution of the difficulty, as presented by the critics, is that
Whitman's claim to equality with sinful persons and his own confession of
an evil nature reflect no discredit on the poet himself since he actually looked
upon everything in the universe as perfect and, in the last analysis, refused
to admit the existence of evil. Thus Allen: "The key to Whitman's attitude
is [his use of the word] *omnes*; he is the poet of *all*— all life, all existence, every
object and particle in the universe equally necessary, perfect and therefore

good."[20] This is a good solution as far as it goes. Whitman himself said, in some lines he never published:

> I am the poet of sin,
> For I do not believe in sin[.][21]

But the question is, *Why* did Whitman not believe in sin? To say that he believed everything *perfect* is not the answer but the question all over again. It does not appear to me that Allen's phrase "equally necessary," in the sense intended, goes very far toward explaining the matter. I do think, however, that in these words, even if Allen himself did not realize it, a hint of the answer is to be found.

In Whitman's view everything *was* "equally necessary" but not in the sense that Allen intends, that everything is needed to make up the whole — not in this sense, but in the sense that everything *is* because it *must* be. All things, that is, are subject to the principle of philosophical Necessity, which Whitman took to mean "that all results, physical, moral, spiritual, everything, every kind, rise out of perpetual flows of endless causes."[22] "The universal and fluid [*sic*] soul," he wrote, "impounds within itself not only all good characters and heros [*sic*], but the distorted characters, murderers, thieves[.]"[23]

> Each of us inevitable,...
> Each of us here as divinely as any is here.[24]

This is the sort of necessity Whitman had in mind, not that each was an indispensable component of the whole, a necessary part, but that each was necessary *as* a part, its existence and its characteristics inevitably what they were. "Do you know," he said one day to Traubel, "my philosophy [note "philosophy"] sees a place and a time for everybody — even Judas Iscariot — yes, for all: all of us are parties to the same bargain: the worst, the best, the middling — all parties to the same bargain. We are as we are, all of us — and that's the very bad and the very good that's to be said."[25]

So we come at last to the only satisfying explanation. When Whitman says, "I do not believe in sin" and "there is in fact no evil," we need only turn for enlightenment to Charles Bray's statement that "The doctrine of Philosophical Necessity assumes that there is no such thing as sin and evil...."[26] And to Bertrand Russell's statement that "the conception of 'sin' is only rational on the assumption of free will, for, on the deterministic hypothesis, when a man does something that the community would wish him not to do, that is because the community has not provided adequate motives to cause him not to do it, or perhaps could not have provided adequate motives."[27] If there is any doubt that Whitman would have endorsed this view, it will be dispelled by a review of one of the conversations recorded by Traubel. Whitman and Traubel and their friend, lawyer Thomas Harned, had been discussing the atrocities of the Civil War prisons. The talk then turned to prisons in general, prisons for the criminal. Traubel relates the conversation as follows:

I said: "Any prison is hard enough to think of: I often wonder if any man was ever bad enough to be put into a prison?" W. looked a bit startled. He asked: "Is that the only thing you've ever wondered?" I asked vehemently: "Did you never wonder some along that line yourself?" He cried: "I have! I have! But, Horace, how in hell did you know it?" I said: "How could anyone know anything about Leaves of Grass and not guess you was guilty?" He then exclaimed: "That's right! that's right!" He asked after a silence: "You've thought no man was ever bad enough to be put into a jail: what have you thought he was bad enough for?" "I have thought he might be bad enough to be put into a hospital — sick enough to be put into a hospital." W. looked at me intently then broke out into a smile: "That's a very striking way to put it: put in that way I say yes, yes, to it: you know, I have often said to you, Tom, and to you, Horace, also, that if I have any doubts at all about Leaves of Grass it is in the matter of the expression of my sympathy for the underdog — the vicious, the criminal, the malignant (if there are any malignant): whether I have made my affirmative feeling about them emphatic enough. You see, Horace, I agree with you fellows who do not believe that the criminal classes so known are the cause of themselves: I see other causes for them: causes as to which they are no more guilty than we are."[28]

Only by a recognition of Whitman's acceptance of this determinist attitude can we understand his sympathy for mankind. "If you and I," wrote Dale Carnegie — "if you and I had inherited the same physical, mental, and emotional characteristics that our enemies have inherited, and if life had done to us what it has done to them, we would act exactly as they do. We couldn't possibly do anything else. Let's be charitable enough to repeat the prayer of the Sioux Indians: 'O Great Spirit, keep me from ever judging and criticizing a man until I have walked in his moccasins for two weeks.' So instead of hating our enemies, let's pity them and thank God that life has not made us what they are. Instead of heaping condemnation and revenge upon our enemies, let's give them our understanding, our sympathy, our help, our forgiveness, and our prayers."[29] Whitman said of Thoreau, "But Thoreau's great fault was disdain — disdain for men (for Tom, Dick and Harry): inability to appreciate the average life — even the exceptional life; it seemed to me a want of imagination. He couldn't put his life into any other life — realize why one man was so and another man was not so: was impatient with other people on the street and so forth."[30] A note which Whitman never published explains his own view:

The secret is here: Perfections are only understood and responded to by perfections.

This rule runs through all and applies to mediocrity, crime and all the rest; each is understood only by the like of itself.

Any degree of development in the soul is only responded to by the similar degree in other souls. One religion wonders at another. A nation wonders *how* another nation can be what it is, wonders how it can like what it likes and dislike what it dislikes; a man wonders at another man's folly and so on. But what a nation likes, is part of the nation; and what it dislikes is part of the same nation; its politics and religion, whatever they are, are inevitable results of the days and events that have preceded the nation, just as much as the condition of the geology of that part of the earth is the result of former conditions.[31]

Physical and moral events are the same, Whitman says (recounting the contribution of Hegel), in that they "fit the mind, and the idea of the all, and are necessary to be so in the nature of things" (see Ch. IV). (Here we have Allen's word "necessary," but in what sense?)

For insight into Whitman's attitude, study Professor Cushman's remark on Spinoza's "mystic ethics":

From the point of view of the philosopher, there is nothing in the world that is morally good or bad,— nothing which merits his hatred, love, fear, contempt, or pity,— since all that occurs is necessary. The philosopher's knowledge of the *determinism* [my italics], of the world lifts him above the usually conceived world of finite things to this *mystic* world [my italics], reconstructed by his intellectual love of nature or God.[32]

There is much anecdotal evidence of Whitman's determinist attitude. Discussing his friend Corning's tendency to overpraise, Whitman finally remarked: "The case is saved if we say Corning is as he is because he must be."[33] And of Comstock, whom he conceded to have been deserving of O'Connor's dispraise, he said: "Of course we should always admit with regard to Comstock that he is what he is for reasons: he is quite honest in all his imbecility."[34] Speaking of what he considered certain faults in doctors and preachers ("what a mass of solid pretense after all!") he ended by acknowledging that his attitude was "unreasonable," that "they can't avoid it — it is the stamp of their circumstance."[35] Discussing an objectionable trait in certain writers, Whitman concluded, "...I confess it seems to me all right — the necessary, the inevitable, thing from their standpoint: and it is from that standpoint they must be judged — not our circumstances, our environment, but theirs...." And Traubel says, "Indeed he thought that 'even the humblest person is entitled to be so judged in connection with the environment to which he has had to conform.'"[36] Edward Wilkins, who served for a time as Whitman's nurse (1888–89), commented on Whitman's attitude of forgiveness: "His common expression in speaking of men and women who have moral faults is, 'It's the critter's way, and he (or she) can't help it,' or 'The critter's bad and he can't help it.'"[37] Traubel remarks in one of his daily entries:

Walt's great phrase of excuse for the prejudices and bigotries which he encounters — for frailties which in themselves are offensive to his perception of justice — is, "they justify themselves — they justify themselves." He first speaks of a writer in a manner the most freely critical and then says: "But she justifies herself by the fact of her temperament and the ways of her life." ... W. has a rather general objection to the clergy. "Their teaching is mostly impudence — their knowledge is mostly ignorance — they are arrogant, spoiled." Yet he suffers them because "they after all justify themselves in the scheme of evolution." He spoke last night of the great social whirl — of "the porcelains, chinas, hangings, laces, fine dinners, equipages, balls, shows, hypocrisies, hard-hartednesses that make it up," arguing: "I hate it — hate it with my body and with the rest of me: but what am I to do? Try to find a place outside the universe for it? It, too, justifies itself, don't you see?"[38]

Whitman's tendency to "justify" must not be considered an indication that he was sentimentally soft toward wrongdoing or that he was indiscriminate in moral judgments. The deed may be condemned and yet the doer be forgiven. "Always remember," he explained to Traubel, "though I hate preaching I do not hate preachers."[39] W. C. Angus of Scotland wrote Whitman in 1888 a commendatory letter in which he said: "Your Specimen Days I regard as the most humane book of the present century. While breathing the spirit of freedom it bears no feeling of ill will against those who wished to keep chains on men because their skins were black." Later, when Traubel was reading the letter over to Whitman, Whitman remarked on these sentences: "Don't carry that inference too far, Angus: I may not hate anybody, but the chains — God damn the chains, I say, no matter where!"[40] The distinction as Whitman expresses it here may seem blunt, but it is one of the most subtle implications of the determinist philosophy. "...let us hate *vice*, not the *vicious*," says Charles Bray, elucidating his determinism. And he continues: "The precautions we take to secure ourselves against that which injures us, are not necessarily connected with our hatred of the injurer."[41] John McTaggart suggests in his chapter on "Free Will" that the determinist may combine "an invariable intolerance of sin with an almost invariable compassion for the sinner." This, he says, was the attitude of Christ.[42] Whitman's feeling for the prostitute ("Miserable! I do not laugh at your oaths nor jeer you"[43]) did not mean that he approved of prostitution. He emphasized in "To Think of Time" that "The difference between sin and goodness is no delusion...." Shelley pointed out that "A Necessarian is inconsequent to his own principles if he indulges in hatred or contempt," but he stressed that "the doctrine of Necessity does not in the least diminish our disapprobation of vice."[44]

Whitman may have been naturally a sympathetic man, but his consciousness of determinism made it all the easier for him to become the hounded slave and "wince at the bite of the dogs,"[45] to see himself in prison "shaped like another man,"[46] to say,

> I walk with delinquents with passionate love,
> I feel I am of them — I belong to those convicts and prostitutes myself,
> And henceforth I will not deny them — for how can I deny myself?[47]

Whitman was expressing patently the determinist view when, on April 19, 1889, he told Traubel: "I always considered how much of a man's self is prenatal, accounted for by surroundings, parentage, birth, circumstances."[48]

If one follows carefully Whitman's remarks as recorded by Traubel he will come upon unmistakable clues to Whitman's belief in determinism, for instance this quaintly amusing story he told about "Sidney Morse's darkey":

> Sidney had a darkey to help him in his work: paid him so much per week: a good enough fellow when he was good but inclined for a splurge now and then. Sidney tells of one of them: he told it to me: a grand spree, lasting a couple of weeks: after the siege was over, after the man had cooled off, Sidney got hold of him, catechized him — asked: why will you do such things? The darkey answered: "I suppose it was all meant!"

Traubel says Whitman repeated the last phrase with infinite humor, "his whole tone and carriage rollicking in response to it." Then he said: "I tell that story because it fits so well here: I suppose *I* was *meant*, too!" Then after a still further reflection: "It was very cute [acute] in the fellow — natural: it may seem very simple — simple, perhaps as he designed it: but it is profound — profound indeed!"[49] On another occasion he remarked:

> Somebody says, and I think it is a wonderfully profound thing, that there is no life, like Burns,' for instance, — like Robert Burns,' the poet's — no life thoroughly penetrated, explicated, understood and gone behind, and that gone behind, and that fact gone behind, but after all, after awhile, you see why it must be so in the nature of things. And that is a splendid explication of Robert Burns. You go behind all, and you realize that, no matter what the blame may be to Robert Burns, somehow or other you feel like excusing and saying that that is the reason why, and that is the reason why, and that is the reason why. See?[50]

The following is a description of Omar Khayyám; but it fits Whitman just as well:

> To him the so-called sins of men were not crimes for which they should be judged and condemned, but weaknesses inherent in their very being and beyond their power to prevent or overcome. He felt for his fellow-creature as few have felt for him. He knew him as few have known him. He knew that

man could not separate himself from all the rest of nature and that the rules and conditions of his being were as fixed and unalterable as the procession of the stars and the succession of the seasons. If we for the nonce leaving aside our righteous sense of indignation, patiently felt for these secret stops that give rise to sins and crimes, we would realize how perfectly the clairvoyant eyes of old Khayyám have penetrated into the heart of things.[51]

As Donaldson has said, Omar's philosophy finds "much similarity" in Whitman's. Donaldson says of the *Rubáiyát* given him by Whitman: "In it he had inserted or pinned many newspaper slips relating to the poet, and marked many passages with a blue pencil" (see Ch. IV).

An opponent of determinism lamented that it makes men "no more justly liable to moral blame or condemnation than the lion, the tiger, the earthquake, or the cyclone" (see Ch. II). Whitman said to Traubel, "Do you know, Horace, it has come to me as a conviction out of long experience that there seem to be some men, some natures, that must develop, must display, the bad, just as the snake gives its poison, just as the tiger exercises its ferocity."[52] Compare Charles Bray: "We guard ourselves sedulously against the poison of the viper and the destructive propensities of the tiger, although, knowing as we do that their power and disposition to injure is the inevitable condition of their nature, we cannot be said to hate them."[53] (Echoes: Whitman, "snake"; Bray, "viper." Whitman, "poison"; Bray, "poison." Whitman, "tiger"; Bray, "tiger.") "The wolf, the snake, the cur" — these were terms Whitman applied to (of all things!) "the modern sportsman," emphasizing what he took to be the faults of baseball pitchers. He said to his friend Thomas Harned: "Tell me, Tom — I want to ask you a question: in base-ball, is it the rule that the fellow who pitches the ball aims to pitch it in such a way the batter cannot hit it? Gives it a twist — what not — so it slides off or won't be struck fairly?" Tom affirmed this. Whitman: "Eh? that's the modern rule then, is it? I thought something of the kind — read the papers about it — it seemed to indicate that there." Then, Traubel says, Whitman denounced the custom roundly: "The wolf, the snake, the cur, the sneak, all seem entered into the modern sportsman — [but then he relented] though I ought not to say that, for the snake is snake because it is born so, and man the snake for other reasons, it may be said."[54] In almost the same terms, Whitman's determinism surfaced in a more serious context. After the Civil War, Whitman said he "could not give" Jefferson Davis his "respect," but he did "not forget that the rattlesnake, the asp, could not help being the rattlesnake, the asp."[55]

We may now read exoneration into those severely self-condemnatory lines in Section 6 of "Crossing Brooklyn Ferry":

I am he who knew what it was to be evil,

. . . .

The wolf, the snake, the hog, not wanting in me

Notice the exact echo of Whitman's baseball condemnation: "The wolf, the snake"/ "The wolf, the snake." But can you appreciate the poem's irony? Whitman confesses, at first:

I am he who knew what it was to be evil, ...

. . . .

Blabb'd, blush'd, resented, lied, stole, grudg'd,
Had guile, anger, lust, hot wishes I dared not speak,
Was wayward, vain, greedy, shallow, sly, cowardly, malignant,

and then, in the next line, seemingly, *seemingly*, he descends to the very depths of his confession of iniquity

The wolf, the snake, the hog, not wanting in me

And this line, utterly self-demeaning, is actually, *actually*, self-forgiving! The wolf, the snake, the hog, are no less to be forgiven than the rattlesnake, the asp, which "could not help being the rattlesnake, the asp." The words have double meaning: Whitman seems to have delighted in ambiguity. There is a better term, and I shall use it, but casting aside its traditional suggestiveness of something risqué: *double-entendre*—I shall say that Whitman was fond of double-entendres.

And he used quite a few of them. When he says "(O admirers, praise not me — you make me wince,/ I see what you do not — I know what you do not)," he is misleading us by pretending to confess secret sins. But he is remembering Epictetus' description of the Stoic determinist: "If any one praises him, in his own mind he condemns the flatterer" (see Ch. IV). When he admits, "I walk with delinquents with passionate love," his words may be literal, but they are also a figurative expression of his determinist attitude. His poetic publication of this ethic without the philosophy which supports it was not a whim. "If I were to write my 'Leaves' over again, I should put in more toleration and receptivity for those we call bad, or the criminal." He says, "I praise no eminent man, I rebuke to his face the one that was thought most worthy." This line from "Myself and Mine" gives the impression that Whitman is arrogant and independent — but, again, he is exercising the tenets of his philosophy. That philosophy had been reinforced by Whitman's study of Epictetus. Whitman's list of Epictetus' characteristics of a wise man (see Ch. IV) began:

He reproves nobody —
Praises nobody
Blames nobody.

I dare say that, until now, very few readers — certainly very few critics —

have understood this aspect of Whitman's idiosyncratic ethical outlook. The redoubtable F. O. Matthiessen lamented: "The Whitman who is most nearly meaningless is the one who could declare at the start of his career and repeat on occasion to the end:

> I am myself just as much evil as good, and my nation is — and I say there is in fact no evil."[56]

Two words explain: *determinism* and *double-entendre*!

As a determinist, Whitman refuses to "call the tortoise unworthy because she is not something else" ("Song of Myself," Sec. 13). Bray brings the same elusive determinism to the surface in an amusing but instructive anecdote: "The gardener turned the toad out of the strawberry bed, where he was doing excellent service by eating the slugs, with the remark, 'I'll larn 'ee to be a tooard.' If necessity or determinism [*sic*] is true have we any of us a more rational cause of enmity."[57] Whitman's tortoise and Bray's toad are equally forgivable. Whitman's prostitute by the same philosophy is also forgivable.

Friedrich Nietzsche, describing the determinist (see Ch. III), says: "...in the same way as he regards plants, so must he regard his own actions and those of mankind." When Traubel asked Whitman, "Are we responsible?" Whitman replied that it was "a great problem" for "is the thistle, the oak plant, responsible for being thistle, oak plant?" It was "a thing to consider" — "the tree a tree — man what he is!"[58] Sri Ramakrishna, discussing the "great and small, strong and weak, good and bad, virtuous and vicious," ends with: "You must have observed that all the trees in a garden are not of the same kind." And at another time, he asked: "Haven't you noticed that there are both sweet and bitter fruits? Some trees give sweet fruit, and some bitter or sour. God has made the mango-tree, which yields sweet fruit, and also the hog plum, which yields sour fruit."[59] In close comparison, Shelley's lines now reveal what may have been a hidden meaning:

>   ...the poison tree,
> Beneath whose shade all life is withered up,
> And the fair oak, whose leafy dome affords
> A temple where the vows of happy love
> Are registered, are equal in thy sight....[60]

These singularly similar metaphors are joined by a duplicate in the question formulated (see Ch. II) by John Dewey: "If the man's nature, original and acquired, makes him do what he does, how does his action differ from that of a stone or tree? Have we not parted with any ground for responsibility?" We need not suppose that Whitman's philosophic acumen was so weak that he did not anticipate Dewey's answer (see Ch. II). In his understanding of determinism and his adoption of it as a practical personal philosophy Whitman was far ahead of his time. And it was on this account perhaps mainly that he chose to withhold from his readers the explanation of what seemed to many of them an eccentric, indeed morally perverted, attitude toward "sin." The world that condemned Whitman's peculiar morality would have condemned the determinism which explains it. But he had hope that "future ages" would understand him: "...I write with reference to being far better understood then than I can possibly be now."[61]

When it is said of Omar Khayyám, "He knew that man could not separate himself from all the rest of nature and that the rules and conditions of his being were as fixed and unalterable as the procession of the stars and the succession of the seasons," we know that this might also be said of Whitman. Indeed Whitman himself, in a trial flight of his verses, asserted it:

> As the turbulence of the expressions of the earth, — as the great heat and the great cold — as the soiledness of animals and the bareness of vegetables and minerals
> Nor more than these were the roughs among men shocking to me[.][62]

Like Haserot, he viewed the behavior of men in the same light as "the motions of the stars, the opening of flowers in the sunlight, the tropisms in butterflies, the responses of animals." See the quote above for the echo: "animals"/ "animals." Whitman would have agreed with Haserot that "a recognition of the deterministic behavior of humans is one of the principal avenues to the overcoming of the barriers of particularity which cut off communication between private persons and private worlds and which makes men act as if they were autonomous individuals not comprehended in a nexus of relations with other things."[63]

> All these separations and gaps shall be taken up and hook'd and link'd together,
> The whole earth, this cold, impassive, voiceless earth, shall be completely justified, ...
> Nature and Man shall be disjoin'd and diffused no more,
> The true son of God shall absolutely fuse them.[64]

Surely this "cold, impassive, voiceless earth" in these lines is philosophically akin to "the great cold" of the "earth" in the trial lines at note 62 above. Remember that for Whitman the earth symbolized determinism (Ch. V).

2 — Equality

> Each of us inevitable, ...
> Each of us here as divinely as any is here.[65]

Determinism was for Whitman, as it will be for anybody who believes in it and understands it, the great Equalizer. It gives one a new way of viewing himself and his fellow men and women. He learns, through contemplating it, to bring down the high and raise up the low. For he sees that the stature and station of every man and woman, though often to be credited as a result of their own wisdom and labors — or debited as due to their laziness or low intelligence, are in the last reckoning a gift of the Universe and inevitably what they are. He who has succeeded or is in certain respects superior deserves, therefore, no fawning praise; he who has failed or is in some way inferior deserves no haughty condemnation. In the matter of merit all are equal. "If there is no such Thing as Free-will in Creatures," says Benjamin Franklin, elucidating his determinism, "there can be neither Merit nor Demerit in Creatures. And therefore every Creature must be equally esteem'd by the Creator."[66] A line in "Myself and Mine" relies on the same philosophy:

> I praise no eminent man, I rebuke to his face the one that was thought most worthy.

The determinist explanation of this line is evident in a conversation related by Bucke in which Whitman "talked of great men generally, and how their apparent greatness is often due to the force of circumstances — often because it is convenient for history to use them as radiating points and illustrations of vast currents of ideas floating in the time, more than to any qualities inherent in themselves."[67]

> The law of heroes and good-doers cannot be eluded,
> The law of drunkards, informers, mean persons, not one iota thereof can be eluded.[68]

Thus does Whitman support poetically a broad democracy. His interpreters, so far as I have determined, have overlooked this support. Whitman stated the same democratic view in prose, in a fragmentary note: "The universal and fluid soul impounds within itself not only all the good characters and heros [sic], but the distorted characters, murderers, thieves[.]"[69] This "fluid soul," this determinism, was the "divine rapport which "equalized"[70] Whitman with all men and women. Contemplating determinism he could say,

> Of criminals — To me, any judge, or any juror, is equally criminal — and any reputable person is also — and the President is also.[71]

Compare these words with those of a famous lawyer: "There is no such thing as a crime as the word is generally understood. I do not believe there is any sort of distinction between the real moral condition of the people in and out of jail. One is just as good as the other." This was a determinist speaking — Clarence Darrow. "In one sense," said Darrow, "everybody is equally good and equally bad."[72] From the same determinist point of view Whitman avowed:

> This is the meal equally set, this the meat for natural hunger,
> It is for the wicked just the same as the righteous, I make appointments with all,
> I will not have a single person slighted or left away,
> The kept-woman, sponger, thief, are hereby invited;
> The heavy-lipp'd slave is invited, the venerealee is invited;
> There shall be no difference between them and the rest.[73]

> Here the profound lesson of reception, nor preference nor denial,
> The black with his woolly head, the felon, the diseas'd, the illiterate person, are not denied; ...
> None but are accepted, none but shall be dear to me.[74]

Whitman's determinism gave him his large sympathy; it inspired in him the broad and generous democracy which the mere mention of his name now recalls to the world. Whitman wrote of himself: "He does not separate the learned from the unlearned, the northerner from the southerner, the white from the black, or the native from the immigrant just landed at the wharf."[75] His determinism made it so, made him think in this way; "...all of us are parties to the same bargain. We are as we are, all of us — and that's the very bad and the very good that's to be said."[76]

> The past is the push of you, me, all, precisely the same....[77]

Charles Bray, in writing about his own determinism, had declared that man is "a mere link in the chain of causation."[78] Whitman, perceiving the democratic import of the same idea, proclaimed "human beings alike, as links of the same chain."[79]

> I do not call one greater and one smaller,
> That which fills its period and place is equal to any.[80]

"...my philosophy sees a place and a time for everybody — even Judas Iscariot...."[81]

> The universe is duly in order, everything is in its place,
> What has arrived is in its place and what waits shall be in its place,
> The twisted skull waits, the watery or rotten blood waits,
> The child of the glutton or venerealee waits long, and the child of the drunkard waits long, and the drunkard himself waits long....[82]

Section 16 of "Song of Myself" says all that needs to be said about Whitman's democracy. The section begins with this line:

> I am of old and young, of the foolish as much as the wise....

And then Whitman makes use of one of his "catalogues," one which must seem pointless to those who have not grasped its rationale. But in magnificent fashion it is a catalogue of democracy, where Whitman assumes identity — and by implication, equality — with all sorts of people: a Southerner, a Northerner, a planter, a Yankee trader, a Kentuckian in deer-skin leggings, a Louisianian, a Georgian, a Hoosier, Badger, Buckeye, citizens of Vermont, Maine, and California — and even extends his democratic hospitality to include one "on Kanadian snowshoes" and "fishermen off Newfoundland." All these give emphasis to Whitman's willingness, his eagerness, to accept all others as his equals.

> Comrade of raftsmen and coalmen, comrade of all who shake hands and welcome to drink and meat,
> A learner with the simplest, a teacher of the thoughtfullest,
> A novice beginning yet experient of myriads of seasons,
> Of every hue and caste am I, of every rank and religion,
> A farmer, mechanic, artist, gentleman, sailor, quaker,
> Prisoner, fancy-man, rowdy, lawyer, physician, priest.

He adds that he is "not stuck up, and am in my place." And finishes the section with:

> (The moth and the fish-eggs are in their place,
> The bright suns I see and the dark suns I cannot see are in their place,
> The palpable is in its place and the impalpable is in its place.)

Thus does he reveal to us, at least to those of us who understand, the philosophic base of his democratic attitude: the "place" of each of us is determined by the unvarying processes of nature, just as much as the place of the moth and the fish-eggs, the bright suns and the dark suns. And, in the final line, "palpable" and "impalpable" give us the clue that Whitman speaks here of the same all-including "physical, moral, spiritual" of his definition of determinism so often harked back to in this book.[83]

Whitman knew "perfectly well" his "own egotism," yet "would fetch you whoever you are flush with myself."[84] His democracy was not a leveling or demeaning democracy — reducing all to mediocrity. In this democracy every individual was divine, and each was as divine as any.

> Each of us inevitable,...
> Each of us here as divinely as any is here.[85]

No sickly humility, no pompous pride, but the simple, calm assurance of one's equality under the divine law with all others — this is the attitude of Whitman's ideal man.

> He says indifferently and alike *How are you friend?* to the President at his levee,
> And he says *Good-day my brother*, to Cudge that hoes in the sugar-field,
> And both understand him and know that his speech is right.[86]

◆ ◆ ◆

I should like to add a postscript to this section on "Equality."

The "Calamus" poems have generally baffled Whitman's critics and they baffle me. There seems to be no way of explaining them other than to accept that they display a homosexual side of Whitman, and there can be no doubt that they do distinctly display a love of man for man. But Whitman's determinism entered into almost every aspect of his attitudes as revealed in his poems, and I would suggest the possibility that Whitman conceived of determinism as a philosophical basis for his display of affection for all men and women. We have seen that his philosophy enabled him to "walk with delinquents with passionate love." If it was Whitman's conversion to determinism that is expressed in "Song of Myself," Sec. 5 — and I think surely it was — then it is certain that the almost mystic illumination of that philosophy gave him the vision "that all the men ever born are also my brothers, and the women my sisters and lovers,/ And that a kelson of the creation is love." See Ch. III, where I pointed out that Whitman's expression of this sentiment echoes Priestley's pronouncement that determinism inspires "the most unbounded benevolence to our fellow-creatures." The third poem in the "Calamus" group might easily be construed as an invitation to the reader to join in homosexuality, albeit at risk and pain. The title of the poem is "Whoever You Are Holding Me Now in Hand." One critic (he shall remain nameless) gives the title as "Whoever You Are Holding My Hand," which suggests a liaison. But the "me" in the title is not the poet, it is his book — and the poem is not about sex, it is about the pains and dangers of adopting the poet's philosophy:

> Who is he that would become my follower?
> Who would sign himself a candidate for my affections?

But "the candidates for my love [note "love"] (unless at most a very few)" will not, says Whitman, "prove victorious." The "very few" here is echoed elsewhere by Whitman — apparently in statements about his *philosophy*. Ch. I: "What lies behind 'Leaves of Grass' is something that *few, very few* ... are at all in a position to seize" (my italics).

Ch. I (when Mrs. Costelloe was "a little afraid" of his "deterministic [*sic*] theories"): "*few* can stomach me whole..." (my italics). It is fairly obvious that Whitman considers anyone "who would sign himself a candidate for my affections," who would be among "the candidates for my love," as prospective sharers of his *philosophy*. The intense love of man-to-man in the "Calamus" poems might, perhaps, be looked at from this *philosophical* point of view.

It may well be that in these poems the same fondness for double-entendres that I called attention to in the section on "Sin" comes into play. I am not sure that this is the case, but consider the following "Calamus" poem in that light. It could just be that Whitman's words have double meaning.

Among the Multitude

Among the men and women the multitude,
I perceive one picking me out by secret and divine signs,
Acknowledging none else, not parent, wife, husband, brother, child, any
nearer than I am,
Some are baffled, but that one is not — that one knows me.
Ah lover and perfect equal,
I meant that you should discover me so by faint indirections,
And I when I meet you mean to discover you by the like in you.

This poem, if one does not go beyond its ostensible meaning, has only ama-
tory or sexual overtones. It seems to suggest an assignation. But considering
what we now know, that Whitman had a secret philosophy which he saw fit
to reveal here and elsewhere only by "indirections," it may be that this poem,
by ambiguity, alludes to that hidden philosophy, which, if that is the case,
one might be able to discover, as Whitman indicates, "by secret and divine
signs." The line "I meant that you should discover me so by faint indirections" may be saying, "By correctly reading the signs, as I intended, you have
discovered the secret meaning of my poems."

The amative aspects of the poem (it should be noted that Whitman
includes both "men and women") could be explained by reference to determinism, with its logical support for compassion and kindness and, by exten-
sion in Whitman's mind, perhaps, pure love. Notice line 5:

Ah lover and perfect equal....

Compare this line with Whitman's statement in "Salut au Monde," Sec. 13:

My spirit has pass'd in compassion and determination around the whole
earth,
I have look'd for equals and lovers and found them ready for me in all lands,
I think some divine rapport has equalized me with them.

Notice that "equals and lovers" here may be equivalent to "lover and perfect
equal" in line 5, above. And, importantly, the last line here, "I think some
divine rapport has equalized me with them," leads us to the thought that *philosophy*, not mere amorousness, is involved. The "divine rapport" is determinism. Notice that the first line quoted here mentions "compassion." The
determinist's universal "love" is, by careful definition, "compassion."

So I would extend these thoughts as a possible beginning-point for a new
interpretation of Whitman's "Calamus" poems.

3 — Evil

Whitman viewed all events, happy and tragic alike, as parts of an infinite
and inevitable series with a nexus of causality. When Whitman's dear friend

O'Connor was lingering in a fatal illness, another friend, Dr. Maurice Bucke, protested, "It's a damn shame a man so young with such genius should be sitting there waiting to die!" Later, when Traubel repeated the remark to Whitman, Whitman replied: "I know how natural it is for a fellow to feel that way: that is always the first emotion: it demands to be uttered: but after that comes the philosophic thought, the conviction, the vision, that there is after all no mystery in this or any other trouble — that there is always a new or distant good cause to explain it: a cause often in the man himself: if not there, then in the father and mother before him — or perhaps even back in their fathers and mothers: but whatever, always the best reason, the profoundest necessity [*sic*], the supremest providence."[87] Whitman always looked to the cause, the "new or distant good cause," the "peerless, passionate, good cause,/ Thou stern, remorseless, sweet idea...." He even wrote a poem dedicating his book to this "good cause."

> *To Thee Old Cause*
>
> To thee old cause!
> Thou peerless, passionate good cause,
> Thou stern, remorseless, sweet idea,
> Deathless throughout the ages, races, lands,
> After a strange sad war, great war for thee,
> (I think all war through time was really fought, and ever will be really
> fought, for thee,)
> These chants for thee, the eternal march of thee.
>
> (A war O soldiers not for itself alone,
> Far, far more stood silently waiting behind, now to advance in this book.)
>
> Thou orb of many orbs!
> Thou seething principle! thou well-kept latent germ! thou centre!
> Around the idea of thee the war revolving,
> With all its angry and vehement play of causes,
> (With vast results to come for thrice a thousand years,)
> These recitatives for thee,— my book and the war are one,
> Merged in its spirit I and mine, as the contest hinged on thee,
> As a wheel on its axis turns, this book unwitting to itself,
> Around the idea of thee.

This is one of Whitman's subtlest poems. It is another of his double-entendres. On one level it salutes the "cause of freedom," or the "cause of justice" — a cause, that is, to which one dedicates oneself or for which one fights. But in its serious meaning the poem goes far beyond this. To interpret it on this shallow level would be to miss entirely its essential greatness. Paradoxically, the *book* is *about* the "old cause," and, "unwitting to itself," the book is a result, a predetermined result, of the "old cause." The "strange sad war" was also predetermined — and, "merged in its spirit," *Whitman himself* was predetermined! Whitman saw his book as the inevitable product of contemporary and preceding events: "I know very well," he wrote, "that my 'Leaves' could not possibly have emerged or been fashion'd or completed, from any other era than the latter half of the Nineteenth Century, nor any other land than democratic America."[88] And he stressed that those very Nineteenth Century events themselves were "inevitable":

> The Nineteenth Century, now well towards its close (and ripening into fruit the seeds of the two preceding centuries) — the uprisings of national masses and shiftings of boundary-lines — the historical and other prominent facts of the United States — the war of attempted Secession — the stormy rush and haste of nebulous forces — never can future years witness more excitement and din of action — never completer changes of army front along the whole line, the whole civilized world. For all these new and evolutionary facts, meanings, purposes, new poetic messages, new forms and expressions, are inevitable.[89]

The "old cause," in a deeper and more significant meaning, is literally "cause" in the cause-effect sense of the word. The "eternal march" of the old cause is another way of referring to the "perpetual flows of endless causes" of Whitman's definition of determinism (see Ch. IV). (Echo: "eternal"/ "endless"; echo: "eternal"/ "perpetual.") The poem is a veiled and indirect reference to determinism. But on even a third level it goes beyond sequential cause and effect: it is a reverent reminder of the "well-kept" ultimate ground of which causation is itself an effect.

The determinist tenor of the poem is Hegelian in its inspiration. "This vast congeries of volitions, interests and activities," says Hegel, "constitute the instruments and means of the World-Spirit for attaining its object ... those manifestations of vitality on the part of individuals and peoples, in which they seek and satisfy their own purposes, are, at the same time, the means and instruments of a higher and broader purpose of which they know nothing.... In relation to this independently universal and substantial existence — all else is subordinate, subservient to it, and the means for its development."[90] Whitman translated Hegel's "World-Spirit" into "old cause." His recognition of the Hegelian idea of an overruling determinism is evident in a note already quoted:

> Wise men say there are two sets of wills to nations and to persons — one set that acts and works from explainable motives — from teaching, intelligence, judgment, circumstance, caprice, emulation, greed, &c. — and then another set, perhaps deep, hidden, unsuspected, yet often more potent than the first, refusing to be argued with, rising as it were out of abysses, resistlessly urging on speakers, doers, communities, *unwitting to themselves* [my italics] — the poet to his fieriest words — the race to pursue its loftiest ideal.[91]

The prose phrase "unwitting to themselves" and the poetic phrase "unwitting to itself" (in the last line but one of "To Thee Old Cause") emphasize in echo the effectiveness of the prose note as an aid in interpreting the poem. Whitman is saying that the war was an inevitable event in a predetermined series of events — that the war was itself the result of causes and would in turn, with all its own "angry and vehement play of causes," produce "vast results to come for thrice a thousand years." This determinist view of the war was reiterated quite literally by Whitman in a conversation with Traubel:

> And by the way, talking of the War — have you seen what Conway has to say about that? It is Conway's opinion that the Rebellion was in great part a war that could have been avoided — a war of the politicians. I want Conway to say it all, of course — preach, write, argue, for his point of view — put in his negative in any form he chooses — but still I am forced to dissent. The War was the boil — that was all: not the root. The War was not the cause of the War: the cause lay deeper — could not have been shifted from its purposes. There are cute [acute] historical writers — very cute ones, the best of the whole group — who trace events in modern history back to the Crusades — establish a definite and conclusive connection. So it must be with our Rebellion: to try to consider it without considering what preceded it is only to dally with the truth.[92]

Here again, then, is confirmation of Whitman's characteristic predisposition to place sin and evil in a determinist context. He had said to Traubel that he agreed that the "criminal classes" are not "the cause of themselves." And now he reasserts the same determinist view by saying that "The War was not the cause of the War." The cause, he says, "lay deeper — could not have been shifted from its purposes." Whitman's universe was one vast inevitability. All events, without exception, were "provided for":

> I do not doubt that the passionately-wept deaths of young men are provided for, and that the deaths of young women and the deaths of little children are provided for,...
> I do not doubt that wrecks at sea, no matter what the horrors of them, no matter whose wife, child, husband, father, lover, has gone down, are provided for, to the minutest points,
> I do not doubt that whatever can possibly happen anywhere at any time, is provided for in the inherences of things,...[93]

It is this determinist attitude that explains a great deal about the serenity and equanimity which contributed so much to Whitman's greatness as a poet and made him so nearly Christlike as a man. Charles Bray says of determinism, "Nothing tends more than this conviction to the calm and quiet which is essential to the formation of that habit of mind upon which the highest happiness depends, and nothing tends more to worry and disquiet than the assumption that things might have been and ought to have been different in the past.[94] Hegel says,

> Without rhetorical exaggeration, a simply truthful combination of the miseries that have overwhelmed the noblest of nations and polities, and the finest exemplars of private virtue,— forms a picture of the most fearful aspect, and excites emotions of the profoundest and most hopeless sadness, counterbalanced by no consolatory result. We endure in beholding it a mental torture, allowing no defence or escape but the consideration that what has happened could not be otherwise; that it is a fatality which no intervention could alter.[95]

One of America's greatest disasters, the Johnstown Flood, occurred on May 31, 1889, Whitman's seventieth birthday. Several times during the next five days, Whitman expressed shock and dismay over the destruction and loss of life: more than 2,000 persons were killed. "It seems to hang over us all like a cloud — a dark, dark, dark cloud." On June 5 a representative from the *New York World* visited Whitman and asked him to write "a threnody on the Johnstown dead." Hesitant at first, Whitman did compose, the next day, "A Voice from Death." Written in only an hour and a half,[96] the poem begins,

> A voice from Death, solemn and strange, in all his sweep and power,
> With sudden indescribable blow — towns drown'd — humanity by thousands slain,
> The vaunted work of thrift, goods, dwellings, forge, street, iron bridge,
> Dashed pell-mell by the blow....

then continues with enumeration of the horrifying and regrettable results:

> Yea, Death, we bow our faces, veil our eyes to thee,
> We mourn the old, the young untimely drawn to thee,
> The fair, the strong, the good, the capable,
> The household wreck'd, the husband and the wife, the forger in his forge,
> The corpses in the whelming waters and the mud,
> The gather'd thousands to their funeral mounds, and thousands never found or gather'd.

Whitman then offers the consolation, which comes, of course, from his long-held philosophy. The second stanza had ended with Death confessing, "I too a minister of Deity." And in the final stanza Whitman recognizes and salutes a "vital, universal, giant force resistless, sleepless, calm,

> Holding Humanity as in thy open hand, as some ephemeral toy,
> How ill to e'er forget thee!

There are touches in the poem of the allegiance to meliorism which dominated Whitman's philosophic outlook:

> E'en as I chant, lo! out of death, and out of ooze and slime,
> The blossoms rapidly blooming, sympathy, help, love....

But this, or any, meliorism bears a troubling incongruity with determinism, which confers upon the mind neither pessimism nor optimism, but equanimity, tranquility, resignation to the inevitable. It is true that many determinists — I can name Whitman, Hegel, Emerson, Bray, Godwin, Priestley — held to a belief in a kind of optimism, a feeling that the working-out of the predetermined scheme was melioristic, would lead to a greater good. But determinism is not, as I see it, a logical ally of meliorism. Strangely, Whitman realized this, in fact stated it. But in the same statement, he reverted to his meliorism by contending that determinism, though of itself amoral, leads "inevitably" to an improved world. That is my understanding of the following remark:

> (In a certain sense, while the Moral is the purport and last intelligence of all Nature, there is absolutely nothing of the moral in the works, or laws, or shows of Nature. Those only lead inevitably to it — begin and necessitate it.)[97]

There is a paradox here, perhaps even a contradiction, that is beyond my ability to resolve. But there is no denying that a sort of joyous anticipation of an improved world is a major element in the thought of *Leaves of Grass*. However, along with this anticipation is a strong resignation — and this *is* logical — to the world as it is, to events as they happen, no matter how awful they may be.

How illuminating it is to compare Whitman with Lincoln! Lincoln, as we have seen (Ch. IV), was a determinist, a man of great equanimity. "Come what would, weal or woe, victory or defeat, life or death, Lincoln was cool and calm, neither despairing nor exulting, praising nor blaming, eulogizing nor condemning."[98] When Whitman was an old man and very sick, though still bravely living on, his friend Traubel said to him, "You are serene: you are almost prosaically poised: then you have faith." Whitman assented, "Yes: perhaps it's the serenity most of all." He laughed, Traubel says, "over my phrase 'prosaically poised.'" And then Whitman explained, "I do not worry: I determine not to worry — let come what may come. Resignation, I may call it: peace in spite of fate." Traubel broke in: "Peace at any price?" Whitman laughed. "Almost that: what the religious people call resignation: the feeling that whatever comes is just the thing that ought to come — ought to be welcomed." And Traubel continues, "But this element in him 'is not explained' by his 'occidental origins':

> His vision drew him into the past. "Somewhere, back, back, thousands of years ago, in my fathers, mothers, there must have been an oriental strain, element, introduced — a dreamy languor, calm, content: the germ seed of it, somehow — of this quality which now turns up in me, to my benefit, salvation." Had this anything to do with fatalism? The Mohammedan tempera-

ment? "No: it antedates all that; we find it in Hindustan, Palestine, all over the East: rich, suffused with the glow of peace: in nations of men: before what we call civilization."[99]

Notice that Whitman's words, "come what may come" and "whatever comes," echo "Come what would" in the description of Lincoln's outlook. Herndon, describing Lincoln's philosophy, says, "Everything, everywhere, is doomed for all time. If a man was good or bad, small or great, and if virtue or vice prevailed, it was so doomed. If bloody war, deathly famine, and cruel pestilence stalked over the land, it was to be and *had come*, and to mourn for this, to regret it, to resist it, would only be flying in the face of the inevitable."[100] Whitman, in one of the collected notes, admonishes, "Do not grumble at any fact or condition whatever. What has been has been well, and what is is well, for nothing but such as they could come out of such as underlay them. They also are to underlie what could be built upon nothing better than them."[101]

Lincoln was one of the greatest exemplars of determinist resignation. Look at photographs of him. There you will see the face of a man who has made truce with inevitability. "He looked out from his noble nature upon the stern realities of life, the ludicrous and the sad, the foolish and the wise, and whispered to himself, 'All this was decreed, it is inevitable, it was to be and now is.'"[102] Whitman also "looked out" in this very same way:

I Sit and Look Out

I sit and look out upon all the sorrows of the world, and upon all oppression and shame,

I hear secret convulsive sobs from young men at anguish with themselves, remorseful after deeds done,

I see in low life the mother misused by her children, dying, neglected, gaunt, desperate,

I see the wife misused by her husband, I see the treacherous seducer of young women,

I mark the ranklings of jealousy and unrequited love attempted to be hid, I see these sights on the earth,

I see the workings of battle, pestilence, tyranny, I see martyrs and prisoners,

I observe a famine at sea, I observe the sailors casting lots who shall be kill'd to preserve the lives of the rest,

I observe the slights and degradations cast by arrogant persons upon laborers, the poor, and upon negroes, and the like;

All these — all the meanness and agony without end I sitting look out upon,

See, hear, and am silent.

Lincoln "looked out ... upon the stern realities of life ... and whispered to himself, 'All this was decreed, it is inevitable, it was to be and now is.'" How well the description fits Whitman! Whitman, thinking back upon is own life, remarked: "I don't spend much of my time with regrets for anything: yet sometimes I regret that I never went to Europe: other times I regret that I never learned to read German or French. No doubt it's all just as well as it is: it all came about according to what they used to describe as 'the ordinances of God': there's no chance in it...."[103] "If a man was good or bad, small or great, and if virtue or vice prevailed, it was so doomed. If bloody war, deathly famine, and cruel pestilence stalked over the land, it was to be and *had come*, and to mourn for this, to regret it, to resist it, would only be flying in the face of the inevitable." Such was Lincoln's philosophy — and Whitman's.

◆ ◆ ◆

David S. Reynolds includes "I Sit and Look Out" among poems which he takes to be Whitman's "negative comments on society and human nature," products of "the bleak years after the 1856 edition." He calls these comments "glum."[104] Henry Alonzo Myers cites "I Sit and Look Out" as "a fair example" of Whitman's occasional "moods of depression."[105] Henry Seidel Canby characterizes it as "a sad and mellower poem ... in which his melancholy doubts of human nature under stress and temptation are imperishably recorded."[106] David B. Baldwin, in his analysis of the poem, says of Whitman, "With rare understatement, he conveys his grief that such negative conditions abide and his dismay that he is helpless in the face of them."[107] These comments serve quite well to show how far astray Whitman's critics can be led by their failure to recognize his determinism. The poem is not "glum," not one of Whitman's "negative comments" nor does it exemplify a "mood of depression" nor is it "sad" or "melancholy" nor does it convey "grief" and "dismay." It is an expression of the consolation and acceptance logically consequent on a belief in determinism. "A Necessarian," says Shelley, "looks with an elevated and dreadless composure upon the links of the universal chain as they pass before his eyes."[108] When he wrote "I Sit and Look Out," this was Whitman's attitude exactly — not sadness and regret.

> From the point of view of the philosopher, there is nothing in the world that is morally good or bad, — nothing which merits his hatred, love, fear, contempt, or pity, — since all that occurs is necessary. The philosopher's knowledge of the determinism [*sic*] of the world lifts him above the usually conceived world of finite things to this mystic world, reconstructed by his intellectual love of nature or God.[109]

VII

The Beautiful Necessity

Let us build altars to the Beautiful Necessity.
— R. W. Emerson, "Fate."

A typical visitor to Whitman's little house on Mickle Street in Camden in the late 1880's would have been met at the door by the housekeeper, Mrs. Davis. If the poet was feeling well enough that day, the admirer — or he may have been only a curiosity seeker — was conducted up the narrow stairs to the big front room on the second floor. A good-natured welcome, a chat of a few minutes or so, a tactful dismissal (if necessary) — that was the routine.

There was one thing about Whitman's room the visitor would not have overlooked nor soon have forgotten: its unashamed disarray. Books, bundles of letters, sheaves of old manuscript, loose photographs, clippings — these cluttered the mantel and shelves and two large tables and lay in piles on the floor. This was Whitman's filing system. He resisted the attempts his housekeeper made to put things in order, and when he could not find anything, he sometimes complained that Mrs. Davis had been "cleaning up again."[1] Once he said, "Mary thinks it an utterly indecent place — disorder added to disorder. But then you remember what some one said writing about the Leaves: 'This book is a confused book — that's its main trouble: the author got mixed up at the start and was never put to order again.' That explains this room."[2]

When reminiscing to Traubel he often interrupted his narrative to explore about in the piles with the point — one writer says the crook — of his cane, looking for some item of documentation. And the search was usually successful — a great wonder indeed, considering that the collection consisted of materials gathered together over a period of some forty years. But sometimes he looked and looked, and looked again, and could not find the precious letter or first draft or proof-sheet or clipping he knew he had saved. There was, for instance, the case of the missing photographs.

159

Had he found the missing pictures yet? "No: not a sign of 'em: but we are to hunt again: Ed says he will go over all the shelves in there once more." I looked questioningly towards the confused table at his elbow. "Would they be likely to be there?" He laughed: "It's not impossible: nothing is impossible with the Lord." When I asked: "You don't put that table on the Lord, surely"—he persisted: "Why not? there is a philosopher somewhere—oh! what is his name? let me see"—it would not come—"anyhow, a wise fellow once asserted something to the effect—I cannot give you his words—that the Lord is no concrete personage, but the essence—the idea back of ideas—through which conditions, events as they were, were justified."[3]

At that point Whitman might very appropriately have quoted to Traubel the following lines from Boethius, of whose philosophy he had early knowledge:

> There the Tigris and Euphrates
>   At one source their waters blend,
> Soon to draw apart, and plainward
>   Each its separate way to wend.
> When once more their waters mingle
>   In a channel deep and wide,
> All the flotsam comes together
>   That is borne upon the tide:
> Ships, and trunks of trees, uprooted
>   In the torrent's wild career,
> Meet, as 'mid the swirling waters
>   Chance their random way may steer.
> Yet the shelving of the channel
>   And the flowing water's force
> Guides each movement, and determines
>   Every floating fragment's course.
> Thus where'er the drift of hazard
>   Seems most unrestrained to flow,
> Chance herself is reined and bitted,
>   And the curb of law doth know.[4]

In "A Voice from Death" Whitman refers to "rushing, whirling, wild debris" (line 5), but the closing lines of that poem tell us that he was reminded, even by that very disorder and apparent chaos, of a hidden and easily forgotten power:

> Thou waters that encompass us!
> Thou that in all the life and death of us, in action or in sleep!
> Thou laws invisible that permeate them and all,
> Thou that in all, and over all, and through and under all, incessant!
> Thou! thou! the vital, universal, giant force resistless, sleepless, calm
> Holding Humanity as in thy open hand, as some ephemeral toy,
> How ill to e'er forget thee!

For I too have forgotten,
(Wrapt in these little potencies of progress, politics, culture, wealth,
inventions, civilization,)
Have lost my recognition of your silent ever-swaying power, ye mighty
elemental throes,
In which and upon which we float, and every one of us is buoy'd.[5]

Whitman did at times forget these all-powerful, determining latencies,
this law, this "vital, universal, giant force." He was distracted by the "little
potencies of progress, politics, culture, wealth, inventions, civilization." But
here, writing about the chaos and tragedy of the Johnstown Flood, he recalls
his determinism. "Float" and "buoy'd" in the last line and "incessant" in
the fourth identify his subject as the determinism which he defined as
"perpetual flows of endless causes" in his Priestley note.[6] What he speaks
of in this poem is that which "lies behind almost every line" of *Leaves of Grass*.[7]

To those unable to detect its presence in Whitman's poems, much
of *Leaves of Grass* will always appear to be, as in line 5 of "A Voice from
Death," just so much "rushing, whirling, wild debris." Whitman's endless heterogeneous lists of things, his "catalogues" as they are called, have been
ridiculed and parodied. Reynolds finds them "tiresomely inclusive."[8] T. W.
Higginson looked upon them as "sandy wastes of iteration."[9] Kenneth Burke
wisely conjectured, "It is possible that, after long inspection, we might find
some 'over-arching' principle of development that 'underlies' his typical lists."[10]
Now we have found it!—determinism.

After visiting a rugged canyon in Colorado, Whitman wrote "Spirit That
Form'd This Scene":

Spirit that form'd this scene,
These tumbled rock-piles grim and red,
These reckless heaven-ambitious peaks,
These gorges, turbulent-clear streams, this naked freshness,
These formless wild arrays, for reasons of their own,
I know thee, savage spirit—we have communed together,
Mine too such wild arrays, for reasons of their own;
Was't charged against my chants they had forgotten art?
To fuse within themselves its rules precise and delicatesse?
The lyrist's measur'd beat, the wrought-out temple's grace—column and
polish'd arch forgot?
But thou that revelest here—spirit that form'd this scene,
They have remember'd thee.

In this poem, by an obvious analogy, Whitman cleverly reveals his poetic
technique. Shelley, in *Queen Mab*, speaks also of a "Spirit." His lines offer
clarification:

A Spirit of activity and life ...
... in the storm of change, that ceaselessly
Rolls round the eternal universe, and shakes
Its undecaying battlement, presides,
Apportioning with irresistible law
The place each spring of its machine shall fill;
So that when waves on waves tumultuous heap
Confusion to the clouds, and fiercely driven
Heaven's lightnings scorch the uprooted ocean-fords,
Whilst, to the eye of shipwrecked mariner,
Lone sitting on the bare and shuddering rock,
All seems unlinked contingency and chance:
No atom of this turbulence fulfils
A vague and unnecessitated task,
Or acts but as it must and ought to act.[11]

"The great poet," Whitman reminded himself in a note, "submits only to himself. Is nature rude, free, irregular? If nature be so, do you too be so. Do you suppose nature has nothing under those beautiful, terrible, irrational forms?"[12] This statement clarifies and is in turn clarified by the lines quoted above from Whitman and Shelley.

Those who have no feeling for, or cannot see, determinism in nature will have no feeling for, and will be unable to see in its wide pervasiveness, the determinism in *Leaves of Grass*. For them it will ever seem that Whitman's style, his form, has too much freedom. (Nietzsche says: "In looking at a waterfall we imagine that there is freedom of will and fancy in the countless turnings, twistings, and breakings of the waves; but everything is compulsory, every movement can be mathematically calculated."[13]) Those, on the other hand, who see nature as a vast (and intricate) inevitability will comprehend that Whitman, in his poetic echoing of the "formless wild arrays" of nature, makes use of a "formless" form which is indispensable as the highest artistic vehicle for the determinist impressions which he sought to present, to convey.

I confess I have stated the case too strongly. One need not *be* a determinist to perceive important determinist nuances in the poems. If one can accept determinism as a hypothesis, not as a fact (my friend says it should be called a theory, not a hypothesis), and understand that Whitman, even if in error, believed in determinism and made use of it, one might, even on this level, outdistance all the confused and stumbling interpreters who have failed to succeed in interpreting. Chapters II and III of this book explain determinism, not as a fact but as a hypothesis (or theory). If one absorbs enough of that explanation, he may be able to grasp the meaning, long hidden, in these lines:

I musing late in the autumn day, gazing off southward,
Held by this electric self out of the pride of which I utter poems,
Was seiz'd by the spirit that trails in the lines underfoot,
The rim, the sediment that stands for all the water, and all the land of the globe.

Fascinated, my eyes reverting from the south, dropt to follow those slender windrows,
Chaff, straw, splinters of wood, weeds, and the sea-glutten,
Scum, scales from shining rocks, leaves of salt-lettuce, left by the tide....

. . . .

I too but signify at the utmost a little wash'd-up drift,
A few sands and dead leaves to gather,
Gather, and merge myself as part of the sands and drift.

. . . .

I too Paumanok,
I too have bubbled up, floated the measureless float, and been wash'd on your shores,
I too am but a trail of drift and debris,
I too leave little wrecks upon you, you fish-shaped island.

. . . .

Me and mine, loose windrows, little corpses,
Froth, snowy white, and bubbles,
(See, from my dead lips the ooze exuding at last,
See, the prismatic colors glistening and rolling,)
Tufts of straw, sands, fragments,
Buoy'd hither from many moods, one contradicting another,
From the storm, the long calm, the darkness, the swell,
Musing, pondering, a breath, a briny tear, a dab of liquid or soil,
Up just as much out of fathomless workings fermented and thrown,
A limp blossom or two, torn, just as much over waves floating, drifted at random....

. . . .

We, capricious, brought hither we know not whence, spread out before you,
You up there walking or sitting,
Whoever you are, we too lie in drifts at your feet.[14]

The "spirit that trails in the lines underfoot" is the same "spirit" that formed the "wild arrays" in Colorado. Just as, for Boethius, "the flotsam comes together/ That is borne upon the tide," so for Whitman, the "wash'd-up drift" is "left by the tide." In neither case is there any real "chance," any exemption from law; for as Boethius says, there is something that "determines/ Every floating fragment's course." Whitman and his poems are parts of the "measureless float," the equivalent of the "perpetual flows of endless causes" in his definition of determinism in the note on Priestley (Ch. IV). He himself, like his poems, signifies "a little wash'd-up drift." Take care not to read into this determinism a note of pessimism; Whitman is not, as most critics no doubt would assume, modestly conceding that he and his poems are of no great moment in the scheme of things.

Whitman felt that "The style of a great poem must flow on 'unhasting and unresting.'"[15] "Most poets," he wrote, "finish specimens of characters — I will never finish single specimens; I will shower them by exhaustless laws as nature does, indicating not only themselves but successive productions out of themselves, later and fresher continually."[16] Here "flow," "exhaustless," and "continually" echo "flows" and "endless" of the aforementioned definition.

It is obvious after analysis, though not always openly evident, that in many of the poems, Whitman was possessed by the spirit of Priestley's "great tenet." Only a little help will reveal this to be the case in the opening lines of "Salut au Monde!"

> Such gliding wonders! such sights and sounds!
> Such join'd unended links, each hook'd to the next,
> Each answering all, each sharing the earth with all.

The "unended links" are surely the "endless causes" of the Priestley note! These lines are a compact description of the subject-matter of *Leaves of Grass*. Nothing stands alone. All is connected with all in a mighty network of Necessity. However heterogeneous the images, however jumbled the objects, however isolated the pictures, everything fits into the scheme; each object, each event, each person, is a manifestation of the mysterious controlling factor which makes things as they are, which minute by minute, age on age, works out the warp and woof of the world's history. "[M]y form," Whitman wrote, "has strictly grown from my purports and facts, and is the analogy of them."[17]

Whitman consciously and deliberately made use of determinism as an artistic principle. How this could be will, I hope, be made clear by this chapter — but I am afraid the way determinism elevates, and indeed even serves as the basis of, art — I am afraid this will not be easy to convey. The quotations later on from Taine and Emerson should be given particular attention.

Amazingly, Whitman anticipated the powerful theory of Hippolyte Taine — by some eighteen years! As early as the writing of his 1855 Preface, Whitman was engrossed with the idea that the ideal poet merges himself with his era, aware that he and his poems are a part of the determinist flow:

The direct trial of him who would be the greatest poet is today. If he does not flood himself with the immediate age as with vast oceanic tides ... and if he be not himself the age transfigured ... and if to him is not opened the eternity which gives similitude to all periods and locations and processes and animate and inanimate forms, and which is the bond of time, and rises up from its inconceivable vagueness and infiniteness in the swimming shapes of today, and is held by the ductile anchors of life, and makes the present spot the passage from what was to what shall be, and commits itself to the representation of this wave of an hour and this one of the sixty beautiful children of the wave — let him merge in the general run and wait his development.[18]

A chapter could be written bringing out the determinism of these lines. The ideal poet would *be* a determinist! He would immerse himself in the determinist matrix, "flood himself with the immediate age." We see now what Whitman may have meant when he said that he would "merge myself as part of the sands and drift."

Whitman's conscious concern with inevitability — or as I have suggested, perhaps his natural inclination to perceive inevitability — elevated his poetry, lifted it to spiritual heights only attainable through his attention to inevitability. The question of his success or failure in conveying a sense of that inevitability to the reader is actually the thesis of this book. In summary it might be said that he succeeded but only in a delicate and impressionistic way. It certainly cannot be said that Whitman's readers have read his poems with the same consciousness of determinism with which they were written. Only a few, as I have indicated, have any sense of Whitman's determinism, as a philosophy, at all. But it is there, and, in a mysterious way it serves as the basis for even the average reader's sense of the greatness of Whitman's poems. In Section 8 of "Crossing Brooklyn Ferry" we find a cleverly veiled statement of this very aspect of Whitman's method. What he had "promised without mentioning it" (his determinism), what he realized "the study could not teach," what could not be conveyed by "preaching," is, by his chosen *indirect* method, "accomplish'd":

We understand then do we not?
What I promis'd without mentioning it, have you not accepted?
What the study could not teach — what the preaching could not accomplish is accomplish'd, is it not?

As Whitman would have confessed, his perceptions of the artistic aspects of determinism were not original with him. Others, as far back as Aristotle (in his *Poetics*), perceived the same aspects.

Hegel's philosophy of art, as such, may have had little influence on Whitman, but his metaphysical emphasis on spirit in his general philosophy probably contributed to Whitman's artistic theory and, as we shall presently see, to the theory of Hippolyte Taine, who, without doubt, strengthened Whitman's theory. The following statement by Hegel so well expresses Taine's concept that it might have been written by Taine:

> The spirit of a people is a definite spirit; its character is determined by the historical stage of their development. This spirit is the basis out of which proceed all the forms of national culture. It is an individuality, which in religion is represented, reverenced, and loved in its essential character; in art, it is exhibited in visible images and forms; in philosophy, it is known and apprehended as thought. The forms which these things take are in inseparable union with the spirit of the people; the substance of which they are formed and their objects are originally the same; hence, only with such a religion can we have such a state; in such a state only such a philosophy and art.[19]

Taine based two of his major works, *Histoire de la littérature anglaise* (1863) and *Philosophie de l'art* (1865–67), on determinism as he conceived of it as an indispensable factor in literature and art. He summed up his philosophy as follows:

> ... we may rest assured that if we desire to comprehend the taste or the genius of an artist, the reasons leading him to choose a particular style of painting or drama, to prefer this or that character or coloring, and to represent particular sentiments, we must seek for them in the social and intellectual conditions of the community in the midst of which he lived.
>
> We have therefore to lay down this rule: that, in order to comprehend a work of art, an artist or a group of artists, we must clearly comprehend the general social and intellectual condition of the times to which they belong. Herein is to be found the final explanation; herein resides the primitive cause determining all that follows it.[20]

As might have been predicted, Whitman accepted Taine's theory with enthusiasm. He even wrote a twenty-page abridgment of parts of *History of English Literature*.[21] Certainly Taine's determinism is what attracted him. In its entry for Taine, *Reader's Encyclopedia* states: "He is known for his emphasis on the role of scientific determinism [*sic*] in literature and history, particularly as exemplified in hereditary and environmental influences."[22] Taine's determinism crops up repeatedly in the thirty-six page Introduction to his *History of English Literature*[23]:

(P. 1) It was perceived that a literary work is not a mere individual play of imagination, the isolated caprice of an excited brain, but a transcript of contemporary manners....

(P. 8) ... the moral constitution of a people or an age is as particular and distinct as the physical structure of a family of plants or an order of animals.

(P. 10) No matter if the facts be physical or moral, they all have their causes; there is a cause for ambition, for courage, for truth, as there is for digestion, for muscular movement, for animal heat.

(P. 12) Here lie the grand causes, for they are the universal and permanent causes, present at every moment in every case, everywhere and always acting, indestructible, and finally infallibly supreme....

(P. 13) As in mineralogy the crystals, however diverse, spring from certain simple physical forms, so in history, civilizations, however diverse, are derived from certain simple spiritual forms.

(P. 31) There are similarly connected data in the moral as in the physical world, as rigorously bound together, and as universally extended in the one as in the other.

(P. 32) Given a literature, philosophy, society, art, group of arts, what is the moral condition which produced it?

Taine's *History of English Literature* was translated in 1871. In 1888 Whitman published, as the Preface to his *November Boughs*, "A Backward Glance O'er Travel'd Roads." There we find evidence of Whitman's agreement with Taine:

> Also it must be carefully remember'd that first-class literature does not shine by any luminosity of its own; nor do its poems. They grow of circumstances, and are evolutionary. The actual living light is always curiously from elsewhere—follows unaccountable sources, and is lunar and relative at the best....
>
> Just as all the old imaginative works rest, after their kind, on long trains of presuppositions, often entirely unmention'd by themselves, yet supplying the most important bases of them, and without which they could have had no reason for being, so "Leaves of Grass," before a line was written, presupposed something different from any other, and, as it stands, is the result of such presupposition. I should say, indeed, it were useless to attempt reading the book without first carefully tallying that preparatory background and quality in the mind.[24]

One needs only a little penetration to see, at more or less removes, the material facts of their country and radius, with the coloring of the moods of humanity at the time, and its gloomy or hopeful prospects, behind all poets and each poet, and forming their birth-marks. I know very well that my "Leaves" could not possibly have emerged or been fashion'd or completed, from any other era than the latter half of the Nineteenth Century, nor any other land than democratic America, and from the absolute triumph of the National Union arms.... As America fully and fairly construed is the legitimate result and evolutionary outcome of the past, so I would dare to claim for my verse.[25]

In "Song of the Redwood-Tree" Whitman salutes the "vital, universal, deathless germs, beneath all creeds, arts, statutes, literatures...." This was 1874, three years after the first Taine translations, before which Taine's ideas probably did not influence Whitman.

The influence of Emerson, even on Whitman's earlier thought, is easier to hypothesize. Emerson's determinism surfaces with significance in his essay "Art," first published in 1841:

> As far as the spiritual character of the period overpowers the artist, and finds expression in his work, so far will it retain a certain grandeur, and will represent to future beholders the Unknown, the inevitable, the Divine. No man can quite exclude this element of Necessity from his labor. No man can quite emancipate himself from his age and country, or produce a model in which the education, the religion, the politics, usages, and arts, of his times shall have no share. Though he were never so original, never so wilful and fantastic, he cannot wipe out of his work every trace of the thoughts amidst which it grew. The very avoidance betrays the usage he avoids. Above his will, and out of his sight, he is necessitated, by the air he breathes, and the idea on which he and his contemporaries live and toil, to share the manner of his times, without knowing what that manner is. *Now that which is inevitable in the work has a higher charm than individual talent can ever give, inasmuch as the artist's pen or chisel seems to have been held and guided by a gigantic hand to inscribe a line in the history of the human race.* [Italics mine.] This circumstance gives a value to the Egyptian hieroglyphics, to the Indian, Chinese, and Mexican idols, however gross and shapeless. They denote the height of the human soul in that hour, and were not fantastic, but sprung from a necessity as deep as the world.[26]

The last two sentences give the clearest insight into the theory. No matter the condition of the work: the gross and shapeless idols mentioned by Emerson, cave paintings crude though they may be, the ballad with no identifiable author, now a piece of folklore — these become art when we lose sight of the seeming freedom which produced them. A spinning wheel or a cobbler's bench is now a work of art; a broken bowl, hurled away as useless, now graces an honored niche in a museum.

Whitman held consistently to the theory as stated here (and elsewhere) by Emerson, and by Taine in his Introductions to the two works mentioned above. "No great poem or other literary or artistic work of any scope, old or new," Whitman wrote, "can be essentially considered without weighing first the age, politics (or want of politics) and aim, visible forms, unseen soul, and current times, out of the midst of which it rises and is formulated...."[27] On January 14, 1890, Horace Traubel heard Daniel G. Brinton lecture on Giordano Bruno at the Contemporary Club in Philadelphia. He took the manuscript copy of the lecture to Whitman, who was too sick to attend. On the 17th Whitman told Traubel he had read the lecture. He gave it high praise: "There is one thing about it I particularly delighted in — a theory of which Taine [*sic*] makes the most of any man I know. The part enacted by environment, surroundings, circumstances, — the man's age, land — all that went before, generations — is today."[28] Whitman's explanation is echoed by every encyclopedia entry for Taine I have seen. *The World Book Encyclopedia* (1993), after mentioning Taine's "application of the philosophy of determinism to art and literature," continues:

> To understand the origin and development of an artist's or writer's work, Taine said we must discover all the significant facts about the person's *race*, (heredity), *milieu* (environment), and *moment* (state of the artistic tradition in which the person worked).

Whitman almost duplicated this when he mentioned, "The part enacted by environment, surroundings, circumstances,— the man's age, land — all that went before...." He "particularly delighted in" the lecturer's reference to Taine's theory. The *World Book* entry states that Taine's works on literature and art "illustrate his deterministic [*sic*] philosophy."

Besides the study of external influences on literary productions, there are to be considered internal relationships which in the best productions place all events and persons in a determinist matrix. Aristotle in his *Poetics* stressed that tragic incidents have their greatest effect when they occur in consequence of logical causes and do not happen of themselves or by chance. Cf. Taine, (P. 10): "No matter if the facts be physical or moral, they all have their causes...." The hero follows an inevitable path to his downfall. Oedipus blames Apollo for his "sore, sore woes." Professor Ledger Wood in his excellent essay on determinism says that historical accounts are judged for their accuracy by reference to the principle of "psychological determinism," *i.e.* historically, people may be expected to have behaved in a predetermined way. The same determinist criterion, says Professor Wood,

> is appealed to even in the evaluation of works of fiction. The novelist or the playwright gives a portrayal of his characters, he places them in definite situations, and then describes how they act. If his account of their behaviour under these precisely defined circumstances violates any of the recognized laws of human motivation, his literary and dramatic artistry is to that extent defective. Thus the principle of psychological determinism serves as a recognized canon on historical, literary, and dramatic criticism, and while this does not "prove" the correctness of psychological determinism, it does afford confirmation of it from an unsuspected quarter.[29]

The writer, however, faces a sublime paradox: he must not present his characters in a deterministic light: they must *seem* to function in perfect freedom. The danger was pointed out by David Castronovo in his article "Novel" in *Collier's Encyclopedia*, 1989:

> ... whether or not free will is an illusion the novelist must assume it is not, otherwise characters will appear to be merely puppets in the novelist's predetermined scheme of things.

The logic of this statement would seem to provide an excuse for Whitman's method, his use of "indirections." In his very first Inscription, he promises to sing the Modern Man "for freest action form'd under the laws divine." It is the old lesson of *Leaves of Grass*: we are free, but at the same time we are a function of the absolute law.

Rightfully, the critics are preoccupied not with internal but with external influences. The value of the historical approach to the study of literature derives almost entirely from the fact that an increased awareness of the environmental and philosophical conditions which produced the works adds to their stature and arouses in us a larger appreciation. David S. Reynolds' fine work *Walt Whitman's America* is quite appropriately subtitled "A Cultural Biography." I am not sure Reynolds appreciates the value of his historical revelations as determinist elements in the birth and growth of *Leaves of Grass*.

"The builder does not build as he chooses," says Paulsen, "but as the age chooses: in the fourteenth century, in the Gothic style: in the sixteenth, Renaissance; in the eighteenth, Rococo."[30] Our appreciation of these architectural marvels is enlarged as our awareness of the historical elements that relate to their creation and to their contemporary physical and spiritual environment increases.

> All architecture is what you do to it when you look upon it;
> (Did you think it was in the white or gray stone? or the lines of the arches and cornices?)
>
> ["A Song for Occupations," Sec. 4.]

The carefully-followed Gothic-style architecture of a great university (here remaining nameless) inspired the following critical comment in a 2005 council meeting in a nearby city: "I don't know how they get away with calling it Gothic. It's fake! It looks like Disney built it." However faithful the reproduction, the result is unsatisfactory. The art is gone, the determinism is gone. The copy was "freely" produced. There is a depth of meaning in Taine's statement "a good cast is not equal to a good statue"![31]

Photographs, which can be taken "at will," generally have less artistic value than do paintings of the same scenes. A photograph of the Bridge at Arles would not be worth much. But Van Gogh's painting would sell for millions. This is not to say that photographs, once the inevitability of their taking or the determinist qualities of their content are discerned, will not on that account alone become true art. All photographs, says Susan Sontag, "by slicing out this moment and freezing it ... testify to time's relentless melt.... Time eventually positions most photographs, even the most amateurish, at the level of art."[32] Time gives us a perception of the determinism of events. We are conscious of their seeming freedom only as we live them, as we experience them as contemporary to us. Photographs capture time and hold its determinism in freeze-frame. This delicate concept was recognized by Dudley and Faricy, who give a forceful presentation of it:

> It seems to be especially true of great photographs that whatever processes have been used between the pressing of the camera button and the final result, the finished photograph is most appealing when it appears to have caught a bit of transient truth, fleeting, unposed — so that the total composition appears to be inevitable.[33]

Many scenes in *Leaves of Grass*, in just this way, capture a photographic segment of transient inevitability. An excellent example is "Sparkles from the Wheel," in which the knife-grinder's wheel throws off sparks which Whitman deftly suggests are symbolic of the children who are watching.

David Reynolds has shown that Whitman's "picture" imagery was influenced by contemporary "genre" paintings.[34] These paintings typically depicted common activities on farms and in other rural settings. They have a distinguishing "freeze-frame" quality, as do the Whitman poems which are reminiscent of them: "The Torch," which captures a nighttime scene of spearing salmon; "A Paumanok Picture," to be quoted at the end of this chapter; "Cavalry Crossing a Ford" and other "Drum Taps" poems; the scene in "Song of Myself," Sec. 10, portraying the marriage of a trapper to a "red girl"; "Twenty Years," about the return of a sailor; "The Ship Starting," a vivid picture of a sailing ship on the "unbounded sea." These poems and the genre pictures they resemble, catch, like the photographs mentioned above, "a bit of transient truth, fleeting, unposed ... inevitable." In his history of art H. W. Janson assigns the same quality to "the genre scenes of Jan Vermeer": "Single figures, usually women, engage in simple everyday tasks.... They exist in a timeless 'still life' world seemingly calmed by some magic spell."[35] Vermeer's "The Artist's Studio" is an excellent example.

I am not sure the paintings of Millet would be "genre," but Whitman liked them very much. He sensed in them "the untold something behind all that was depicted — an essence, a suggestion, an indirection, leading off into the immortal mysteries."[36] What Whitman was here groping to explain was that Millet enabled him to perceive things *sub specie aeternitatis*, to use Spinoza's idea and his phrase. The following explication by Joseph Ratner of what Spinoza meant is admirably applicable to our present study:

> It is the nature of reason to see things under the form of eternity. And we can apprehend the infinite essence of God or Nature because every particular finite thing is a determinate expression of the infinite.... Thus from the comprehension of any particular thing, we can pass to a comprehension of the infinite and eternal.
> This is most commonly understood, curiously enough, not in religion, but in art. The ecstatic power of beauty makes the soul lose all sense of

time and location. And in the specific object the soul sees an infinite meaning. Indeed, one can almost say that the more specific or limited the artistic object, the more clearly is the absolute or infinite meaning portrayed and discerned.... It is for this reason Spinoza says the more we understand particular things the more do we understand God.[37]

The key to the explanation is Ratner's phrase "a determinate expression of the infinite"—which brings the focus, again, to determinism.

Undoubtedly there are in most literary or linguistic products, and even in the products of the pictorial and plastic arts, certain elements of universality and timelessness which abstract them from the conditions of their production. The Venus de Milo or Keats's "St. Agnes' Eve" would be beautiful to us even if we knew not whence they came. It appears, however, when we look upon the matter from this point of view, that the principle of Necessity is still visible though operative in a different way. Through the genius of the artist, events and objects and people can be emancipated from their temporal relationships in such a way that we for the moment lose sight of their *immediate* causal histories and rise to the perception of a higher aspect of the Necessity under which they exist — or, to use Spinoza's phrase again, we see them *sub specie aeternitatis*. If we but see far enough into Walt Whitman's method, we see that that is just what he does in *Leaves of Grass*: he presents scenes, objects, and persons under the aspect of eternity. Van Gogh came close to this idea when he wrote his brother, "I want to paint men and women with that something of the eternal which the halo used to symbolize."[38] In an 1889 *Century Magazine* article, Whitman read a quotation from Millet which he found "deeply impressive": "One must be able to make use of the trivial for the expression of the sublime."[39] Emerson says, "All human activities are sublime when seen as emanations of a Necessity contradistinguished from the vulgar Fate by being instant and alive, and dissolving man as well as his works in its flowing beneficence."[40] "For me," Whitman wrote, "I see no object, no expression, no animal, no tree, no art, no book, but I see, from morning to night, and from night to morning, the spiritual."[41]

The beginning of the solution to the puzzle of Whitman's style lies in the realization that he was profoundly conscious of determinism. With that realization, the reader will begin to understand the poetic rationale of Whitman's catalogues, of passages like the following:

> I see African and Asiatic towns,
> I see Algiers, Tripoli, Derne, Mogadore, Timbuctoo, Monrovia,
> I see the swarms of Pekin, Canton, Benares, Delhi, Calcutta, Tokio,
> I see the Kruman in his hut, and the Dahoman and Ashantee-men in their huts.
> I see the Turk smoking opium in Aleppo,
> I see the picturesque crowds at the fairs of Khiva and those of Herat,

I see Teheran, I see Muscat and Medina and the intervening sands, I see the caravans toiling onward,

I see Egypt and the Egyptians, I see the pyramids and obelisks,

I look on chisell'd histories, records of conquering kings, dynasties, cut in slabs of sand-stone, or on granite-blocks,

I see at Memphis mummy-pits, containing mummies embalm'd, swathed in linen cloth, lying there many centuries,

I look on the fall'n Theban, the large-ball'd eyes, the side-drooping neck, the hands folded across the breast.[42]

"Each of us inevitable," declares Whitman in the next section of the poem, making explicit the hidden determinism which elevates the people, towns, objects, and events to a spiritual level, so that we see them under the aspect of eternity. I have not stressed enough this important duality in Whitman's poems. They are filled with images of the physical and actual, but Whitman was never unaware of the spiritual, which he believed ruled "unseen," "hidden," "universal."[43] This all-important duality has never been more clearly perceived than by Donald Hall:

> The familiar doubleness is here — "the world I see," and "the Invisible World" — and emphasis falls upon the latter phrase as it must. Many of Whitman's admirers, I think, consider that he chiefly concerns himself with the world he sees. They speak of his catalogues, his multiplication of *things*. Yet, the seen world hardly exists for him, because he spiritualizes everything.... [His] songs, when the truth is out, are all dedicated to the Invisible World. Appearances in poetry are the colors and shapes of spirit by which Whitman brings us into the Invisible World, which he insists is also ours if we will only discover it.[44]

Nothing so valuable has ever been said about Walt Whitman. If one can understand Hall's statement and see in it a reflection of Whitman's determinism, that is all one needs for the fullest appreciation of the poems.

Now for an experiment. Read the following poem thinking all the while of the determinist theory of art given in this chapter. This is a typical short Whitman poem. It describes a predetermined event, suspended in time. Even the minutest details of the coloration and spotting of the fish drawn up on the shore — are predetermined.

A Paumanok Picture

Two boats with nets lying off the sea-beach, quite still,

Ten fishermen waiting — they discover a thick school of mossbonkers — they drop the join'd seine-ends in the water,

The boats separate and row off, each on its rounding course to the beach, enclosing the mossbonkers,

The net is drawn in by a windlass by those who stop ashore,

Some of the fishermen lounge in their boats, others stand ankle-deep in the water, pois'd on strong legs,

The boats partly drawn up, the water slapping against them,
Strewed on the sand in heaps and windrows, well out from the water, the
green-back'd spotted mossbonkers.

◆ ◆ ◆

In the tumbled books and papers on the floor and on the tables in his
room; in the "formless wild arrays" of a canyon in Colorado; in the "rushing, whirling, wild debris" of the Johnstown Flood; in the slender windrows
washed up by the sea (the fish, above, lie in "windrows"); in all these, and
everywhere he looked, he saw, he sensed the presence of something which mysteriously and unaccountably makes things as they are, a hidden Necessity
which dwells in all the parts of nature and in the thoughts and works of men.
He looked into the past and saw this same Necessity shaping its way to the
future, fashioning, moulding, casting men and nations and events as it went.
And from these perceptions came inspiration for his poetry.

> Beginning my studies the first step pleas'd me so much,
> The mere fact consciousness, these forms, the power of motion,
> The least insect or animal, the senses, eyesight, love,
> The first step I say awed me and pleas'd me so much,
> I have hardly gone and hardly wish'd to go any farther,
> But stop and loiter all the time to sing it in ecstatic songs.[45]

Whitman had caught a soul-sight of determinism, he had discovered the
Beautiful Necessity. And this divine Necessity, in itself indescribable, is
reflected, through the genius and poetic artistry of Walt Whitman, subtly
and sometimes quite obviously, as the major theme in *Leaves of Grass*.

> Sometimes it is so delicately expressed as to be easily passed over:
> Each moment and whatever happens thrills me with joy,
> I cannot tell how my ankles bend, nor whence the cause of my faintest
> wish,
> Nor the cause of the friendship I emit, nor the cause of the friendship I
> take again.

> That I walk up my stoop, I pause to consider if it really be,
> A morning-glory at my window satisfies me more than the metaphysics of
> books.

> To behold the day-break!
> The little light fades the immense and diaphanous shadows,
> The air tastes good to my palate.

> Hefts of the moving world at innocent gambols silently rising freshly
> exuding,
> Scooting obliquely high and low.[46]

Whitman's friend Dr. Maurice Bucke said of him: "All natural objects seemed to have a charm for him; all sights and sounds, outdoors and indoors, seemed to please him."[47] Emerson had the explanation:

> There is no need for foolish amateurs to fetch me to admire a garden of flowers, or a sun-gilt cloud, or a waterfall, when I cannot look without seeing splendor and grace. How idle to choose a random sparkle here or there, when the indwelling necessity plants the rose of beauty on the brow of chaos, and discloses the central intention of Nature to be harmony and joy.
> Let us build altars to the Beautiful Necessity.[48]

I had not noticed, but within this quotation lies the explanation, the exoneration, of Whitman's often criticized helter-skelter imagery. Throughout *Leaves of Grass*, "the indwelling necessity plants the rose of beauty on the brow of chaos."

VIII

The Indefinable It

Something there is more immortal than even the stars.
 —"On the Beach at Night."

Leaves of Grass at first sight is, and for some never ceases to be, a poem of particulars. It sings "the simple separate person"; it celebrates "identity," the isolation and independence of individual beings, objects, existences; it pictures events in flashes. In doing all this it ignores, apparently, the thought that nothing, after all, really stands alone.

But Whitman's genius, as perhaps does all genius, springs from the trick of recognizing connection in the apparently disconnected. One who looks hard enough for the central message of *Leaves of Grass* will find at last that beyond Whitman's deftly presented particulars there is a universal which gives them their existence. No object, no person, in the poems is to be looked upon as representative merely of that individuality, or individualness, in which it is presented. Whitman's objects and persons and events, are in a profound sense to be taken as nothing more than reminders of an eternal ground of being in which they are all united.

A vast similitude interlocks all,
All spheres, grown, ungrown, small, large, suns, moons, planets,
All distances of place however wide,
All distances of time, all inanimate forms,
All souls, all living bodies though they be ever so different, or in different worlds,
All gaseous, watery, vegetable, mineral processes, the fishes, the brutes,
All nations, colors, barbarisms, civilizations, languages,
All identities that have existed or may exist on this globe, or any globe,
All lives and deaths, all of the past, present, future,

176

This vast similitude spans them, and always has spann'd
And shall forever span them and compactly hold and enclose them.[1]

It would be easy to attribute Whitman's perception of this important Unifier (once one has understood that he did perceive it) to what so many of his interpreters have called his mysticism.

Swiftly arose and spread around me the peace and knowledge that pass all the argument of the earth,
And I know that the hand of God is the promise of my own,
And that all the men ever born are also my brothers, and the women my sisters and lovers,
And that a kelson of the creation is love....

This passage, from Section 5 of "Song of Myself," is often quoted as representing an outright mystical visionary experience by Whitman. There is no firm argument against the possibility that Whitman did as the passage suggests, experience a sudden luminous, mystical vision of reality. W. T. Stace, in his excellent discussion of mysticism,[2] states that the mystic experiences "union with God," "the peace which passes all understanding," and a heightened "love for our fellow men." These three elements are clearly found in the lines from Section 5. Stace emphasizes as an outstanding result of mystical experiences the perception of the "unity in all things." Whitman's understanding of this important concept can be found in several places in his poems. It is particularly evident in the lines quoted above, in which "A vast similitude interlocks all." It is natural to assume that Whitman was a mystic, that his ideas came to him through a direct perception of reality or through an intuitive grasp of truth.

But it is my thesis that Whitman's philosophical ideas made him *seem* a mystic. I have shown already, in Chapter III, how magnificent and inspiring determinism can be. In the cold light of logic or the harsh glare of scientific truth it may seem a bare and unconsoling theory. Even when it is given a broad philosophic interpretation, it often seems mundane and uninspiring. But when one brings to it more than mere intellectualism, when one gives his heart and soul to it, or sees that it *is* his heart and soul — then what may have seemed a terrible philosophy assumes a kindlier mien, gives strength and offers freedom, brings peace and speaks love, to and through its new-found friend. This higher or deeper insight is not easily reached, and the circumstance under which it *is* reached does border upon the mystical:

It is, alas! only in occasional seasons of retirement from the world, in the happy hours of devout contemplation, that, I believe the most perfect of our race can fully indulge the enlarged views, and lay himself open to the genuine feelings, of the Necessarian principles; that is, that he can *see every thing in God*, or in its relation to him. Habitually and constantly, to realize these views, would be always to *live in the house of God*, and within the *gate of heaven*; seeing the plain finger of God in all events, and as if the angels of God were constantly descending to earth, and ascending to heaven before our eyes.[3]

These glowing words, written by a man whom Whitman admired, Joseph Priestley, remind us of the famous Section 5 of "Song of Myself," quoted in part above, wherein it was revealed to the poet that "the hand of God is the promise of my own." It is reasonable to suppose that the two men had the same vision — and in Priestley's case it was the vision of a devout determinist, as his words above prove.

　　In this chapter we turn once more to determinism for insight into Whitman's mind and meanings. Let us consider, first, an idea developed by Spinoza, who stands perhaps greatest and grandest among the determinists. Josiah Royce, in the following description of Spinoza's concept of "Substance," gives us a point of reference.

　　He calls the supreme nature of things the universal "Substance" of all the world. In it are we all; it makes us what we are; it does what its own nature determines; it explains itself and all of us; it isn't produced, it produces; it is uncrate, supreme, overruling, omnipresent, absolute, rational, irreversible, unchangeable, the law of laws, the nature of natures; and we — we, with all our acts, thoughts, feelings, life, relations, experiences — are just the result of it, as the diameters are results of the nature of a circle. Feel, hope, desire, choose, strive, as you will, all is in you because this universal "substance" makes you what you are, forces you into this place in the nature of things, rules you as the higher truth rules the lower, as the wheel rules the spoke, as the storm rules the raindrop, as the tide rules the wavelet, as autumn rules the dead leaves, as the snowdrift rules the fallen snowflake; and this substance is what Spinoza calls God.[4]

Whitman could have been referring to Spinoza when he remarked to Traubel, "…there is a philosophy somewhere — oh! what is his name? let me see … anyhow, a wise fellow once asserted something to the effect — I cannot give you his words — that the Lord is no concrete personage, but the essence — the idea back of ideas — through which conditions, events as they were, were justified."[5] For Royce the Substance is "supreme, overruling." Whitman's *Old Cause* is "stern, remorseless." (See "To Thee Old Cause," Ch. VI) Whitman identifies the Cause as the "orb of many orbs," recasting poetically Royce's "law of laws, the nature of natures." Here, Whitman refers to "the essence — the idea back of ideas" and, in "Chanting the Square Deific," to "the essence of forms." It is odd that both Royce and Whitman employ the figure of a *wheel*: Royce: "as the wheel rules the spoke"/Whitman (in "To Thee Old

Cause"): "As a wheel on its axis turns." The descriptions of the philosophy somehow elicited all these echoes.

Royce, continuing, gives a forceful presentation of other implications of Spinoza's "Substance" concept:

> We fancy our past wholly past, and our future wholly unmade ... it is not so. For the eternal substance there is no before and after; all truth is truth. "Far and forgot to me is near," it says. In the unvarying precision of the mathematical universe, all is eternally written.
>
> "Not all your piety nor wit
> Can lure it back to cancel half a line,
> Nor all your tears wash out one word of it."
>
> What will be for endless ages, what has been since time began, is in the one substance completely present, as in one scroll may be written the joys and sorrows of many lives, as one earth contains the dead of countless generations, as one space enfolds all the limitless wealth of figured curves and of bodily forms.[6]

Some of these ideas are in "Starting from Paumanok," Sec. 12:

> And I will thread a thread through my poems that time and events are compact,
> And that all the things of the universe are perfect miracles, each as profound as any.
>
> I will not make poems with reference to parts,
> But I will make poems, songs, thoughts, with reference to ensemble,
> And I will not sing with reference to a day, but with reference to all days,
> And I will not make a poem nor the least part of a poem but has reference to the soul,
> Because having look'd at the objects of the universe, I find there is no one nor any particle of one but has reference to the soul.

Do not be misled by Whitman's "soul"; it is not soul in the usual sense. Whitman again uses "soul," quite tellingly, in the last stanza of "Chanting the Square Deific":

> Santa Spirita, breather, life,
> Beyond the light, lighter than light,
> Beyond the flames of hell, joyous, leaping easily above hell,
> Beyond Paradise, perfumed solely with mine own perfume,
> Including all life on earth, touching, including God, including Saviour and Satan,
> Ethereal, pervading all, (for without me what were all? what were God?)
> Essence of forms, life of the real identities, permanent, positive, (namely the unseen,)
> Life of the great round world, the sun and stars, and of man, I, the general soul,

Here the square finishing, the solid, I the most solid,
Breathe my breath also through these songs.

Referring to "Passage to India" in a footnote to his 1876 Preface, Whitman expressed the conviction that "the unseen soul govern[s] absolutely at last."[7] Whitman's "unseen soul," "general soul," "Santa Spirita"—all are equivalent to Spinoza's Substance, all identical with determinism. We have stumbled onto the long-sought answer to the mystery of Whitman's "Square"!

Three of the sides are 1) God the relentless controller; 2) God the consoler or Christ; and 3) Satan, the defiant commissioner of sin and evil. But the fourth side, "Santa Spirita," "the general soul," puzzlingly includes the other three—"including God, including Saviour and Satan." The mystery is solved in this way: the fourth, all-including, side, Santa Spirita, is determinism; the other three sides are aspects of determinism. But how can God be an aspect of determinism! Is God *subject* to determinism!? To suggest this, as Whitman does ("without me ... what were God?"), is heretical. But Whitman was not alone in this heresy. Nietzsche speaks of "that indomitable Moira [fate], which rules even the Gods."[8] In the first century, Seneca made the same assertion: "Both Gods and men are bound by the same chain of necessity" (see Ch. V). Shelley, necessitarian, admirer and translator of Spinoza, makes the impious statement that "admitting the existence of this hypothetic being, He is also subjected to the dominion of an immutable necessity."[9] This idea, the same in Whitman, Nietzsche, Seneca, and Shelley, is indeed a daring concept: that beyond God is something (Whitman's Santa Spirita, Nietzsche's Moira, Seneca's and Shelley's necessity) under which even God is subsumed! Even Spinoza felt that "Things could not have been produced by God in any manner or order other than that in which they were produced." But he denied that he considered God to be subject to fate.[10]

In "Chanting the Square" (above), the great determiner is "beyond Paradise," "beyond the light." It is "the general soul," the "essence of forms," the equivalent, as I have indicated, of Spinoza's Substance. Another equivalent is the "vast similitude" in "On the Beach at Night Alone" Varying the terminology even further, Whitman uses "float":

I too Paumanok,
I too have bubbled up, floated the measureless float, and been wash'd on your shores,
I too am but a trail of drift and debris....

I too but signify at the utmost a little wash'd-up drift,
A few sands and dead leaves to gather,
Gather, and merge myself as part of the sands and drift.[11]

Interesting, the echo: Whitman, "dead leaves"/Royce, "dead leaves." Royce's "wavelet" is echoed in the seventh "Fancies at Navesink" poem, where Whitman compares his "three-score years of life" to

> ... some drop within God's scheme's ensemble — some wave, or part of wave,
> Like one of yours, ye multitudinous ocean.

Whitman's "drop" here almost matches Royce's "raindrop" in his statement that the Substance rules one "as the storm rules the raindrop." The ocean here and in the lines above may stand for the Substance. In those lines Whitman "floated the measureless float," borne along, surely, by the "perpetual flows of endless causes" with which he defined determinism (see Ch. IV). Note the similarity: "measureless float"/ "perpetual flows." Flowing waters seem to equate the Substance also — as in "A Voice from Death":

> Thou waters that encompass us!
> Thou that in all the life and death of us, in action or in sleep!
> Thou laws invisible that permeate them and all,
> Thou that in all, and over all, and through and under all, incessant!
> Thou! thou! the vital, universal, giant force resistless, sleepless, calm.
> Holding Humanity as in thy open hand, as some ephemeral toy,
> How ill to e'er forget thee!
>
> For I too have forgotten,
> (Wrapt in these little potencies of progress, politics, culture, wealth, inventions, civilization,)
> Have lost my recognition of your silent ever-swaying power, ye mighty, elemental throes,
> In which and upon which we float, and every one of us is buoy'd.

In the last line here, again: "float." "Float" recurs, along with flowing waters (here "current"), in Whitman's most magnificently determinist poem, "Crossing Brooklyn Ferry." Here we find "similitudes" echoing the "vast similitude" of lines quoted above:

> The simple, compact, well-join'd scheme, myself disintegrated, every one disintegrated yet part of the scheme,
> The similitudes of the past and those of the future...
> The current rushing so swiftly and swimming with me far away,
> The others that are to follow me, the ties between me and them...
>
> . . . .
>
> I too had been struck from the float forever held in solution [Cf. I too have ... floated the measureless float"],
>
> . . . .
>
> What is more subtle than this which ties me to the woman or man that looks in my face?

Which fuses me into you now, and pours my meaning into you?

For emphasis I repeat, from the penultimate line, "What is more subtle...?" Whitman was puzzled as all have been to whom the concept came, as to the nature of this great Connector. He confesses in "Song of Myself," Sec. 20:

... I do not know what it is — but I know it is in me,

. . . .

I do not know it — it is without name — it is a word unsaid,
It is not in any dictionary, utterance, symbol.

And again:

O Thou transcendent,
Nameless....[12]

And again:

Haply God's riddle it, so vague and yet so certain....

It is

That which eludes this verse and any verse,
Unheard by sharpest ear, unform'd in clearest eye or cunningest mind....

It is

Open but still a secret, the real of the real, an illusion,
Costless, vouchsafed to each, yet never man the owner....[13]

Sufficient contemplation of causation leads us finally to the conclusion that there is something *beyond* causation, something of which causation itself is an effect. As Hume pointed out, all we know of causation is that it entails invariability of sequence; that is, a particular kind of event is invariably followed by another particular kind of event. We can never detect anything in the "cause" which necessitates the "effect." We formulate natural "laws" which state, "If this happens, then that will happen," but in doing so we have not explained *why* if this happens then that will happen. We merely know (or really we merely expect) that, given the first event, the second event will occur. We do not know *why* the second event occurs. "This is universally true," says Paulsen: "the laws of nature do not compel things to act in a certain way; these laws are the expression of the spontaneous activity of the things. They do not explain *why* things behave as they do, but simply state in a general formula *how* they behave. They do not solve the riddle; they are the riddle themselves."[14] ("Haply God's riddle," said Whitman.) We are driven at last to the conclusion that there is something, beyond the causal sequence, which maintains the constancy of the causal sequence. Spinoza's concept of this was described by Royce as "the law of laws, the nature of natures." "[T]he real of the real," says Whitman — and "the idea back of ideas."

For practical purposes we speak of "this" as the cause of "that"; for the purposes of philosophic analysis we speak of "this" as the antecedent and "that" as the consequent; and the philosophic conclusion is that "we never see any principle or virtue by which one event is conjoined to, or made the antecedent of, another."[15] In Hindu philosophy one theory maintains that "the causal operation is itself an effect."[16] Professor Ewing speaks of "Kant's conviction that the rationale, the real ground of the causal connection always belongs to the noumenal sphere and is for this very reason unknowable."[17] "We have rejected," says Inge, "the notion that one event is the cause of another. The cause of any event is the will of a spiritual being, of a mind which has willed it to happen in a certain series."[18] "It is possible (and I for one should maintain)," says Rashdall, "that even in mechanical action the real and ultimate cause of the event is not the previous event or any mysterious necessity of thought which requires that like physical antecedents should have like physical consequents, but the Will of God which within the region of Mechanics works invariably (we have every reason to believe) according to this law of uniform succession."[19] Charles Bray, in the book which, as I have shown, influenced Emerson and bears so many parallels in phrase and thought to Whitman, *The Philosophy of Necessity*, concludes: "...God, therefore, must not be considered as only the first of a series of causes, but as the all-pervading influence which maintains the connection between all antecedents and consequents."[20] Leibniz, according to Paulsen, believed that "the bond which exists between cause and effect is not an accidental and particular bond: it is the universal and essential bond which binds together all the elements of existence. The latter are not foreign or external to each other; they are members of one being: God is the bond which unites all things in essence; his is the being in whom all are one."[21] Einstein made his stance clear when he declared, "Now I believe that events in nature are controlled by a much stricter and more closely binding law than we suspect to-day, when we speak of one event being the *cause* of another" (see Ch. II). Ben-Gurion said of Einstein, "Even he, with his great formula about energy and mass, agreed that there must be something behind the energy."[22]

It might be wise to point out that in some of these examples God is given anthropomorphic qualities which would not be necessary in the functions posited. Call it God, if you will — but it is not necessary to personalize "it" to assign to it its proper function as derived in the thought of the authors quoted in the preceding paragraph. This question aside, it should be agreed that I have shown in what direction the contemplation of causation can lead; and we may now see how this whole analysis applies to Whitman's thought.

Though he often mentions God, Whitman usually relies on symbolic or figurative synonyms in his poetic allusions to the God concept.

It, magnificent, beyond materials, with continuous hands sweeps and provides for all.[23]

Here Whitman uses "it," these lines reflecting the contention of Kant that "the real ground of the causal connection always belongs to the noumenal sphere." (Whitman's "beyond materials" equates Kant's "noumenal sphere.") David Hume uses impersonal synonyms in his statement that "The scenes of the universe are continually shifting, and one object follows another in an uninterrupted succession; but the power or force, which actuates the whole machine, is entirely concealed from us, and never discovers itself in any of the sensible qualities of body."[24] In the following poem Whitman uses the same synonyms, "power" and "force." Hume's force is "entirely concealed"' Whitman's is "unseen."

You Tides with Ceaseless Swell

You tides with ceaseless swell! you power that does this work!
You unseen force, centripetal, centrifugal, through space's spread,
Rapport of sun, moon, earth, and all the constellations,
What are the messages by you from distant stars to us? what Sirius'? what Capella's?
What central heart — and you the pulse — vivifies all? what boundless aggregate of all?
What subtle indirection and significance in you? what clue to all in you? what fluid, vast identity? ·
Holding the universe with all its parts as one — as sailing in a ship?

This "fluid, vast identity,/ Holding the universe with all its parts as one" is the same as the "vast similitude" which will forever "hold and enclose" all. Note the echoes: "vast"/ "vast"; "Holding"/ "hold"; "sun, moon"/ "suns, moons."

The poem which immediately precedes the poem just quoted gives further evidence that Whitman was, like Hume and the others, puzzled about the nature of the cause-effect nexus:

Had I the Choice

Had I the choice to tally the greatest bards,
To limn their portraits, stately, beautiful, and emulate at will,
Homer with all his wars and warriors — Hector, Achilles, Ajax,
Or Shakspere's woe-entangled Hamlet, Lear, Othello — Tennyson's fair ladies,
Meter or wit the best, or choice conceit to wield in perfect rhyme, delight of singers;
These, these, O sea, all these I'd gladly barter,
Would you the undulation of one wave, its trick to me transfer,
Or breathe one breath of yours upon my verse,
And leave its odor there.

The philosophy in this poem is expressed in the following statement by Durant

Drake: "In short, causality is one fact, invariability of recurrence is another fact — even if the two facts actually always go together. To explain a given case of cause-and-effect by saying that it is a case of a given natural law is not to *explain* it at all. Why it should happen thus over and over again is, indeed, a question; but a more ultimate question is why it happens *once*. If we could understand a single case of causation, we should doubtless see why it *always* happens that way — if it does."[25] Now we see why Whitman considered the understanding of the "undulation of one wave" so valuable and why he speaks of the "trick" of such an undulation. Drake: "If we could understand a *single case* [italics mine] of causation...." Of course, the waves, for Whitman, symbolized all causes. This poem of Whitman's shows that he had mastered the finest point of the determinist philosophy. There is more philosophy in *Leaves of Grass* than the critics have dreamt of! "What the process of causation is in itself," says Fiske, "we cannot know. We can know it only as it is presented to our consciousness, as the unconditional invariable sequence of events."[26] Like Whitman's waves. Again Fiske says: "The attempt to detect the *oculta vis* or hidden energy in the act of causation, is but the fruitless attempt to bind in the chains of some thinkable formula that universal Protean Power, of whose multitudinous effects we are cognizant in the sequence of phenomena, but which in its secret nature must ever mockingly elude our grasp."[27]

> That which eludes this verse and any verse,
> Unheard by sharpest ear, unform'd in clearest or cunningest mind....

So begins "A Riddle Song." It is a riddle which no man or woman has ever solved.

> Haply God's riddle it, so vague and yet so certain....

This line and others in the poem make it clear that the answer to the riddle is itself a riddle. The poem is actually an ingenious *double* riddle — the first, answerable; the second, beyond all human ability to answer. Ironically, Whitman's interpreters have been unable to answer even the first riddle.

> Two little breaths of words comprising it,
> Two words, yet all from first to last comprised in it.

What are the two words? W. S. Kennedy suggested "the Ideal."[28] Floyd Stovall agreed: "The two words that explain the riddle are probably *the ideal*."[29] *Walt Whitman Review* reported other answers: C. Scott Pugh argued extensively for "the end";[30] Louise M. Kawada countered with "the truth."[31] Not to be outdone for inanity, Emory Holloway demurred: "I think 'One-self' closer to the mark."[32] (Does "One-self" count as only *one* word?) Dr. Bucke made some sense when he submitted "'good cause' or 'old cause' or some other words meaning the same thing —?—."[33] At least he didn't waste his first word with "the."

For more than a century the first of the two words has lain undetected right there in the riddle itself: "first."

Two little breaths of words comprising it,
Two words, yet all from first to last comprised in it.

And with an understanding of determinism, one easily finds the second word: "cause." The answer is—*First Cause!*

The First Cause was not considered by Whitman as first in a linear time sense. In his view the First Cause is not some remote (personal) Being or some far-off event 'way back at the beginning of things; it is a living presence around us and within us. Determinism taught Whitman that the First Cause is inscrutable and, though always present, always hidden in the most profound sense of being hidden. There is comfort in the concept that this living presence will last beyond us, through eternity. In "On the Beach at Night" Whitman has the father tell his weeping child, "Something there is more immortal than even the stars."

This mysterious "something"—this "indefinable it"—figured prominently in Albert Einstein's religious outlook. He expressed his poignant awareness of it as follows:

To know that what is impenetrable to us rally exists manifesting itself as the highest wisdom and the most radiant beauty which our dull faculties can comprehend only in their most primitive forms—this knowledge, this feeling, is at the center of true religiousness.[34]

Varuna, Yaweh, Aton, Re, T'ien, Brahma, Zeus, Allah, God—it has been named ten thousand names and worshiped in a thousand different ways since man became man. The Idea, the Unconditioned, the Logos, the Unmanifest, the Absolute, the Substance—these have been efforts to describe it.

Lao Tze called it Tao:

The Tao that can be told of
Is not the Absolute Tao;
The Names that can be given
Are not Absolute Names.[35]

"And what," asks one interpreter, "is the explanation of the Tao? Its definition has baffled all students because Tao is itself undefinable, like the Ineffable of all doctrines and philosophies, which cannot be set into the confines of a category. Hence some men have called it God; some have called it the Word or the Way; some have spoken of it as the Logos or Brahman. In effect, They are the one—the Cosmic Impulse, the Primary Cause from which all emanates and toward which all strive."[36]

Father of All! in ev'ry Age,
In ev'ry Clime ador'd,
By Saint, by Savage, and by Sage,
Jehovah, Jove, or Lord!

Thou Great First Cause, least understood....

Thus does Pope pay homage to it in "The Universal Prayer."[37] Whitman marvels in "A Riddle Song" how "the bright fascinating lambent flames of it, in every age and land, have drawn men's eyes...." Is the duplication coincidental? Whitman: "in every age and land"; Pope: "in ev'ry Age, / In ev'ry Clime." And Pope gives us the answer to Whitman's riddle: "First Cause."

Emerson made the following entry in his journal: "I have puzzled myself like a mob of writers before me in trying to state the doctrine of Fate for the printer. I wish to sum the conflicting impressions by saying that all point at last to an Unity which inspires all, but disdains words and passes understanding.... The *First Cause* [my italics]; as soon as it is uttered, it is profaned."[38] We turn to the *Bhagavad Gita* and find that it is "indefinable, unshown ... everywhere present, inconceivable."[39] It is spoken of in the Upanishads as "neti, neti" — which means "not that, not that."[40] "It is not simple consciousness nor is It unconsciousness. It is unperceived, unrelated, incomprehensible, uninferable, unthinkable, and indescribable."[41] Sri Ramakrishna worshiped it as Kali, "the Mother of the Universe":

O Kali, my Mother full of Bliss!...
Eternal One! Thou great *First Cause* [my italics] clothed in the form of the Void!...
Thou art the Mover of all that move, and we are but thy helpless toys;
We move alone as Thou movest us and speak as through us thou speakest.[42]

Shelley had it in mind when he wrote *Queen Mab*:

Spirit of Nature! All-sufficing Power,
Necessity! thou mother of the world![43]

Herbert Spencer, English philosopher born a year later than Whitman, recognized it as "an Infinite and Eternal Energy, from which all things proceed"[44]: "Force, as we know it, can be regarded only as a certain conditioned effect of the Unconditioned Cause — as the relative reality indicating to us an Absolute Reality by which it is immediately produced."[45] Spencer elucidates further: "Thus the consciousness of an Inscrutable Power manifested to us through all phenomena has been growing ever clearer; and must eventually be freed from its imperfections. The certainty that on the one hand such a Power exists, while on the other hand its nature transcends intuition and is beyond imagination, is the certainty toward which intelligence has from the first been progressing."[46] Wordsworth sensed its presence in

> The light of setting suns,
> And the round ocean and the living air,
> And the blue sky, and in the mind of man.

He describes it as

> A motion and a spirit, that impels
> All thinking things, all objects of all thought,
> And rolls through all things.[47]

Hazlitt wrote of these lines: "Perhaps, the doctrine of what has been called philosophical necessity was never more finely expressed.... There can be no doubt that all that exists, exists by necessity; that the vast fabric of the universe is held together in one mighty chain, reaching to the 'threshold of Jove's throne'; that whatever has a beginning, must have a cause; that there is no object, no feeling, no action, which, other things being the same, could have been otherwise; that thought follows thought, like wave following wave; that chance or accident has no share in any thing that comes to pass in the moral or the physical world; that whatever is, must be; that whatever is to be will be necessarily."[48] Wordsworth expands the idea in another poem:

> An *active* Principle:— howe'er removed
> From sense and observation, it subsists
> In all things, in all natures; in the stars
> Of azure heaven, the unenduring clouds,
> In flower and tree, in every pebbly stone
> That paves the brooks, the stationary rocks,
> The moving waters, and the invisible air.
> Whate'er exists hath properties that spread
> Beyond itself, communicating good,
> A simple blessing, or with evil mixed;
> Spirit that knows no insulated spot,
> No chasm, no solitude; from link to link
> It circulates, the Soul of all the worlds,
> This is the freedom of the universe;
> Unfolded still the more, more visible,
> The more we know; and yet is reverenced least,
> And least respected in the human Mind,
> Its most apparent home.[49]

Whitman:

> Indifferently, 'mid public, private haunts, in solitude,
> Behind the mountain and the wood,
> Companion of the city's busiest streets, through the assemblage,

It and its radiations constantly glide.

In looks of fair unconscious babes,
Or strangely in the coffin'd dead,
Or show of breaking dawn or stars by night,
As some dissolving delicate film of dreams,
Hiding yet lingering.

Two little breaths of words comprising it,
Two words, yet all from first to last comprised in it.[50]

Lao Tze:

There is a thing inherent and natural,
Which existed before heaven and earth.
Motionless and fathomless,
It stands alone and never changes;
It pervades everywhere and never becomes exhausted.
It may be regarded as the Mother of the Universe.
I do not know its name.
If I am forced to give it a name,
I call it Tao, and I name it as supreme.[51]

Again — Whitman:

There is something that comes to one now and perpetually,
It is not what is printed, preach'd, discussed, it eludes discussion and print,
It is not to be put in a book, it is not in this book,
It is for you whoever you are, it is no farther from you than your hearing
and sight are from you,
It is hinted by nearest, commonest, readiest, it is provoked by them.[52]

Similarly,

Without peeping out of the window
One can see the Tao of heaven.[53]

Yet, paradoxically,

Tao cannot be heard ... that which is heard is not Tao. Tao cannot be
seen; that which is seen is not Tao. Tao cannot be told; that which can be
told is not Tao.[54]

This, then, is the Riddle which answers, but does not answer, Whitman's
"Riddle Song."

That which eludes this verse and any verse,
Unheard by sharpest ear, unform'd in clearest eye or cunningest mind,
Nor lore nor fame, nor happiness nor wealth,

And yet the pulse of every heart and life throughout the world inces-
santly,
Which you and I and all pursuing ever ever miss,
Open but still a secret, the real of the real, an illusion,
Costless, vouchsafed to each, yet never man the owner,
Which poets vainly seek to put in rhyme, historians in prose,
Which sculptor never chisel'd yet, nor painter painted
Which vocalist never sung, nor orator nor actor ever utter'd,
Invoking here and now I challenge for my song.

◆ ◆ ◆

On the evening of September 28, 1890, the aging and ailing Whitman
joined his friends at Tom Harned's house in Camden for camaraderie and a
delightful dinner. Present were Harned and his wife Augusta, their daughter
Anna, Tom Donaldson, Horace Traubel with Anne Montgomerie, later to be
his wife, John Clifford, and John Burroughs (the naturalist). Anna served
whiskey toddies to Burroughs and Whitman and later to her father, lawyer
Tom Harned. These toddies, which Whitman always enjoyed, may have been
instrumental in bringing forth probably the most valuable statement he ever
made about his poems. Here is Traubel's entry:

> At one point in the dinner, he sat with a piece of chicken on his fork and
> entered into quite a talk about the "meanings" of "Leaves of Grass," that "it
> can never be understood but by an indirection," and adding, "It stands first
> of all for that something back of phenomena, in phenomena, which gives it
> all its significance, yet cannot be described — eludes definition, yet is the
> most real thing of all." Then finishing his bite and passing to another sub-
> ject.[55]

IX

The Greater Religion

Know you, solely to drop in the earth the
germs of a greater religion,
The following chants each for its kind I sing.
— "Starting from Paumanok."

"The New Theology — heir of the West — lusty and loving, and won-
drous beautiful."[1] Such were the terms Whitman used to describe the "greater
religion." In 1884 Whitman talked to Edward Carpenter about what
"lies behind" *Leaves of Grass*. In the course of the conversation Whitman
expressed the opinion that "there are truths which it is necessary to envelop
or wrap up." "I replied," Carpenter says, "that all through history the
old mysteries, or whatever they may have been called, had been held back,
and added that probably we had something yet to learn from India in these
matters." And Whitman said, "I do not myself think there is anything
more to come from that source; we must rather look to modern science to
open the way. Time alone can absolutely test my poems or any one's."[2] A dozen
years previously, in the 1872 Preface, Whitman had prophesied the new religion:

> With Science, the Old Theology of the East, long in its dotage, begins to
> die and disappear. But (to my mind) Science — and may be such will prove
> its principal service — as evidently prepares the way for One indescribably
> grander — Time's young but perfect offspring — the New Theology — heir of
> the West — lusty and loving, and wondrous beautiful.[3]

With these convictions Whitman could proclaim in "Passage to India":
"Passage to more than India!"[4] A pioneer passage, accomplished through the
labors of science, prepares the way for the spiritual passage, which is to be
effected through the work of "the true son of God, the poet":

191

Then not your deeds only O voyagers, O scientists and inventors, shall be
justified,
All these hearts as of fretted children shall be sooth'd,
All affection shall be fully responded to, the *secret* [my italics] shall be
told,
All these separations and gaps shall be taken up and hook'd and link'd
together,...
Nature and Man shall be disjoin'd and diffused no more,
The true son of God shall absolutely fuse them.[5]

Just what was to be the part which science would play in shaping the
new religion? This is a question which can only be answered by reference to
Whitman's awareness of the progressive fulfillment by science of the idea of
determinism. He saw very clearly even in his own day the increasing tendency
on the part of science to place man among the other objects of Nature, to
treat his actions as no less subject to determinist law than the forces which
make the sea flow or the globe revolve.

Whitman could not have anticipated the disturbing gradual weakening of
the scientific reputation of determinism, beginning in 1900 and culminating in
1927 in the work of Werner Heisenberg, whose theory, later prejudicially named
the Principle of Indeterminacy, provided hope for many — scientists and laymen alike — who desperately sought to overthrow determinism. Determinism
has not been disproved by science, but it has been displaced in some modern
formulations by the use of quantum-inspired statistics.

Albert Einstein, in the latter part of his life and until his death, concentrated his efforts on the development of an interpretation that would provide
a scientific reassignment of determinism to its former status or, indeed, replace
it by an even stronger determinism. I emphasized in Chapter II that Einstein
felt that "events in nature are controlled by a much stricter and more closely
binding law than we suspect to-day, when we speak of one event being the
cause of another." He never lost faith in determinism. In a letter to Max Born,
Dec. 12, 1926, he had written:

Quantum mechanics is certainly imposing. But an inner voice tells me that
it is not yet the real thing. The theory says a lot, but does not really bring
us any closer to the secret of the Old One. I, at any rate, am convinced that
He does not throw dice.[6]

This last remark is often repeated as "God does not play dice with the world."

Max Planck's formulation of the quantum theory eventuated, ironically,
in the flurry of modern arguments against the very determinism in which he
continued firmly to believe. In his book *Where Is Science Going?* Planck considers the evidence of the applicability of determinism in the humanist sciences and comes to the following conclusion:

Under these circumstances it is obvious that we cannot erect a definite boundary and say: Thus far but no farther. The principle of causality must be held to extend even to the highest achievements of the human soul. We must admit that the mind of each one of our greatest geniuses — Aristotle, Kant or Leonardo, Goethe or Beethoven, Dante or Shakespeare — even in the most profound workings of the soul, was subject to the causal fiat and was an instrument in the hands of an almighty law which governs the world.[7]

If we leave aside the intricacies of the scientific arguments and look at practical evidence, it will be clear that there has been no real interruption of the trends towards strengthening the determinist stance. Broad practical applications of determinism are producing results which Whitman would have found gratifying. Mind-altering drugs now widely used could have helped his neurotic sister Hannah lead a normal life. In social work and in law the determinist influences of heredity and environment are at last being given recognition — a recognition which was heretofore made impossible by a prevalent ethical narrowness and an uncultured vengefulness both feeding from a root of free will-ism. In 1951 — the statement seems remarkably prescient — Stuart Hampshire outlined some modern meanings of Spinoza's determinism:

> ... *in proportion as* our scientific knowledge, or knowledge of causes, increases, we necessarily abandon the primitive conception of human beings as free and self-determining in their choices.... [We] think of human beings as self-determining and free agents, to be distinguished in this respect from all other beings in Nature, only in so far as we are ignorant of the causes of their behaviour, and in so far as our scientific knowledge is incomplete.... As psychology in its various branches progresses, ... the line drawn in our common-sense speech and thought between a disease or pathological condition, for which the sufferer is not responsible, and wickedness, which the agent could have avoided, is gradually effaced in one case after another; young criminals are reclassified as juvenile delinquents, whose anti-social behaviour can be cured by the appropriate treatment, but cannot usefully and reasonably be blamed, with the purely moral implications which formerly attached to such blame; the very words — "anti-social" in place of "bad," "delinquent" in place of "criminal" and so on — show the gradual erosion of the old common-sense attitude, as scientific knowledge advances.[8]

We now see the wisdom and foresight of Whitman when he said to Traubel: "I agree with you new fellows who do not believe that the criminal classes so known are the cause of themselves" (see Ch. VI). And we understand that this was a determinist speaking, a determinist wise enough to anticipate the beneficial consequences of his philosophy.

More of us now agree with Whitman that a nation's "politics and religion, whatever they are, are inevitable results of the days and events that have preceded the nation" Ch. IV). Few of us now would oppose William H. Halverson's statement that "an immediate and steadily growing quantity of scientific evidence appears to bear out the hypothesis that this is an orderly universe, that every event has a cause, that everything that occurs is an inevitable consequence of antecedent causes."[9]

In greater and greater numbers we are beginning to understand and accept Freud's pronouncement that "determinism in the psychic realm is carried out uninterruptedly."[10] The "first and foremost" principle of psychoanalysis, says Jacob Arlow, "is the principle of determinism":

> Psychoanalytic theory assumes that mental events are not random, haphazard, accidental, unrelated phenomena. Thoughts, feelings, and impulses are events in a chain of causally related phenomena. They result from antecedent experiences in the life of the individual.[11]

In 1953 Francis Crick went into a Cambridge pub and announced that he and James Watson had "found the secret of life." Probably few heads turned. Crick and Watson, in that now long-ago year, had discovered the double-helix structure of deoxyribonucleic acid — DNA. With the patient efforts of many scientists over many years, that discovery has led to amazing developments. Biotechnology, a $30-billion-a-year industry, has produced more than 150 drugs and vaccines. Doctors use genetic analysis to detect diseases, and gene therapy to treat diseases. Genetic engineering enables farmers to grow bigger tomatoes and raise crops with less use of pesticides. Police now routinely use DNA evidence to solve (and re-solve) crimes. On June 26, 2000, came the stunning announcement by geneticists that they had virtually completed assembly of what is called "the book of life" — an achievement considered as important as man's walk on the moon or as the discovery of the microscope. Studies of the brain and operations on the brain reveal unmistakable mental and behavioral responses to its physical functions.

We are witnessing the fulfillment of Whitman's prophecy that "Nature and Man shall be disjoin'd and diffused no more." This line states the central theme of "Passage to India." Out of India itself came a remarkable restatement of that theme, employing the term "modern science" just as Whitman would have employed it:

> The same "eternal laws of iron" rule men as every other created object in the universe. Modern science, thus, demonstrates the truth which the *Rishis* of old intuitively apprehended and *secretly* [my italics] proclaimed thirty centuries ago on the banks of the Ganges: "They who see but One in the changing manifoldness of the universe, unto them belongs Eternal Truth, unto none else."[12]

Rabindranath Tagore, modern Hindu philosopher and poet, speaking of "the Rishis of India," remarks: "These ancient seers felt in the serene depth of their mind that the same energy which vibrates and passes into the endless forms of the world manifests itself in our inner being as consciousness; and there is no break in unity. For these seers there was no gap in their luminous vision of perfection."[13]

Carpenter, we remember, had called Whitman's attention to "the old mysteries" and had suggested that probably "we had something yet to learn from India in these matters." But Whitman said, no, he did not think there was anything more to come from that source, that "we must rather look to modern science to open the way." Whitman evidently felt that whatever truths the old theologies may have contained could be re-substantiated by science. The old forms of religion had served their purpose, had lived out their usefulness. A new religion was coming and science would "open the way." Certainly science was not to be all. It was to be the work of the poet to show the religious significance of the findings of science. Whitman said: "I can see what science sees — what it says can be seen: but there is much beyond that: I see that too."[14] Science was to clear the passage:

> I should be inclined to say the supreme value, the highest service, science is rendering to thought, today, in our world, is in clearing the way, pioneering, opening roads: untilling, in fact, some things instead of tilling them: sweeping away, destroying, burning, the underbrush. Oh! think of what it has done in untilling alone — what a precious force it has exerted in untilling! Take the instance of what is called the theological, what people call the religious world — the world of belief, so-called: think of it: of what it has swept away there: the slag, the waste, the filth: the loathsome prisons, bitternesses, barbarisms! Even today its task is not done: see how much lingers still in some places: the cruel anathema not only of words but of deeds: how the traditions are still harped on, made much of, in pulpits — even in the press: how they threaten, slander, browbeat.[15]

Science, casting aside the idea of an anthropomorphic God, would discredit the established religious attitudes. Science would make acceptable the concept of the oneness of nature. The new religion would emphasize that this oneness includes man. A modern endorsement of this view appeared in a 2001 magazine article:

> Science will not *replace* religion. Rather it will be a major part of the intellectual basis of whatever worldview does replace it. The failure to recognize that humans are indeed a part of nature is one of the great shortcomings of revealed religions.[16]

This statement bears out Whitman's prediction in "Passage to India" that "Nature and Man shall be disjoin'd and diffused no more." This indeed

would be a Passage to India. "In the west," says Tagore, "the prevalent feeling is that nature belongs exclusively to inanimate things and to beasts,
that there is a sudden unaccountable break where human-nature begins.
According to it, everything that is low in the scale of beings is merely nature,
and whatever has the stamp of perfection on it, intellectual or moral, is
human-nature. It is like dividing the bud and blossom into two separate
categories, and putting their grace to the credit of two antithetical principles. But the Indian mind never has any hesitation in acknowledging its kinship with nature, its unbroken relation with all."[17] Whitman saw that science, aided by the work of the poet, was to bring about the acceptance by
the Western mind of this very belief in the oneness of man with nature. This
was to be the Passage to India, the first step in the establishment of the new
religion.

> America needs, and the world needs, a class of bards who will, now and
> ever, so link and tally the rational physical being of man, with the ensem-
> bles of time and space, and with this vast and multiform show, Nature, sur-
> rounding him, ever tantalizing him, equally a part, and yet not a part of
> him, as to essentially harmonize, satisfy, and put at rest. Faith, very old,
> now scared away by science, must be restored, brought back by the same
> power that caused her departure — restored with a new sway, deeper, wider,
> higher than ever.[18]

"Passage to more than India!" And out of India now comes an echo of Whitman's prophetic line. "Through our progress in science," says Tagore, "the
wholeness of the world and our oneness with it is becoming clearer to our
mind. When the perception of unity is not merely intellectual, when it opens
out our whole being into a luminous consciousness of the all, then it becomes
a radiant joy, an overspreading love."[19]

Whitman saw that science was developing toward these ends. We, of
course, are in a position to observe that science has taken at least the first
steps toward the verification of Whitman's predictions:

> Recent psychology, in large measure through the influences of Freud, has
> achieved a more penetrating analysis of human motivation by bringing to
> the fore certain hitherto obscure factors which are operative in volition. The
> psychology of the subconscious by filling in apparent gaps in the psycholog-
> ical causation of volition has furthered the case for determinism.... The
> more we know about the physiological and neural processes which go on
> inside the human organism ... the more evident it becomes that there is no
> break in the continuous chain of causation.[20]

The "gaps" mentioned here by Professor Ledger Wood are the same "gaps"
which Whitman had in mind in writing "Passage to India," wherein he avers
that "these separations and gaps [sic] shall be taken up and hook'd and link'd

together." Tagore said the Rishis saw "no gap"; he himself saw no "unaccountable break." Science would show that as Professor Wood says, "there is no break in the continuous chain of causation." "The principle of causality must be held to extend even to the highest achievements of the human soul." "The same 'eternal laws of iron' rule men as every other created object in the universe." "Nature and Man shall be disjoin'd and diffused no more."

In Horace Traubel's priceless reports of Whitman's conversations there is a page-long presentation of Whitman's vehemently stated views on religion and science. Adherents to present-day orthodoxy may be shocked by Whitman's bluntness, but here is that valuable presentation of his views:

W. was considerably amused by an announcement in today's Press that preachers would tomorrow discuss the question, why so many pews were empty. "It seems to me a very plain case," he said, "a case easily explicated to any one who cares to see. The simple truth is, from time immemorial theology has built itself upon mythology — and now the time has come when that mythology can no longer be believed — believed by any one of any account. We need a reconstruction — *are having* a reconstruction in fact — of theology, so to call it — perhaps properly so to call it. I have heard it said that the church and genius are divorced — the church and the masses, too — and when we ask why, the preacher will say, from pride in the genius, stupidity in the others — that contrariety is at fault whatever. Damn the preachers! What do they know or care to know? The churches have constructed a god of moral goodness — wholly, solely, moral goodness — and that is its weakness. For if there is one thing that is *not* true, that is the thing: not but that moral goodness has its part. See what we get out of science, democracy, the modern — on this point! According to such a standard of moral goodness — the standard of the churches — probably nine-tenths of the universe is depraved — probably nine-tenths denied a right in the scheme of things — which is ridiculous, outright: might have satisfied an older intelligence, but will not ours. Our time, land, age, the future — demands readjustment — demands the fuller recognition of democracy — the *ensemble*: these have hardly been recognized at all in the old theology. What can science have to do with such a spectre as the present church? All their methods are opposed — must be opposed — utterly opposed: for one means restriction, the other freedom: the church — ill-adjustment, science — harmony."[21]

Rash as these statements may seem, they are affirmed by quite similar statements by Emerson and by Albert Einstein. Einstein, one of the greatest modern scientists, was — I will not let you forget — a determinist. Whitman, as a determinist, could not but have looked to science, especially to the future development of science, for the verification and exoneration of his philosophy. He looked on science, in spite of, or indeed because of, its antagonism to established religious forms, as holding greatest promise in the evolution of a religion surpassing all others. And he felt that the evolution, the revolution, was already beginning to take place:

> The whole mass of people are being leavened by this spirit of scientific wor-ship — this noblest of religions coming after all the religions that came before. After culture has said its last say we find that the best things yet remain to be said: that the heart is still listening to have brain things said to it — the faith, the spirit, the soul of man waiting to have such things of faith, spirit, the soul said to it. Books won't say what we must have said: try all that books may they can't say it. The utmost pride goes with the utmost resignation; science says to us — be ready to say yes yes whatever happens, whatever don't happen: yes, yes, yes. That's where science becomes reli-gion — where the new spirit utters the highest truth — makes the last demonstration of faith; looks the universe full in the face — its bad in the face, its good — and says yes to it.[22]

Thus Whitman clearly states that the new religion will have science as a factual basis. Emerson also, looking hopefully toward the future, felt that "the scientific mind must have a faith, which is science." He, too, predicted the new religion:

> We say, the old forms of religion decay, and that a scepticism devastates the community. I do not think it can be cured or stayed by any modification of theologic creeds, much less by theologic discipline.... Let us replace sentimentalism by realism and *dare to uncover* [my italics] those sim-ple and terrible laws which, be they seen or unseen, pervade and govern....
> ...Man is made of the same atoms as the world is, he shares the same impressions, pre-dispositions, and destiny. When his mind is illuminated, when his heart is kind, he throws himself joyfully into the sublime order, and does, with knowledge, what the stones do by structure.
> The religion which is to guide and fulfil the present and coming ages, whatever else it be, must be intellectual. The scientific mind must have a faith, which is science. "There are two things," said Mahomet, "which I abhor, the learned in his infidelities, and the fool in his devotions." Our times are impatient of both, and especially of the last. Let us have nothing now which is not its own evidence. There is surely enough for the heart and imagination in the religion itself. Let us not be pestered with assertions and half-truths, with emotions and snuffle.
> There will be a new church founded on moral science, at first cold and naked, a babe in a manger again, the algebra and mathematics of ethical law, *the church of men to come* [my italics], without shawms, or psaltery, or sackbut; but it will fast enough gather beauty, music, picture, poetry.[23]

"The church of men to come" — how brave this prophecy must have been in the days of Emerson and Whitman. Indeed it can only be made in ours by holding firmly to the courage supplied by honest conviction. For even today such a religion seems far off, and to most people it must seem, to use Emerson's phrase, "cold and naked." How few today are able to grasp the beauty of it or thrill to its magnificent conceptions!

Albert Einstein, the great mathematical physicist, was one of these few — Albert Einstein, whose miraculous mind probed deeper into the awe-inspiring arcana of nature than perhaps the mind of any person who ever lived. The scope of his vision was like that of the mystics. Significantly, he seems to have felt that he was not alone among his colleagues in his remarkable religious perceptions:

> ... the scientist is possessed by the sense of universal causation. The future, to him, is every whit as necessary and determined as the past.... His religious feeling takes the form of a rapturous amazement at the harmony of natural law, which reveals an intelligence of such superiority that compared with it, all the systematic thinking and acting of human beings is an utterly insignificant reflection.[24]

Whitman's close friend Dr. R. M. Bucke noted in Whitman's character a mysterious element which he termed Cosmic Consciousness. Though Bucke may have been correct in explaining this element as a mysticism which he believed certain persons in the course of the mental evolution of the race achieve, I believe it was a direct result of Whitman's determinism. Like Einstein, Whitman was "possessed by the sense of universal causation." In his book *Cosmic Consciousness* Bucke wrote of Whitman: "His favorite occupation seemed to be strolling or sauntering about outdoors by himself, looking at the grass, the trees, the flowers, the vistas of light, the varying aspects of the sky, and listening to the birds, the crickets, the tree-frogs, the wind in the trees, and all the hundreds of natural sounds. It was evident that these things gave him a feeling of pleasure far beyond what they give to ordinary people. Until I knew the man it had not occurred to me that anyone could derive so much absolute happiness and ample fulfilment from these things as he evidently did."[25] Because of his determinism Whitman viewed the world with Einstein's "rapturous amazement."

In his essay "Cosmic Religion" Einstein explains that there are two lower stages of religious development: the primitive stage, in which fear of a whimsical and willful God is predominant; and the social or moral stage, requiring belief in a loving and consoling God who deals out rewards and punishments. In the concept of both of these stages, says Einstein, God is anthropomorphic. Einstein then goes on to say:

> Only exceptionally gifted individuals or especially noble communities rise *essentially* above this level; in these there is found a third level of religious experience, even if it is seldom found in a pure form. I will call it the cosmic religious sense....

How can this cosmic religious experience be communicated from man to man, if it cannot lead to a definite conception of God or to a theology? It seems to me that the most important function of art and of science is to arouse and keep alive this feeling in those who are receptive.

Thus we reach an interpretation of the relation of science to religion which is very different from the customary view. From the study of history, one is inclined to regard religion and science as irreconcilable antagonists, and this for a reason that is very easily seen. For any one who is *pervaded with the sense of causal law in all that happens, who accepts in real earnest the assumption of causality* [my italics], the idea of a Being who interferes with the sequence of events in the world is absolutely impossible. Neither the religion of fear nor the social-moral religion can have any hold on him. A God who rewards and punishes is for him unthinkable, because *man acts in accordance with an inner and outer necessity, and would, in the eyes of God, be as little responsible as an inanimate object is for the movement which it makes.*[26] [The italics are mine.]

Whitman whispers, in a line now to become famous, "(I reckon I behave no prouder than the level I plant my house by, after all.)"[27] Think of the little bubble in Whitman's level when you reread Einstein's last sentence.

Other similarities are equally startling. Whitman speaks of "the Kosmic Spirit, which must henceforth, in my opinion, be the background and underlying impetus, more or less visible, of all first-class songs."[28] Einstein, in the passage quoted, asserts that the communication of the cosmic religious feeling is "the most important function of art and of science." Fully agreeing, Whitman mentions "the Spiritual, the Religious — which it is to be the greatest office of Scientism, in my opinion, and of future Poetry also, to free from fables, crudities and superstitions, and launch forth in renewed Faith and Scope a hundred fold."[29]

Stressing that science "opens the way" to the new religion, Whitman indicates that the fruition will be slow but certain:

To me, the crown of Savantism is to be, that it surely opens the way for a more splendid Theology, and for ampler and diviner Songs. No year, nor even century, will settle this. This is a phase of the Real, lurking behind the Real, which it is all for.[30]

Please understand the import of this last sentence: Whitman is saying that the new religion is *a part of the predetermined scheme,* "Time's young but perfect offspring." The scope of his vision lets him see far into the boundless future; he waits with a determinist's patience the arrival of the New Theology. I wonder if he ever thought about the irony: the new religion, which would be confirmed by the determinism of science, would *itself* be predetermined!

The new religion has far to go to reach its full meaning and a broad acceptance. It depends for its life on determinism, the determinism accepted by Emerson, defended by Planck and Einstein, and affirmed by Tagore and Sri Ramakrishna, the determinism from which Whitman sought sustenance and to which he went for inspiration in the writing of *Leaves of Grass*.

◆ ◆ ◆

In a letter to Horace Traubel on June 12, 1889, Gabriel Sarrazin confided a valuable understanding of Walt Whitman:

He is really the only one who has clearly seen that man is an indivisible fragment of the Universal Divinity.... This view of which Whitman has been in this century the practicing apostle, this view will renovate the world.[31]

Notes

References to Whitman's poems, unless otherwise expressed, will be to Leaves of Grass *(Philadelphia: David McKay, 1891–92).*

Chapter I

1. H. L. Traubel, *With Walt Whitman in Camden*, III, 276. For publisher and date, see my bibliography. Hereafter *WWC*.

2. *Critical Kit-Kats* (London: William Heinemann, 1913), 96. When Dr. Richard Maurice Bucke, friend and bibliographer of Whitman, was asked by Karl Knortz to explain some passages in *Leaves of Grass*, he replied, "Why who can understand it? it will be a hundred years, perhaps, before any one understands it."—Quoted by Knortz in "Walt Whitman," in *In Re Walt Whitman*, ed. H. Traubel et al. (Philadelphia: David McKay, 1893), 220. Standish O'Grady felt that "there is an undertone of meaning in Whitman which can never be fully comprehended."—"Walt Whitman, The Poet of Joy," in *In Re WW*, 362. "That book," said Whitman, "has an amazing elusiveness: I am still looking for some of its meanings myself."—*WWC*, I, 162.

3. *WWC*, VII, 391.

4. *Ibid.*, I, 96. Discussing Heine: "Heine! Oh how great! The more you stop to look, to examine, the deeper seem the roots, the broader and higher the umbrage."—*Ibid.*, 461.

5. *Ibid.*, VII, 156. For Whitman's use of "indirections" see "When I Read the Book," "Among the Multitude," "Myself and Mine," "On the Beach at Night," "Laws for Creations."

6. "Walt Whitman and His Poems," in *In Re Walt Whitman*, ed. H. L. Traubel et al. (Philadelphia: David McKay, 1893), 19.

7. Entry, "Religion," in *Walt Whitman: An Encyclopedia*, ed. J. R. LeMaster and D. D.

Kummings (New York and London: Garland, 1998), 583.

8. *WWC*, II, 234.

9. *Days with Walt Whitman* (2nd ed.; London: George Allen & Unwin, 1906), 43.

10. "Notes and Fragments," ed. R. M. Bucke, in *The Complete Writings of Walt Whitman*, ed. R. M. Bucke et al. (New York and London: G. P. Putnam's Sons, 1902), IX, 12–13. This note as published omits the words "of the old or its adaptation to the modern and to," which I have added in conformity with the original, a facsimile of which was included in the Detroit Public Library exhibit of the Charles E. Feinberg collection in 1955. The phrase "must not say originalities" was first written by Whitman "might almost say originalities." Whitman struck through the words "might almost" and wrote in "must not" above them for the final version. With "fruitage" in the final sentence compare: "Thou but the apples, long, long a-growing,/ The fruit [*sic*] of the Old ripening to-day in thee."—"Thou Mother with Thy Equal Brood," Sec. 3.

11. Whitman, "Immortality," in *In Re WW*, 350. This article, pp. 349–51 in *In Re*, comprises a news reporter's draft of part of a discussion between Whitman and Ingersoll at the 1890 birthday dinner for Whitman. The published draft "contains only two or three changes, made by Whitman himself"—ed.'s note p. 349.

12. *WWC*, VI, 440.

13. *Ibid.*, II, 71.

14. *Ibid.* V, 311.

15. *Ibid.*, I, 156–57.

16. *Inclusive Edition: Leaves of Grass*, ed. E.

Holloway (Garden City, N. Y.: Doubleday, Doran, 1945), 513.

17. Whitman's advertisement in his *As a Strong Bird on Pinions Free*, 1872, in Esther Shephard, *Walt Whitman's Pose* (New York: Harcourt, Brace, 1936), 363.

18. R.M. Bucke, *Walt Whitman* (Philadelphia: David McKay, 1883), 66. Whitman explained to Traubel: "I do not teach a definite philosophy.... I but outline, suggest, hint — tell what I see — then each may make up the rest for himself.... The last thing the world needs is a cut and dried philosophy, and the last man to announce a cut and dried philosophy would be Walt Whitman." — *WWC*, V, 310–11.

19. *American Renaissance* (New York: Oxford UP, 1964), 526.

20. "The Philosopher," in *Walt Whitman, Man, Poet, Philosopher* (Washington: Library of Congress, 1955 [Reprint; Norwood, 1971]), 35.

21. *Walt Whitman Handbook* (Chicago: Packard, 1946), 240.

22. *Pragmatism* (London: Longmans, Green, 1910), 116.

23. *Leaves of Grass, 1855 Version* (Ann Arbor Media Group [Ann Arbor, Mich.: Borders Classics, 2003]), 18. *Nota bene*: This source does not, as do editions by Holloway, Stovall, Untermeyer, Miller, and probably others, commit the error of including the word "to" in the phrase "nearer [to] the beginning." The "no result exists" statement was omitted, as were many other parts of the 1855 Preface, when it was reprinted in the 1892 ed. of Whitman's prose. Some of the omitted parts were converted to poetry.

24. p. 276.

25. *The Solitary Singer: A Critical Biography of Walt Whitman* (New York: Macmillan, 1955), 135, 187.

26. *Ibid.*, 166.

27. "Philosopher," in *WW, Man, Poet, Philos.*, 46.

28. "Mysticism," in *WW: Encyclopedia*, 445.

29. *Walt Whitman, Representative Selections*, ed. Floyd Stovall (Rev. ed.; New York: American Book, 1939), 461 (note). I would suggest Hegel as a source for some of the ideas in Stovall's note, but I suspect he did not fully grasp Hegel's meanings. For Hegel's explanation see Ch. IV. Stovall's modifier "rational" points to Kant and Boethius as sources.

30. Paul A. Bennett, *Books and Printing* (New York: World, 1951), 359.

31. Samuel L. Clemens (pseud. Mark Twain), *Mark Twain in Eruption: Hitherto Unpublished Pages about Men and Events*, ed. Bernard DeVoto (1st ed.; New York and London: Harper & Brothers, 1940), 240–41.

32. "Song of the Open Road," Sec. 11.

33. *The English Works of Thomas Hobbes*, ed. W. Molesworth (London: John Bohn), V (1840), 25. The treatise appears in Vol. IV, (1840), 229–78.

34. Bertrand Russell, *A History of Western Philosophy* (New York: Simon and Schuster, 1945), 593.

35. G. F. Leibniz, Letter, May, 1671, in *Philosophical Papers and Letters*, trans. and ed. W. Loemker (Chicago: U of Chicago P, 1956), I, 226–28.

36. Benedict de Spinoza, *Spinoza's Short Treatise on God, Man, and His Well-Being*, trans. and ed. A. Wolf (London: Adam and Charles Black, 1910), Bk. II, Ch. XXVI, p. 149.

37. *Spinoza* (Harmondsworth, Middlesex: Penguin Books, 1951), 152–53. The phrase "hideous hypothesis," source not given, appears on p. 149.

38. "Samples of My Common-place Book," in *Specimen Days*, in *Complete Prose Works* (Philadelphia: David McKay, 1892), 183–85. Whitman listed some two dozen "samples" in a footnote (pp. 183–84), including, on p. 184, the Epictetus quotation, or rather paraphrase.

39. *Enchiridion*, Sec. XLVI, in *Moral Discourses of Epictetus*, trans. Elizabeth Carter, ed. W. Rouse ("Everyman's Library," No. 404 [London: J. M. Dent & Sons; New York: E. P. Dutton, 1950]), 271. Carter's translation appeared in 1758, 1759, 1807 (4th ed.); other pre–*Leaves of Grass* edns. were by M'Cormac, 1844, and Long, 1848. Of the trans. I have seen, Carter's has most Whitman echoes.

40. *WWC*, II, 72. Floyd Stovall, in *The Foreground of Leaves of Grass* (Charlottesville: UP of Virginia, 1794), 174, found Whitman's reminiscence "puzzling" because, he submitted, there were no translations at that time (1835) for Whitman to have seen. But note the dates of Carter's early translations. Carter's 4th ed., 1807, came twenty-eight years before Whitman's discovery of his cherished Epictetus.

41. *Discourses*, trans. Carter, Bk. IV, Ch. VIII, Sec. 7, p. 240.

42. "Song of Myself," Sec. 25.

43. *Discourses*, trans. Carter, Bk. IV, Ch. VIII, Sec. 7, p. 240.

44. Variorum Readings, by O. L. Triggs, in *Inclusive Edition: Leaves of Grass*, ed. E. Holloway (Garden City, N. Y.: Doubleday, Doran, 1945), 578.

45. "A Backward Glance O'er Travel'd Roads," *Leaves of Grass*, 1891–92, p. 434. This essay was published as the Preface to Whitman's *November Boughs*, 1888. Included at the very end of the poems in the 1891–92 ed.

46. See "Phrenological Notes on W. Whitman, by L. N. Fowler, July, 1849," in Edward Hungerford, "Walt Whitman and His Chart of Bumps," *American Literature*, II, (1931), 363. On a scale of 1 through 7, Whitman's "Cautiousness" was rated by Fowler 6 (large).

47. Quoted in Esther Shephard, *Walt Whitman's Pose* (New York: Harcourt, Brace, 1936), 369, from a sale catalogue "of the Bucke collection at Sotheby's in London, May, 1935, p. 34." — Shephard's note, p. 436.

48. *Leaves of Grass* (Boston: Thayer and Eldridge, 1860–61), 421.

49. Above, n. 43.

50. Above, n. 11.

51. *Walt Whitman: The Complete Poems*, ed. F. Murphy (London: Penguin, 2004), xxvi.

52. "Notes and Frags.," in *Comp. Writings*, IX, p. 5.

53. "Debris," *Leaves of Grass*, 1860–61 ed.

54. *An 1855–56 Notebook Toward the Second Edition of "Leaves of Grass,"* ed. H. Blodgett and W. White (Carbondale, Ill.: Southern Illinois UP, 1959), pp. 5–6.

55. *Ench.*, Sec. XXII, in *Moral Discourses*, trans. Carter, 261.

56. "Song of the Open Road," Sec. 11.

57. Above, n. 44.

58. "Song of Myself," Sec. 25.

59. Above, n. 43.

60. "Scented Herbage of My Breast." This poem is in the "Calamus" section. The "freeze" metaphor as used by Epictetus was employed in almost an identical sense by Whitman in a conversation with Traubel: "...it was the original policy of the critics, the professional literaturers, to ignore me — to freeze me out." "When they found they could not freeze you out they tried to burn you out." "Exactly — exactly: but neither heat nor could has killed our bud: the Leaves have lasted, lasted, seasons in and out, hates in and out." — *WWC*, I, 127. The possibility is obvious, as I have pointed out, that the root-plant metaphor in Epictetus helped to inspire the curious title *Leaves of Grass*. Notice that "Herbage," in the title above, carries out the "grass" metaphor.

61. "Calamus, No. 13," 1860 ed. Though I am greatly puzzled by the "Calamus" poems, I would suggest that the calamus root symbolizes Whitman's concealed philosophy. That philosophy, determinism, may well have served in Whitman's mind as a rational basis for a broad love of mankind. This interpretation of "Calamus" is, I hasten to admit, confused by the homosexual overtones which are undeniably present in these poems. It may be that Whitman's penchant for indirectness prompted him to shield his philosophic love (which I would define as actually compassion) by a sexual imagery.

62. "Song of the Open Road," Sec. 10.

63. *Days with WW*, 91–92. Cf. a note in Whitman's handwriting referenced "George Sand. *Consuelo*, Vol. 5, p. 164": "The unknown refused to explain himself. 'What could I say to you that I have not said in another (my own) language? Is it my fault that you have not understood me? You think I wished to speak to your senses, and it was my soul spoke to you. What do I say! It was the soul of the whole of humanity that spoke to you through mine.'" — "Notes and Frags.," in *Comp. Writings*, IX, 19.

64. "A Thought on Shakspere," in *November Boughs*, in *Comp. Prose*, 392.

65. Quoted, R. Asselineau, "Walt Whitman's Style: From Mysticism to Art," in *Whitman: A Collection of Critical Essays* ed. H. Pearce (Englewood Cliffs, N. J.: Prentice-Hall, 1962), 93 (note), from review by Aubrey De Vere, "Modern Poetry and Poets," *Edinburgh Review* (Oct., 1849), 123.

66. Quoted by Floyd Stovall, *The Foreground of "Leaves of Grass"* (Charlottesville: UP of Virginia, 1974), 278, from Whitman's clipping of a review by J. Whelpley of a trans. by W. Ross of G. E. Lessing's *Laoccoön, or the Secret of Classic Composition in Poetry, Painting, and Statuary*, in *American Whig Review*, XIII (Jan., 1851), 17–26.

67. R. Wellek and A. Warren, *Theory of Literature* (New York: Harcourt, Brace, 1949), 123.

68. "Freedom," in *Collect* in *Comp. Prose*, 336. This paragraph will be discussed later.

69. Arthur Schopenhauer, *The World as Will and Idea*, trans. R. Haldane and J. Kemp (3rd ed.; London: Kegan Paul, 1891), I, Bk. IV, Sec. 55, p. 372.

70. David Hume, *An Enquiry Concerning Human Understanding*, Sec. VIII, Part I, in *The English Philosophers from Bacon to Mill*, ed. E. Burtt (New York: Modern Library, 1939), 641.

71. Joseph Priestley, *The Doctrine of Philosophical Necessity Illustrated*, in *The Theological and Miscellaneous Works, &c., of Joseph Priestley*, ed. J. Rutt (no place or publisher listed [printed by G. Smallfield, Hackney]), III (n.d.), 506.

72. *Modern Man: His Belief and Behavior* (New York and London: Alfred A. Knopf, 1936), 18.

73. Quoted in Carpenter, *Days with WW*, 72–73, from R. M. Bucke, "Memories of Walt Whitman," in *Walt Whitman Fellowship Papers* (Philadelphia, 1894), 42.

74. "Myself and Mine."

75. *Fatalism or Freedom: A Biologist's Answer* (New York: W. W. Norton, 1926), 83.

76. "Whoever You Are Holding Me Now in Hand."

77. "Notes and Frags.," in *Comp. Writings*, IX, 160.

78. Friedrich Nietzsche, *Human-All-Too-Human*, Part I, trans. Helen Zimmern, in *The Complete Works of Friedrich Nietzsche*, ed. O. Levy (Edinburgh and London: T. N. Foulis), VI (1909), Div. II, Sec. 107, p. 107.

79. *The Philosophy of Necessity* (London: Longman et al., 1841), I, vi (pref.).

80. *Ibid.*

81. *Phases of Opinion and Experience During a Long Life; An Autobiography* (London: Longmans, Green, 1885), 15–16.

82. *Pragmatism*, 117.

83. "You Fellons on Trial in Courts."

84. *WWC*, IV, 488–89. The reference to Whitman's "deterministic theories (further elaborated by Doctor Bucke)" is a tantalizing clue. I have not found, in the Bucke writings I have reviewed, any mention of Whitman's determinism by name.

85. G. W. Allen, *Waldo Emerson: A Biography* (New York: Viking, 1981), 547. Interpreting James's view, Allen assigns to him the opinion that determinism is a "pessimistic philosophy."—*Ibid.*, 436. It is not clear that Allen himself does not agree with that prejudicial assessment.

86. *American Criticism* (Boston and New York: Houghton Mifflin, 1928), 213. The other quote is from 203.

87. *Walt Whitman — Poet of Science* (Morningside Heights, N. Y.: King's Crown, 1951), 119.

88. *Ibid.*, 119–20.

89. *Ibid.*, 126.

90. *Whitman* (New York: Macmillan, 1938), 213–14.

91. *Walt Whitman, Thinker and Artist* (New York: Philosophical Library, 1952), 16.

92. *Ibid.*, 210.

93. *Walt Whitman an American* (Boston: Houghton Mifflin, 1943), 266.

94. "Song of Myself," Sec. 20.

95. *The Poetry of Stephen Crane* (New York: Columbia UP, 1957), 215–16.

96. *Walt Whitman's America: A Cultural Biography* (New York: Knopf, 1995).

97. Letter, Mar. 24, 1999, to the author, quoted with written consent of Mr. Reynolds.

Chapter II

1. "Thoughts on Various Subjects," in *The Works of Alexander Pope, Esq., in Verse and Prose,* ed. W. Bowles (London: J. Johnson, 1806), VI, 411.

2. *A Dissertation on Liberty and Necessity, Pleasure and Pain* (London: Published by the author, 1725 [Reprint, New York: Facsimile Text Society, 1930]), 32.

3. L. Susan Stebbing, *Philosophy and the Physicists* (London: Methuen, 1937), 212.

4. Quoted in Ronald W. Clark, *Einstein: The Life and Times* (New York and Cleveland: World, 1971), 346–47, from *Saturday Evening Post*, Oct.26, 1929, p. 17 ff.

5. *The Doctrine of Philosophical Necessity Illustrated*, in *The Theological and Miscellaneous Works, &c., of Joseph Priestley*, ed. J. Rutt (No place or publisher listed [Printed by G. Smallfield, Hackney]), III (n.d.), 462.

6. *Rubáiyát of Omar Khayyám*, trans. Edward FitzGerald (Complete ed.; New York: Thomas Y. Crowell, 1921). In the five original editions of the Rubáiyát this is sequentially the 53rd, 70th, 73rd, 73rd, 73rd stanza.

7. *Leviathan*, Ch. 21, in *The English Philosophers from Bacon to Mill*, ed. E. Burtt (New York: Modern Library, 1939), 196–97.

8. Letter, Oct. 1674, in *Philosophy of Benedict de Spinoza*, trans. R. Elwes (New York: Tudor, 1934), 396.

9. Letter to Blyenbergh, Jan. 28, 1665, *Ibid.*, 346.

10. *An Essay Concerning Human Understanding*, Bk. II, Ch. 21, in *The Works of John Locke* (11th ed.; London: W. Otridge, 1812), I, 232.

11. David Hume, *An Inquiry Concerning Human Understanding*, Sec. VIII, Part I, in *Eng. Philos.*, ed. Burtt, 643.

12. *Ibid.*, 644.

13. *Outlines of Cosmic Philosophy* (Boston and New York: Houghton Mifflin, 1902), III, 265–66. The only indeterminist that I know of who has squarely faced the *a priori* consequences is William James. But his non-logical pragmatism provides a lame answer. See James's "The Dilemma of Determinism," in his *Essays on Faith and Morals* (New York, London, Toronto: Longmans, Green, 1943), 179–80. Perhaps James picked up "Dilemma" from Fiske's "dilemma" in the part quoted.

14. Benedict de Spinoza, *The Philosophy of Spinoza, Selected from His Chief Works*, ed. J. Ratner (New York: Modern Library, 1927), xxxix (introd.).

15. "Hellenistic and Roman Schools of Philosophy," in *A History of Philosophical Systems*, ed. V. Ferm (New York: Philosophical Library, 1950), 124.

16. *The Freedom of Man* (New Haven: Yale UP, 1936), p. 1.

17. Carl Grabo, *Prometheus Unbound: An Interpretation* (Chapel Hill: U of North Carolina P, 1935), 166–67.

18. G. W. Leibniz, *Theodicy: Essays on the Goodness of God, the Freedom of Man, and the Origin of Evil*, ed. A. Farrer, trans. E. Huggard (New Haven: Yale UP, 1952), 153.

19. Arthur Schopenhauer, *The World as Will and Idea*, trans. R. Haldane and J. Kemp (3rd ed.; London: Kegan Paul, 1891), I, Bk. IV, Sec. 55, p. 389.

20. Friedrich Nietzsche, *Human-All-Too-Human*, Part II, trans P. Cohn, in *The Complete Works of Friedrich Nietzsche*, ed. O. Levy (Edinburgh and London: T. N. Foulis), VII (1911), Div. II, Sec. 61, p. 118.

21. *Theodicy*, 153.

22. "I Lived in the Garden of Allah," in Dale Carnegie, *How to Stop Worrying and Start Living* (New York: Simon and Schuster, 1951), 249.

23. *The Koran*, trans. George Sale (London and New York: Frederick Warne, 1891), Ch. II, p. 52.

24. *Ibid.*, 69.

25. R. W. Emerson, "Fate," in *The Conduct of Life*, in *Ralph Waldo Emerson, Essays & Lectures*, ed. J. Porte (New York: Library of America, 1983), 954.

26. William Sloane Kennedy, letter, May 26, 1889, honoring Whitman on his birthday, in *Camden's Compliment to Walt Whitman, May 31, 1889*, ed. H. Traubel (Philadelphia: David McKay, 1889), 58.

27. *A Concise Introduction to Philosophy* (4th ed.; New York: Random House, 1981), 251. Halverson gives a thorough treatment of determinism; he assumes the role of each contender and argues each aspect with entertaining perspicacity.

28. Sir Arthur Eddington, "Physics and Philosophy," in *Philosophy*, VIII (1933), 41.

29. In Max Planck, *Where Is Science Going?* (1st ed.; New York: W. W. Norton, 1932), 201 (epilogue).

30. *Ibid.*, 202–203 (epilogue). Einstein recognized the advances of modern physics but was never satisfied with the claims for the overthrow of determinism: "Probably never before has a theory been evolved which has given a key to the interpretation and calculation of such a heterogeneous group of phenomena of experience as has the quantum theory. In spite of this, however, I believe that the theory is apt to beguile us into error in our search for a uniform basis for physics, because, in my belief, it is an *incomplete* representation of real things.... The incompleteness of the representation is the outcome of the statistical nature (incompleteness) of the laws." — Albert Einstein, *Out of My Later Years* (Rev. reprint ed.; Secaucas, N. J.: Citadel, 1956), 88.

31. *How Free Are You? The Determinism Problem* (2nd ed.; Oxford: Oxford UP, 2002), 73–74.

32. A. E. Briggs, *Walt Whitman: Thinker and Artist* (New York: Philosophical Library, 1952), 78.

33. *Unpopular Essays* (New York: Simon and Schuster, 1950), 53.

34. R. H. Popkin and A. Stroll, *Philosophy Made Simple* ("Made Simple Books" [2nd ed.; New York: Broadway Books, 1993]), 119.

35. *A System of Ethics*, ed. and trans. F. Thilly (New York: Charles Scribner's Sons, 1911), 459–60.

36. *The Problem of Freedom* (Boston and New York: Houghton Mifflin, 1911), 62.

37. W. T. Stace, *Religion and the Modern Mind* (Philadelphia and New York: J. B. Lippincott, 1952), 257–58.

38. Albert G. Ramsperger, "Determinism," in *Collier's Encyclopedia* (New York: Macmillan; London and New York: P. F. Collier, 1989), VIII, 158.

39. *Human Society in Ethics and Politics* (London: George Allen & Unwin, 1954), 97–98.

40. *The Uncollected Poetry and Prose of Walt Whitman*, ed. E. Holloway (Garden City, N. Y., and Toronto, Ont.: Doubleday, Page, 1921), II, 71.

41. "Religion as the Basis of the Postulates of Freedom," in *Freedom: Its Meaning*, ed. Ruth N. Anshen (1st ed.; New York: Harcourt, Brace, 1940), 477.

42. *Essays on the Logic of Being* (New York: Macmillan, 1932), 537–38.

43. "Philosophies of Freedom," Lecture XI in *Freedom in the Modern World*, ed. H. Kallen (New York: Coward-McCann, 1928), 239.

44. William Godwin, *Enquiry Concerning Political Justice*, ed. F. Priestley (Toronto: U of Toronto P, 1946), I, Bk. IV, Ch. VIII, p. 392.

45. Denis Diderot, Letter to Landois, quoted in Dugald Stewart, *Dissertation Exhibiting the Progress of Metaphysical, Ethical, and Political Philosophy*, Part II, Sec. 4, in *The Collected Works of Dugald Stewart*, ed. W. Hamilton (Edinburgh: Thomas Constable), I, (1854), 311–12.

46. *Doct. Of Philos. Neces.*, in *Works*, III, 509. Cf. Whitman: "I walk with delinquents with passionate love...." — "You Felons on Trial in Courts."

47. Benedict de Spinoza, *Ethic*, trans. W. White (London, etc.: Humphrey Milford, Oxford UP, 1927), Part II, Prop. XLIX, p. 103.

48. W. G. Everett, *Moral Values: A Study of*

the Principles of Conduct (New York: Henry Holt, 1918), 374. Everett's Ch. XII (pp. 335–76) gives an excellent account of determinism.

49. "Relig. as Basis of Freedom," in *Freedom*, ed. Anshen, 477.

50. *Fate and Freedom: A Philosophy for Free Americans* (New York: Simon and Schuster, 1945), 166–67.

51. Above, n. 29, text.

52. *Ethic*, trans. White, Part II, Prop. XLVIII, p. 94.

53. *Tractatus Theologico-Politicus*, Ch. XX, in *The Chief Works of Benedict de Spinoza*, trans. R. Elwes (Rev. ed.; London: George Bell and Sons), II (1898), 258–61.

54. *Philos. Of Spinoza*, ed. Ratner, xliii (introd.).

55. W. H. Herndon, *The Hidden Lincoln: From the Letters and Papers of William H. Herndon*, ed. E. Hertz (New York, Viking, 1938), 167.

56. David Bidney, *The Psychology and Ethics of Spinoza: A Study in the History and Logic of Ideas* (New Haven: Yale UP, 1940), 302.

57. Herndon, *Hidden Lincoln*, 167.

58. *Ibid.*, 265–66.

59. S. F. Gingerich, *Essays in the Romantic Poets* (New York, Macmillan, 1924), pp. 8–9.

60. *Shelley's Religion* (Minneapolis: U of Minnesota P, 1936), 143.

61. *Ibid.* More apropos, see ensuing lines 48–90, wherein Shelley praises "Freedom" five times — but without relinquishing his determinism.

62. *Ibid.*, 136–37. Barnard footnotes his quotations from Godwin: "*Political Justice*, I, 384 (Book IV, Chapter 7)" and "*Ibid.*, p. 385."

63. "The believer in free-will, can expostulate with, or correct, his pupil, with faint and uncertain hopes, conscious that the clearest exhibition of truth is impotent, when brought into contest with the unhearing and indisciplinable faculty of will; or in reality, if he were consistent, secure that it could produce no effect. The necessarian on the contrary employs real antecedents, and has a right to expect real effects." — Godwin, *Pol. Justice*, ed. Priestley, I, Bk. IV, Ch. VIII, p. 390.

64. *The Fundamental Questions of Philosophy* (London: Routledge & Kegan Paul, 1951), 189.

65. *Physics and Philosophy* (Cambridge: Cambridge UP; New York, Macmillan, 1943, 206.

66. J. S. Mill, *A System of Logic* (8th ed.; London, New York, etc.: Longmans, Green, 1919), Bk. VI, Ch. XI, Sec. 3, p. 611.

67. *Ibid.*

68. *On Liberty*, Ch. I, in *Eng. Philos.*, ed. Burtt, 958–59.

69. Albert Einstein, *The World As I See It* (New York: Covici-Friede, 1934), 238.

70. *Ibid.*, 240–41.

71. *Democratic Vistas*, in *Collect*, in *Complete Prose Works* (Philadelphia: David McKay, 1892), 228.

Chapter III

1. Benedict de Spinoza, *The Philosophy of Spinoza*, ed. J. Ratner (New York: Modern Library, 1927), xxxv–xxxvi (introd.).

2. Benedict de Spinoza, *Ethic*, trans. W. White (London, etc.: Humphrey Milford, Oxford UP, 1927), Part V, Prop. XLII, p. 283. From Spinoza's Latin, "*Omnia praeclara tam difficilia quam rara sunt*," "praeclara" is translated as "excellent" or "noble."

3. Johann Gottlieb Fichte, *The Vocation of Man*, Bk. I, in *The Popular Works of Johann Gottlieb Fichte*, trans. W. Smith (London: John Chapman), I (1848), 396–97.

4. *The Doctrine of Philosophical Necessity Illustrated*, in *The Theological and Miscellaneous Works, &c., of Joseph Priestley*, ed. J. Rutt (No place or publisher listed [Printed by George Smallfield, Hackney]), III (n.d.), 454–55 (pref.).

5. *Autobiography* (New York: Columbia UP, 1924), 118–20.

6. *Life of John Stuart Mill* (London: Walter Scott; New York: Thomas Whittaker, 1889), 56.

7. Bertrand Russell, "A Free Man's Worship," in *Mysticism and Logic and Other Essays* (London: Longmans, Green, 1919), 52.

8. Thomas Carlyle, *Sartor Resartus*, ed. C. Harrold ("Doubleday-Doran Series in Literature" [1st ed.; Garden City, N. Y.: Doubleday, Doran, 1937]), 164.

9. *Ibid.*, 168.

10. *An Essay on Burns*, ed. J. Abernethy ("Maynard's English Classic Series," No. 70 [New York: Maynard, Merrill, 1912]), 47.

11. Bertrand Russell, "Worship," in *Myst. and Logic*, 52–53.

12. Friedrich Nietzsche, *Human-All-Too-Human*, Part I, trans. Helen Zimmern, in *The Works of Friedrich Nietzsche*, ed. O. Levy (Edinburgh and London: T. N. Foulis), VI (1909), Div. II, Sec. 107, pp. 107–109.

13. G. W. F. Hegel, *The Logic of Hegel*, trans. W. Wallace (Oxford: Clarendon P, 1874), Sec. 147, pp. 231–32. There is a danger in presuming that the "renunciation" spoken of by Hegel, the resignation in determinism, signifies a complete giving up of the ego. Properly, it is rather the giving up of *egotism*, the ego remaining intact and functioning healthily as the mediator between the superego and the id as described in

Freudian psychology. H. A. Reyburn says of Hegel's view of freedom: "This conception must not be mistaken for that of mere resignation.... Resignation is the mere surrender of a self that does not find itself again. The concrete will does not abandon itself to an independently existing plan, for the plan exists *only in it* [my italics]. It is active, not passive; it conceives and carries out the greatest purposes, for they are those of the whole world."—*The Ethical Theory of Hegel: A Study of the Philosophy of Right* (Oxford: Clarendon P, 1921), 114).

14. Arthur Schopenhauer, *The World as Will and Idea*, trans. R. Haldane and J. Kemp (3rd ed.; London: Kegan Paul et al., 1891), I, Bk. IV, Sec. 55, p. 395.

15. Albert Einstein, "The World As I See It," from *Mein Weltbild*, ed. C. Seelig, in *Ideas and Opinions by Albert Einstein*, new trans. and rev. by Sonja Bargmann (New York: Bonanza Books, 1954), 8–9. Orig. pub. in *Forum and Century*, Vol. 84, pp. 193–194. In keeping with his determinist philosophy, Einstein stated: "*The true value of a human being* is determined primarily by the measure and the sense in which he has attained liberation of the self."—*Ibid.*, 12.

16. *Moral Discourses of Epictetus*, trans. Elizabeth Carter, ed. W. Rouse (London: J. M. Dent & Sons; New York: E. P. Dutton, 1950), Bk. IV, Ch. I, Sec. 14, p. 212.

17. Hegel, *Logic*, 59.

18. *Ibid.*, 243. This quotation and the one preceding are not from Hegel's ms. but are from editorial interpolations "made up of the notes taken in lecture by the editor (Henning) and by Professors Hotho and Michelet. These notes for the most part connect the several sections, rather than explain their statements. Their genuineness is vouched for by their being almost verbally the same with other parts of Hegel's own writing."—Wallace's pref., p. vi.

19. Rabindranath Tagore, *Sadhana: The Realisation of Life* (New York: Macmillan, 1914), 103. By an interesting coincidence this book is dedicated to a great admirer and friend of Walt Whitman: Ernest Rhys.

20. R. W. Emerson, "Fate," in *The Conduct of Life*, ed. S. Mittell (Washington, D.C.: National Home Library Foundation, 1935), 16.

21. *Doct. of Necessity*, in *Works*, III (n.d.), 454 (pref.).

22. *Remarks on Dr. Beattie's Essay on the Nature and Immutability of Truth*, in *Works*, III (n.d.), 94.

23. *Doct. of Necessity*, in *Works*, III (n.d.), 518.

24. *Ibid.*, 451 (dedication).

25. "Fate," in *Cond. of Life*, 31. With Emerson's "it disdains words and passes understanding" compare "the peace of God, which passeth all understanding"—Philippians, 4:7.

26. "Essay on Christianity," in *The Works of Percy Bysshe Shelley in Verse and Prose*, ed. H. Forman (London: Reeves and Turner, 1880), VI, 343–44.

27. *Ethic*, trans. White, Part II, Prop. XLIX, pp. 102–103.

28. *The Story of Philosophy* (New York: Simon and Schuster, 1926), 204–205.

29. "Song of Myself," Sec. 43.

30. *The Roots of Whitman's Grass* (Rutherford, Madison, Teanek: Fairleigh Dickinson UP, 1970), 25. The evaluation "worse than mediocre" is from Harvey O'Higgins, "Alias Whitman," *Harper's Magazine* (May, 1929).

31. "Psychological Approaches," in *Walt Whitman: An Encyclopedia*, ed. J. LeMaster and D. Kummings (New York and London: Garland, 1998), 562.

32. "A Brief Biography," in *A Historical Guide to Walt Whitman*, ed. D. Reynolds (New York, etc.: Oxford UP, 2000), 30.

33. *The Foreground of Leaves of Grass* (Charlottesville: UP of Virginia, 1974), 13.

34. "Notes and Fragments," in *The Complete Writings of Walt Whitman*, ed. R. M. Bucke et al. (New York and London: G. P. Putnam's Sons, 1902), IX, 160–61.

35. "Whoever You Are Holding Me Now in Hand."

36. Above, n. 20.

37. Above, n. 9.

38. Arthur Schopenhauer, *The World as Will and Idea*, in *The Works of Schopenhauer*, ed. W. Durant (abridged ed.; New York: Frederick Ungar, 1961), I, Bk. IV, Sec. 70, pp. 245–46. It appears that J. Sibree was the translator, though the translator's name is not given. To make clearer what I take to be Schopenhauer's meaning, I have relocated "so intensely" in the last sentence.

39. Justin Kaplan, *Walt Whitman, a Life* (New York: Simon and Schuster, 1980), 80.

Chapter IV

1. *Moral Discourses of Epictetus*, trans. Elizabeth Carter, ed. W. Rouse ("Everyman's Library," No. 404 [London: J. M. Dent & Sons; New York: E. P. Dutton, 1950]), Bk. IV, Ch. I, Sec. 14, p. 212.

2. H. L. Traubel, *With Walt Whitman in Camden*, I, 337. For publisher and date, see my bibliography. Hereafter *WWC*.

3. *Ibid.*, III, 373.

4. *Walt Whitman the Man* (New York: Francis P. Harper, 1896), 115–17.

5. *WWC*, I, 422–23.

6. *Ibid.*, IV, 451–52.

7. *Ibid.*, III, 186.

8. *Ibid.*, IV, 67.

9. *In Re Walt Whitman*, ed. H. Traubel et al. (Philadelphia: David McKay, 1893), 158.

10. *WWC*, II, 72.

11. *In Re WW*, 158.

12. *WWC*, I, 207.

13. *Ibid.*, III, 253.

14. *Ibid.*, 184.

15. *Ibid.*, II, 64.

16. *Ibid.*, IV, 371.

17. *Ibid.*, II, 71–72.

18. *The Thoughts of the Emperor M. Aurelius Antoninus*, trans. G. Long (2nd ed.; London: Bell and Daldy, 1869), Bk. IV, Sec. 23, p. 98. Traubel reports that on August 21, 1888, Whitman was downstairs looking for "Symonds' Greek Literature and a copy of Marcus Aurelius." — *WWC*, II, 229. Five days later Whitman told Traubel, "To-day, however, I have been reading Virgil and Marcus Aurelius." — *Ibid.*, 264. Who would not guess that Whitman's most notorious line was inspired by the first sentence of Bk. V, Sec. 28, of Long's translation? Marcus Aurelius: "Art thou angry with him whose arm-pits stink?" Whitman, "Song of Myself," Sec. 24: "The scent of these arm-pits aroma finer than prayer...." Note the hyphen in "arm-pits."

19. *Discourses*, trans. Carter, Bk. II, Ch. XVI, Sec. 4, p. 103.

20. *Ibid.*, Bk. II, Ch. XXIII, Sec. 4, p. 126.

21. *Ibid.*, Bk. II, Ch. XIV, Sec. 2, p. 95. See also Bk. II, Ch. XVII, Sec. 2, p. 105; Bk. III, Ch. V, Sec. 1, p. 143; Bk. IV, Ch. VII, Sec. 2, p. 233; and *Enchiridion*, Sec. LII, p. 274.

22. John Ferguson, "Ancient Greece," in *Religions of the World: From Primitive Beliefs to Modern Faiths*, ed. G. Parrinder (1st U. S. ed.; New York: Grosset & Dunlap, 1971), 135.

23. Epictetus, Fragment CXXXI, in *Discourses*, trans. Carter, 196.

24. "A Song of the Rolling Earth," Sec. 1.

25. *Thoughts of Aurelius*, trans. Long, Bk. X, Sec. 5, p. 172.

26. *Ibid.*, Bk. IV, Sec. 26, p. 99.

27. Above, n. 6.

28. Frederick Pollock, "Marcus Aurelius and the Stoic Philosophy," *Mind*, IV (1879), 55.

29. S. E. Frost, Jr., *The Basic Teachings of the Great Philosophers* (Garden City, N. Y.: Halcyon House, 1948), 146–47.

30. Charles Hartshorne and W. L. Reese, eds., *Philosophers Speak of God* (Chicago: U of Chicago P, 1953), 165.

31. *The Uncollected Poetry and Prose of Walt Whitman*, ed. E. Holloway (Garden City, N. Y., and Toronto, Ont.: Doubleday, Page, 1921), II, 94. The bracketed word, "ignorant," was crossed out by Whitman in the ms. This "Description of a Wise man" has parallels in Whitman's "Song of the Open Road." Parts (or lines) 1–3 of the description are echoed in Sec. 2, lines 3–9, of the poem. Part 7 parallels Sec. 1, line 4, of the poem. Parts 6 and 10 parallel Sec. 5, line 15. The poem has numerous parallels to the Stoic teachings of Epictetus, Marcus Aurelius, and Seneca.

32. W. H. Herndon, *The Hidden Lincoln; from the Letters and Papers of William H. Herndon*, ed. E. Hertz (New York: Viking, 1938), 266.

33. W. E. Barton, *Abraham Lincoln and Walt Whitman* (Indianapolis: Bobbs-Merrill, 1928), 170.

34. Roy P. Basler, ed., *Abraham Lincoln: His Speeches and Writings* (Cambridge, Mass.: Da Capo P, 2001), 187–88.

35. Herndon, *Hidden Lincoln*, 167–68.

36. *Ibid.*, 407.

37. "The Teacher," in *Camden's Compliment to Walt Whitman, May 31, 1889*, ed. H. Traubel (Philadelphia: David McKay, 1889), 41. This speech by Garland (pp. 40–42), prepared for Whitman's 70th birthday celebration, was not delivered because of lack of time. The echoes between Garland's statement and the preceding one by Herndon are fascinating: "cause" / "caused"; "past ... past" / "past ... past"; "future" / "future"; "infinite ... infinite" / "infinite ... infinite."

38. Herndon, *Hidden Lincoln*, 265–66.

39. *Ibid.*, 195. In a letter to J. W. Weik, Jan. 15, 1886, Herndon confessed that he, too, was a determinist, "believing in an infinite Energy, Universal Soul [cf. Whitman's "universal" and "soul"], God.... This infinite energy has *no pets*, rules mind and matter by laws, absolute, universal, and eternal. Now you have my philosophy and religion." — *Ibid.*, 135.

40. *Intimate Character Sketches of Abraham Lincoln* (Philadelphia and London: J. B. Lippincott, 1924), 57. Vivian R. Pollak: "Alas, the tale is a hoax, according to William E. Barton.... Barton claims that Rankin was never one of Lincoln's law clerks." Pollak cites Barton, *Lincoln and Whitman*, 90–94. — "Whitman Unperturbed...," in *The Centennial Essays: Walt Whitman*, ed. E. Folsom (Iowa City: U of Iowa P, 1994), 45 (note).

41. *WWC*, III, 360.

42. Herndon, *Hidden Lincoln*, 142.

43. "Salut au Monde," Secs. 11, 13.

44. *WWC*, V, 227, and I, 22.

45. Herndon, *Hidden Lincoln*, 142–43.

46. *Lincoln and Whitman*, 154.

47. *Ibid.*

48. Ellen F. Frey, ed., *Catalogue of the Whitman Collection in Duke University Library, Being a Part of the Trent Collection Given by Dr. and Mrs. Josiah C. Trent* (Durham, N. C.: Duke U Library, 1945), Sec. I, Sub-sec. II, Item 5, p. 30.

49. "Notes and Fragments," ed. R. M. Bucke, in *The Complete Writings of Walt Whitman*, ed. R. M. Bucke et al. (New York and London: G. P. Putnam's Sons, 1902), IX, 129. I have verified the accuracy of Bucke's transcription by comparison with the original note in the Trent Collection at Duke University. For Priestley's own definition of necessity, see Ch. V.

50. *WWC*, IV, 341. Whitman referred to Benjamin Harrison, because of his windy and empty inauguration speech, as the Gas President.

51. *Ibid.*, 62. Traubel says, "I called it freedom 'except to jump out of your skin.'" And he says that Whitman, laughing gently, said, "Yes."—*Ibid.*

52. L. Susan Stebbing, *Philosophy and the Physicists* (London: Methuen, 1937), 212.

53. *The Philosophy of Necessity; or, The Law of Consequences; as Applicable to Mental, Moral, and Social Science* (London: Longman, 1841), I, 183. Cf. Whitman's close parallel: "Causes, original things, being attended to, the right manners unerringly follow."—*Democratic Vistas* in *Complete Prose Works* (Philadelphia: David McKay, 1892), 233. Echo: "inevitably follow"/ "unerringly follow."

54. Above, n. 50.

55. *WWC*, II, 205. Whitman told Traubel he "often read" the *Free Inquirer.—Ibid.*

56. *WWC*, II, 204. Whitman probably heard Frances Wright speak during her second tour, which began in May, 1836, and lasted for some three years. The first tour extended from July, 1828, to July, 1830. See W. R. Waterman, *Frances Wright* (New York: Columbia UP, 1924), 136 and 224.

57. *WWC*, II, 205.

58. *Ibid.*, 500.

59. *Ibid.*, 445.

60. *Ibid.*

61. *Whitman* (New York: Macmillan, 1938), 165. Cf. Whitman: "A vast similitude interlocks all,/ All spheres, grown, ungrown, ... / All gaseous, watery, vegetable, mineral processes, the fishes, the brutes...."—"On the Bach at Night Alone." Echoes: "sidereal heavens"/ "spheres"; "gases"/ "gaseous"; "vegetables"/ "vegetable"; "ani-

mal kingdoms"/ "the fishes, the brutes." Sherwood Smith was probably not correct in his contention that "Though Whitman greatly admired Volney, he was far from complete acceptance of Volney's mechanistic cosmology...."—Entry, "Volney, Constantin," in *Walt Whitman: An Encyclopedia*, eds. J. LeMaster and D. Kummings (New York and London: Garland, 1998), 755. Abraham Lincoln as a young man also read Volney—see Herndon, *Hidden Lincoln*, 64.

62. First published in London in 1822, the book was titled *A Few Days in Athens, Being the Translation of a Greek Manuscript Discovered in Herculaneum*. Whitman remarked to Traubel: "The book is not great but it is interesting, even fascinating—written, I think, in her eighteenth year—immature, perhaps, crude, but strong."—*WWC*, II, 205. W. R. Waterman suggests that the book, called "Epicurus" in Ms., was written when Frances Wright was 19.—*Wright*, 25.

63. Letter to Menoeceus, in *The Extant Writings of Epicurus*, trans. C. Bailey, in *The Stoic and Epicurean Philosophers*, ed. W. Oates (New York: Random House, 1940), 33.

64. *Hellenistic Philosophies* (Princeton: Princeton UP; London: Humphrey Milford, Oxford UP, 1923), 49.

65. Vatican Collection, Fragment IX, in *Extant Writings*, in *Philosophies*, ed. Oates, 40.

66. *A Few Days in Athens, Being the Translation of a Greek Manuscript Discovered in Herculaneum* (New York: Peter Eckler, 1822), 122. This ed. was "republished from the original London ed."

67. *Ibid.*, 145–46.

68. Above, n. 49.

69. "Notes and Frags.," in *Comp. Writings*, IX, 173.

70. *Enquiry Concerning Political Justice*, ed. F. Priestley (Toronto: U of Toronto P, 1946), I, Bk. IV, Ch. VIII, p. 384.

71. Perry Miller, ed., *The Transcendentalists: An Anthology* (Cambridge, Mass.: Harvard UP, 1967), 75 (headnote).

72. *Phrenology, or the Doctrine of the Mental Phenomena* (2nd American ed.; Boston: Marsh, Capen and Lyon, 1833), II, 117–18.

73. Quoted from Whitman's column "Notices of New Books," *Brooklyn Daily Eagle*, Nov. 16, 1846, by Edward Hungerford, "Walt Whitman and His Chart of Bumps," *American Literature*, II (Jan. 1931), 357.

74. *The Philosophy of Necessity; or, The Law of Consequences; as Applicable to Mental, Moral, and Social Science*, 2 vols. (London: Longman, Orme, Brown, Green, and Longmans, 1841).

75. *Phases of Opinion and Experience During*

a Long Life, An Autobiography (London: Longmans, Green, 1885), 97.

76. *Ibid.*, 23.

77. *Ibid.*, 55.

78. "Old Actors, Singers, Shows, &c., in New York," in *Good-Bye My Fancy*, in *Complete Prose Works* (Philadelphia: David McKay, 1892), 513.

79. *Philos. of Neces.*, I, 298–99.

80. "Song of Myself," Sec. 22.

81. *Philos. of Neces.*, I, 298.

82. "To Think of Time," Sec. 7.

83. "Years of the Modern."

84. *Philos. of Neces.*, I, 299.

85. "Song of Myself," Sec. 52.

86. Preface, *Leaves of Grass, 1855 Version* (Ann Arbor Media Group [Ann Arbor, Mich.: Borders Classics, 2003]), 12.

87. *Philos. of Neces.*, I, 298.

88. *Ibid.*, 297.

89. Preface, *1855 Version*, Borders, 13.

90. *Philos. of Neces.*, I, 299.

91. *Autobiography* (Boston and New York: Houghton, Mifflin, 1904), 156.

92. Bray, *Phases*, 72.

93. *Emerson at Home and Abroad* (Boston: James R. Osgood, 1882), 339.

94. Letter to E. W. Emerson, Dec. 17, 1871, in *The Letters of Ralph Waldo Emerson*, ed. R. Rusk (New York: Columbia UP, 1939), VI, 187.

95. *Phases*, 91. Compare the two titles. 1st ed.: *The Philosophy of Necessity; or, The Law of Consequences; as Applicable to Mental, Moral, and Social Science.* 2nd ed.: *The Philosophy of Necessity; or, Natural Law; as Applicable to Moral, Mental, and Social Science.* In the 1st ed. the phrenological section came first — thus "Mental." In the 2nd ed. the Necessity section was placed first — thus "Moral." This subtle shifting indicates that by 1863 Bray had somewhat succumbed to the failing popularity of phrenology. But his belief in Necessity remained as strong as ever.

96. A search of library catalogues reveals the following partial bibliography for Charles Bray: *The Philosophy of Necessity* (1st ed.; London: Longman et al., 1841), 2 vols.; 2nd ed., 1863, 1 vol. *The Education of the Feelings* (2nd ed.; London: Longman et al., 1849), 163 pp.; 3rd ed., 1860; 4th ed., 1872. *On Force, Its Mental and Moral Correlates; and on That Which Is Supposed to Underlie All Phenomena* (London: Longman et al., 1866), 164 pp. *The Science of Man: A Bird's Eye View of the ... Field of Anthropology* (London: Longmans, 1868), 44 pp. *A Manual of Anthropology, or Science of Man, Based on Modern Research* (London and Coventry: Longmans, 1871), 381 pp.; 2nd ed., 1883. *Illusion and Delusion; or, Modern Pantheism versus Spiritual-*

ism (London and Edinburgh, 1873). *"The Reign of Law" in Mind as in Matter and Its Bearing on Christian Dogma and Moral Responsibility* (London: J. Scott, 1874). *Phases of Opinion and Experience During a Long Life; An Autobiography* (London: Longmans et al., 1885).

97. *Letters of Emerson*, ed. Rusk, III, 170 (footnote).

98. *Philos. of Neces.*, 298.

99. "Fate," in *Cond. of Life*, 31. Bray's faith in phrenology may have had an effect on Emerson. Emerson remarks (p. 22): "Very odious, I confess, are the lessons of Fate. Who likes to have a dapper phrenologist pronouncing on his fortunes?" And (p. 5): "The gross lines are legible to the dull: the cabman is phrenologist so far: he looks in your face to see if his shilling is sure."

100. *WWC*, IV, 478.

101. *Walt Whitman: Complete Poetry and Selected Prose and Letters*, ed. E. Holloway (1st ed.; London: Nonesuch P, 1938), 548–54.

102. Notes and Frags., in *Comp. Writings*, IX, 208.

103. *Philos. and the Physicists*, 211.

104. Letter, May, 1835, in Thomas Carlyle, *Sartor Resartus*, ed. C. Harrold (1st ed.; Garden City, N. Y.: Doubleday, Doran, 1937), 314 (appen.).

105. WW the Man, 134–35.

106. *Philos. and the Physicists*, 212.

107. This stanza and the rest which follow are quoted from the third ed., 1872 (the ed. owned and marked by Whitman), as included in *The Rubáiyát of Omar Khayyám*, trans. Edward FitzGerald (Complete ed.; New York: Thomas Y. Crowell, 1921). The stanzas as printed in Donaldson's *Walt Whitman the Man* contain several errors, apparently made by Donaldson in transcription, or in relying on his memory, and do not conform with the 1872 ed. nor any of the four other eds. (1859, 1868, 1879, 1889).

108. David S. Reynolds, *Walt Whitman* ("Lives and Legacies" series [Oxford, N. Y., etc.: Oxford UP, 2005]), 94.

109. *Uncollected* ed. Holloway II, 71.

110. *WWC*, VII, 429.

111. Henry Thoreau, *Familiar Letters* (Boston: Houghton Mifflin, 1894), 347. Quoted in G. Allen, *Walt Whitman Handbook* (Chicago: Packard, 1946), 457–58.

112. *WW Handbook*, 457.

113. *Radhakrishnan Comparative Studies in Philosophy*, ed. W. Inge et al. (London: George Allen and Unwin, 1951), 352. For Kant's view of free will, see Ch. II.

114. *Ibid.*, 354.

115. In *Leaves of Grass* (Philadelphia: David McKay, 1891–92), 432–33. "A Backward Glance," published as the Preface to *November Boughs*, 1888, was included after the very end of the poems in the 1891–92 ed.

116. *Ibid.*, 432.

117. *The Roots of Whitman's Grass* (Rutherford, Madison, Teanek: Fairleigh Dickinson UP, 1970).

118. *WWC*, 332.

119. Lily Adams Beck (pseud. E. Barrington), *The Story of Oriental Philosophy* (New York: Cosmopolitan Book, 1928), 168.

120. Above, n. 49.

121. *Orient. Philos.*, 344.

122. *Days with WW* (2nd ed.; London: George Allen & Unwin, 1906), 100–101. On pp. 94–99 Carpenter quotes also Whitman parallels to the Upanishads and to *Bhagavad Gita*.

123. *The Wisdom of Laotse*, trans. and ed. L. Yutang (New York: Modern Library, 1948), p. 7. Whitman is mentioned also on p. 16.

124. *Ibid.*, 211. From Ch. 41. (The chapter numbers vary in different translations.)

125. Eileen Thompson et al., eds., *Prentice Hall Literature: World Masterpieces* (Englewood Cliffs, N. J.; Needham, Mass.: Prentice Hall, 1991), 209. From commentary (ed. not named) on excerpts from *Tao Te Ching*, trans. D. Lau (Penguin Classics, 1963).

126. *Wisdom*, trans. Yutang, 186. From Ch. 34.

127. Mahendranath Gupta, *The Gospel of Sri Ramakrishna*, trans. Swami Nikhilananda (New York: Ramakrishna-Vivekananda Center, 1942), 35, 39 (introd.).

128. *Ibid.*, 98, 159, 176, 193, 209, 211, 245, 384, 451, 616, 632, 633, 634, 678, 804, 818, 891, 893. For some of the many other indications of Ramakrishna's determinism, see comments such as "God alone is the Doer" and "everything happens by God's will" on pp. 31, 142, 157, 169, 174, 201, 208, 220, 223, 236, 250, 265, 269, 369, 395, 609, 637, 648, 679, 699, 783, 791, 794, 900. The index lists only three pertinent pages, under "free will."

129. *Ibid.*, 379.

130. *Ibid.*, 893–94.

131. *Ibid.*, 893.

132. *Ibid.*, 223.

133. G. W. F. Hegel, *Lectures on the Philosophy of History*, trans. J. Sibree (London: Bell & Daldy, 1872), p. 8.

134. *Ibid.*, 26.

135. *Ibid.*, 22.

136. "Notes and Frags.," in *Comp. Writings*, IX, 193.

137. *Ibid.*, 192 (editor Bucke's note).

138. *WWC*, VII, 76. The date 1848 is probably erroneous (1st ed. was 1847; 2nd ed. 1849).

139. *Ibid.*, 111.

140. *Ibid.*, VI, 225. Traubel may have erred in stating 1848.

141. "Notes and Frags.," in *Comp. Writings*, IX, 171–72.

142. "Poetry To-Day in America — Shakspere [*sic*] — The Future," in *Collect*, in *Comp. Prose Works*, 299 (footnote).

143. *Ibid.*

144. *Ibid.*, 299–300. For a poetic translation of the final paragraph see "Pioneers! O Pioneers!"

145. "Notes and Frags.," in *Comp. Writings*, IX, 173.

146. Above, n. 49.

147. "Notes and Frags.," in *Comp. Writings*, IX, 118.

148. G. W. F. Hegel, "Introduction to the Philosophy of History," trans. anonymous, in F. H. Hedge, ed., *Prose Writers of Germany* (2nd ed.; Philadelphia: Carey and Hart, 1849), 454.

149. *WWC*, I, 14. Whitman to Sidney Morse: "Civilization and culture come like the weather, from countless sources."— Quoted in Sidney Morse, "My Summer with Walt Whitman, 1887," in *In Re WW*, 387. Compare also a remark in a letter by Whitman to Mrs. W. D. O'Connor: "Nelly, your last letter is very blue, mainly about political and public degradation. Sumner's death and inferior men etc., being rampant etc. I look on all such sates of things exactly as I look on a cloudy and evil state of weather, or a fog, or a long sulk meterological — it is a natural result of things, a growth of something deeper, has its uses and will hasten to exhaust itself and yield to something better."— Quoted, p.217, Roger Asselineau, *The Evolution of Walt Whitman* (Cambridge, Mass.: Belknap P of Harvard UP, 1960), from a letter, March 22, 1874, Berg Collection of the New York Public Library.

150. *Philos. of Hist.*, trans. Sibree, 27 (introd.).

151. *1855 Version*, Borders, 13.

152. *Walt Whitman; Thinker and Artist* (New York: Philosophical Library, 1952), 58.

153. "In Former Songs," in Poems Excluded, in *Leaves of Grass and Other Writings*, ed. M. Moon (New York, London: W. W. Norton, 2002), 538.

154. *Philos. of Hist.*, trans. Sibree, 58 (introd.).

155. "Notes and Frags.," in *Comp. Writings*, IX, 172.

Chapter V

1. *Leaves of Grass, 1855 Version* (Ann Arbor Media Group [Ann Arbor, Mich.: Borders Classics, 2003]), 19.

2. "Notes and Fragments," ed. R. Bucke, in *The Complete Writings of Walt Whitman*, ed. R. Bucke et al. (New York and London: G. P. Putnam's Sons, 1902), IX, 193.

3. See Ch. IV, n. 144, text.

4. "A Backward Glance O'er Travel'd Roads," in *1855 Version*, Borders, 145. "A Backward Glance," reprinted here in the 2003 Borders ed., was first published in 1888 as the preface to *November Boughs*. It was included at the very end of the poems in the 1891–92 ed.

5. *The Doctrine of Philosophical Necessity Illustrated*, in *The Theological and Miscellaneous Works, &c., of Joseph Priestley*, ed. J. Rutt (No place or publisher listed [Printed by George Smallfield, Hackney]), III (n.d.), 462.

6. "Assurances."

7. Quoted in L. Susan Stebbing, *Philosophy and the Physicists* (London: Methuen, 1937), 160, from *Theorie analytique des probabilities* (3rd ed.; Paris, 1820).

8. "Starting from Paumanok," Sec. 7.

9. "Song of the Broad-Axe," Sec. 4.

10. *1855 Version*, Borders, 18.

11. M.C. Boatright, "Whitman and Hegel," *Studies in English*, No. 9 (U of Texas Bulletin, July 8, 1929), 136.

12. *Pragmatism* (London: Longmans, Green, 1910), 116.

13. "Notes and Frags.," in *Comp. Writings*, IX, 12–13. Whitman makes use of the "fruitage" idea in Sec. 3 of "Thou Mother with Thy Equal Brood." There he addresses the "living present brain, heir of the dead, the Old World brain" and ends his apostrophe with a variation of the fruit figure: "Thou but the apples, long, long a-growing,/ The fruit of the Old ripening to-day in thee."

14. *Pragmatism*, 116.

15. "Song of Myself," Sec. 43.

16. "Passage to India," Sec. 1.

17. J. G. Fichte, *The Vocation of Man*, Bk. I, in *The Poplar Works of Johann Gottlieb Fichte*, trans. W. Smith (London: John Chapman), I (1848), 376. (Notice the pre–*Leaves of Grass* date.)

18. "Song of the Open Road," Sec. 12.

19. Sec. 1.

20. Preface, 1872, to *As a Strong Bird on Pinions Free*, in *Inclusive Edition: Leaves of Grass*, ed. E. Holloway (Garden City, N. Y.: Doubleday, Doran, 1945), 508.

21. See Ch. IV, n. 49.

22. *Ibid.*, n. 145.

23. *Ibid.*, n. 147.

24. "Notes and Frags.," in *Comp. Writings*, IX, 21.

25. R. W. Emerson, "Worship," in *The Conduct of Life*, ed. S. Mittell (Washington, D. C.: National Home Library Foundation, 1935), 137.

26. "Notes and Frags.," in *Comp. Writings*, IX, 141.

27. "Song of the Open Road," Sec. 9.

28. "Notes and Frags.," in *Comp. Writings*, IX, 160–61. The hiatus is Whitman's.

29. See Ch. IV, n. 49.

30. *The Philosophy of Necessity* (London: Longman et al., 1841), I, vi (pref.).

31. "A Song of the Rolling Earth," Sec. 3.

32. The lines cited are from Sec. 3; the first is line 19, and the other two are lines 13 and 14. Another line (Sec. 1, line 19) affirms the "push" concept discussed above: "It [the earth] has all attributes, growths, effects, latent in itself from the jump...."

33. L. Annaeus Seneca, "Of Providence," Ch. 5, in *Seneca: Moral Essays*, trans. J. Basore (London: William Heinemann; New York: G. P. Putnam's Sons), I (1928), pp. 37, 39 (parallel text).

34. Benedict de Spinoza, *The Ethics*, Part II, Prop. XLVIII, in *Philosophy of Benedict de Spinoza*, trans. R. Elwes (New York: Tudor, 1934), 118.

35. See Ch. IV, n. 36.

36. Quoted in Charles Bray, *Phases of Opinion and Experience During a Long Life: An Autobiography* (London: Longmans, Green, 1885), 92.

37. "Song of Myself," Sec. 45.

38. *1855 Version*, Borders, 10.

39. "A Backward Glance O'er Travel'd Roads," *1855 Version*, Borders, 141 (footnote).

40. W. G. Everett, *Moral Values: A Study of the Principles of Conduct* (New York: Henry Holt, 1918), 35–36.

41. Above, n. 10.

42. A. W. Benn, *The History of English Rationalism in the Nineteenth Century* (London, etc.: Longmans, Green, 1906), I, 434.

43. Henry Home (Lord Kames), *Essays on the Principles of Morality and Natural Religion* (1st ed.; Edinburgh: A Kincaid and A. Donaldson, 1751), 157.

44. H. L. Traubel, *With Walt Whitman in Camden*, IV, 389. For publisher and date, see my bibliography. Hereafter *WWC*. Whitman expected his poems "to be perceived with the same perception that enjoys music, flowers and the beauty of men and women."—"Notes and Frags." In *Comp. Writings*, IX, 173.

45. Sec. 44. Cf. Emerson: "The book of Nature is the book of Fate. She turns the gigantic pages,—leaf after leaf,—never re-turning one. One leaf she lays down, a floor of granite; then a thousand ages, and a bed of slate; a thousand ages, and a measure of coal; a thousand ages, and a layer of marl and mud; vegetable forms appear; her first misshapen animals, zoophyte, trilobium, fish; then, saurians,—rude forms, in which she has only blocked her future statue, concealing under these unwieldy monsters the fine type of her coming king. The face of the planet cools and dries, the races meliorate, and man is born."—"Fate," in *Cond. of Life*, ed. Mittell, 12. Whitman's "carbon" duplicates Emerson's "coal." Emerson's "saurians ... monsters" become Whitman's "monstrous sauroids." Emerson announces: vegetable forms appear," and Whitman echoes, "vegetables." And Whitman's "long slow strata" are articulated in Emerson's passage with granite, slate, coal, marl and mud being deposited successively, interspersed by "a thousand ages," "a thousand ages," "a thousand ages." Emerson restated this passage in poetry in "Song of Nature."

46. David S. Reynolds, *Walt Whitman's America: A Cultural Biography* (New York: Alfred A. Knopf, 1995), 305.

47. J. G. Fichte, *Vocation of Man*, Bk. I, in *Popular Works*, trans. Smith, I (1848), 381–83.

48. P. B. Shelley, note on *Queen Mab*, Sec. VI, line 198, in *The Complete Poetical Works of Percy Bysshe Shelley*, ed. T. Hutchinson (London, New York, etc.: Henry Frowde, Oxford UP, 1912), 799.

49. *Walt Whitman Handbook* (Chicago: Packard, 1946), 238.

50. *A System of Logic* (8th ed.; London, New York, etc.: Longmans, Green, 1919), Bk. VI, Ch. II, Sec.1, p. 547. The question of Mill's influence on Whitman seems unsettled. In the first paragraph of *Democratic Vistas* (1871) Whitman begins his "speculations" with a brief analysis of "John Stuart Mill's profound essay on Liberty in the future."—*Democratic Vistas*, in *Complete Prose Works*, (Philadelphia: David McKay, 1892), 203. But in 1888 he told Traubel, "I have never read Mill—I know nothing about him but his name."—*WWC*, I, 182.

51. Above, n. 10.

52. Floyd Stovall recognized the determinism of this particular poem, remarking in a note that "Whitman's philosophy had a place for necessity as well as for freedom." —*Walt Whitman: Representative Selections*, ed. Stovall (Rev. ed.; New York, etc.: American Book, 1939), 461 (notes).

53. *The Moral Nature of Man* (New York: Ronald P, 1952), 209.

54. Sec. 1.

55. *History of the Intellectual Development of Europe* (4th ed.; New York: Harper & Brothers, 1865), 621. Whitman's "Pioneers" was published in the same year, 1865. The ultimate source may have been Hegel.

56. Sec. 1.

57. *1855 Version*, Borders, 10.

58. Sec. 5.

59. Above, n. 5.

60. "Passage to India," Sec. 5.

61. "With Antecedents," Sec. 3.

62. *An Enquiry Concerning Human Understanding*, Sec. VII, Part I, in *The English Philosophers from Bacon to Mill*, ed. E. Burtt (New York: Modern Library, 1939), 624.

63. *Ibid.*, 625.

64. "Fancies at Navesink" [II]: "Had I the Choice."

65. Sec. 2.

66. Sec. 8.

67. "Fate," in *Conduct of Life*, ed. Mittell, 26.

68. "Fancies at Navesink" [III]: "You Tides with Ceaseless [*sic*] Swell."

69. "Carlyle from American Points of View," in *Specimen Days*, in *Complete Prose Works* (Philadelphia: David McKay, 1892), 174.

70. Below, n. 113.

71. "Song of the Universal," Sec. 3.

72. *Moral Discourses*, trans. Elizabeth Carter, ed. W. Rouse (London: J. M. Dent & Sons; New York: E. P. Dutton, 1950), Bk. I, Ch. XII, Sec. 2, pp. 30–31.

73. Above, Ch. IV, n. 7.

74. *Ibid.*, n. 25.

75. "To Think of Time," Sec. 7. In a rare instance of critical insight G. W. Allen interpreted these very lines as "spiritual determinism." See Ch. I, n. 27.

76. P. H. T. Holbach (Baron d'), *The System of Nature; or, Laws of the Moral and Physical World*, trans. H. Robinson (Boston: J. P. Mendum, 1889), I, 114–15.

77. "Fate," in *Conduct of Life*, ed. Mittell, 23.

78. *Pragmatism*, 117.

79. "The Bible as Poetry," in *November Boughs*, in *Comp. Prose*, 379–80.

80. *A Few Days in Athens* (New York: Peter Eckler, 1822), 149.

81. *Moral Values*, 342.

82. *God and Evil* (1st ed.; New York and London: Harper & Brothers, 1943), 120.

83. "Starting from Paumanok," Sec. 12.

84. "The Heraclitan Obsession of Walt Whitman," *The Personalist*, XV (1934), 134.

85. "Whitman's 'Long Journey' Motif," *Journal of English and Germanic Philology*, XXXVIII (1939), 77.

86. "Heraclitan Obsession," 138.

87. *Ibid.*, 133–34.

88. *Ibid.*, 133.

89. Friedrich Nietzsche, *Human-All-Too-Human*, Part II, trans. P. Cohn, in *The Complete Works of Friedrich Nietzsche*, ed. O. Levy (Edinburgh and London: T. N. Foulis), VII (1911), Div. II, Sec. 11, p. 191.

90. As expressed by Diogenes Laertius, *Lives and Opinions of Eminent Philosophers*, Bk. 4. Quoted in *Selections from Early Greek Philosophy*, ed. M. Nahm (3rd ed.; New York: Appleton-Century-Crofts, 1947), 96.

91. *The Thoughts of the Emperor M. Aurelius Antoninus*, trans. G. Long (2nd ed.; London: Bell and Daldy, 1869), Bk. V, Sec. 23, p. 114.

92. Quoted from Lucius Annaeus Seneca, *Of Providence*, Ch. 5, in William Enfield, *The History of Philosophy* (Dublin: P. Wogan et al., 1792), I, 356.

93. See Ch. IV, n. 49.

94. "Heraclitan Obsession," 134.

95. "Long Journey," 77.

96. See Ch. IV, n. 49.

97. The dates given are those of earliest known publication as determined by Holloway in his *Inclusive Edition: Leaves of Grass*. For "Passage to India" the date is that of *composition* as determined by Holloway. My text for all these passages is the 1891–92 ed. of *Leaves of Grass*. Triggs's variorum readings, in Holloway, show little variation in these passages after original publication.

98. See, above, n. 69, text.

99. *WW's America*, 226.

100. Above, n. 92.

101. Below, n. 113, text.

102. These lines comprise the poem "Then Last of All."

103. *WWC*, V, 434.

104. *Ibid.*, VI, 159. Using the same figure, Whitman spoke of "how the deep currents flow and flow and flow and flow…. Every new case is the continuation of a thousand — of tens of thousands, of streams that pulse on away from human sight or even human imagination…. People think an event consists of itself alone — but what event is there but involves a thousand elements scarcely dreamed of?" — *Ibid.*, 297.

105. See Ch. IV, n. 49.

106. "Song of Myself," Sec. 51.

107. *Religio Medici*, ed. W. Greenhill (London: Macmillan, 1950), 13.

108. Sec. 5.

109. *Walt Whitman Reconsidered* (New York: William Sloane Associates, 1955), 104.

110. Preface, 1876, in *Comp. Prose*, 285–85 (footnote).

111. "One's-Self I Sing."

112. See Ch. IV, n. 51. Cf., Ch. IV, nn. 149, 150.

113. In *Collect*, in *Comp. Prose*, 336–37. Originally published in *Specimen Days and Collect* (Philadelphia: Rees Welsh, 1882–83). The part omitted, at the ellipsis, is as follows: "More precious than all worldly riches is Freedom — freedom from the painful constipation and poor narrowness of ecclesiasticism — freedom in manners, habiliments, furniture, from the silliness and tyranny of local fashions — entire freedom from party rings and mere conventions in Politics — and better than all, a general freedom of One's-Self from the tyrannic domination of vices, habits, appetites, under which nearly every man of us, (often the greatest brawler for freedom,) is enslaved. Can we attain such enfranchisement — the true Democracy, and the height of it?" These two sentences, though they show an impassioned concern for freedom in the practical sense, are not in keeping with the philosophical tenor of the paragraph.

114. Above, Ch. IV, Sec. 7, text.

115. G. W. F. Hegel, *Lectures on the Philosophy of History*, trans. J. Sibree (London: Bell & Daldy, 1872), 41 (introd.).

116. *Ibid.*, 27.

117. See respectively, above, text, nn. 113, 113, 111, 110.

118. Above, n. 110.

119. *WWC*, III, 276.

120. Edward Carpenter, *Days with Walt Whitman* (2nd ed.; London: George Allen & Unwin, 1906), 43.

121. *Ibid.*

122. *WW Reconsidered*, 104.

123. G. W. F. Hegel, *Lectures on the Philosophy of Religion*, trans. E. Speirs and J. Sanderson (London: Kegan Paul et al., 1895), II, 291.

124. "Song of Myself," Sec. 20.

125. "Song of the Open Road," Sec. 5.

126. "Stoicism," in *Western Philosophy and Philosophers*, ed. J. Urmson (New York: Hawthorne Books, 1965), 375. Chrysippus' "road appointed by fate," along which we "run willingly," is the same as Whitman's "long brown path … leading wherever I choose" in "Song of the Open Road," Sec. 1. In that poem can be found echoes of other Stoics: Seneca, Marcus Aurelius, Epictetus. There are at least eight echoes of Epictetus' *Discourses* and *Enchiridion*. For instance, Whitman's "open air," Sec. 4, line 11, echoes "open air" in Epictetus' *Discourses*, Bk. IV, Ch.1, Sec. 5.

127. Friedrich Nietzsche, *The Joyful Wisdom*, trans. T. Common, in *The Complete Works of Friedrich Nietzsche* (Edinburgh and London: T. N. Foulis), X (1910), Bk. IV, Sec. 310, p. 243.

128. "With Husky-Haughty Lips, O Sea!"
129. "Fancies at Navesink" [VIII]: "Then Last of All."
130. Preface, 1872, to *As a Strong Bird on Pinions Free*, in *Inclus. Ed., Leaves of Grass*, ed. Holloway, 508.
131. Quoted in Ernest Jones, *Sigmund Freud: Life and Work* (London: Hogarth P, 1954), I, 401. No ref. given. Probably from Tylor's *Primitive Culture*, 1871, or his *Anthropology*, 1881. N. B.: The name is Tylor, not Taylor.
132. *Syst. Of Nature*, trans. Robinson, 346.
133. *Ibid.*, 234.
134. Max Planck, *Where Is Science Going?*, trans. J. Murphy (1st ed.; New York: W. W. Norton, 1932), 155–56.

Chapter VI

1. "Starting from Paumanok," Sec. 7.
2. "Walt Whitman and His Poems," in *In Re Walt Whitman*, ed. H. Traubel et al. (Philadelphia: David McKay, 1893), 19.
3. Quoted in Clara Barrus, *Whitman and Burroughs, Comrades* (Boston and New York: Houghton Mifflin, 1931), 17.
4. *Walt Whitman* (Philadelphia: David McKay, 1883), 69.
5. *Walt Whitman the Man* (New York: Francis P. Harper, 1896), 118–19.
6. Letter, Apr. 12, 1902, to J. T. Trowbridge. Quoted in R. A. Coleman, "Further Reminiscences of Walt Whitman," *Modern Language Notes*, LXIII (Apr., 1948), 268. Compare Herndon on Lincoln: "...take him all in all, he was one of the best, wisest, greatest, and noblest of men in all the ages."—*The Hidden Lincoln*, ed. E. Hertz (New York: Viking P, 1938), 91.
7. *Leaves of Grass*, ed. D. McKay (Philadelphia: David McKay, 1900), iv (pref.).
8. "Personal Memories of Walt Whitman," in *Whitman in His Own Time*, ed. J. Myerson (Iowa City: U of Iowa P, 2000), 273. From *Bookman* XLVI (Dec., 1917), 404–413.
9. H. L. Traubel, *With Walt Whitman in Camden*, III, 318. For publisher and date, see my bibliography. Hereafter *WWC*.
10. *WW*, 59.
11. "Song of Myself," Sec. 22.
12. "You Felons on Trial in Courts."
13. "Thoughts, No. 1," in 1860 ed. *Leaves of Grass*. This poem was later titled "Of the Visages of Things." Rejected, 1871.
14. *Degeneration*, trans. from German (New York: D. Appleton, 1895), Ch. VI, p. 231.
15. R. M. Bucke, *Cosmic Consciousness* (12th ed.; New York: E. P. Dutton, 1946), 237.

16. *WWC*, III, 494–95.
17. *Ibid.*, IV, 389.
18. H. L. Traubel, "Walt Whitman at Date," in *In Re WW*, 136.
19. *WWC*, IV, 389.
20. G. W. Allen, *Walt Whitman Handbook* (Chicago: Packard, 1946), 273.
21. *The Uncollected Poetry and Prose of Walt Whitman*, ed. E. Holloway (Garden City, N. Y., and Toronto, Ont.: Doubleday, Page, 1921), II, 71.
22. See Ch. IV, n. 49.
23. *Uncollected*, ed. Holloway, II, 65–66. This quotation and the one above are from "the earliest Whitman notebook extant, containing the date 1847."—Holloway's footnote, p. 63.
24. "Salut au Monde!" Sec. 11.
25. *WWC*, I, 82.
26. *The Philosophy of Necessity* (2nd ed., rev.; London: Longman et al., 1863), 32. Ebron Classics replica, undated.
27. *Human Society in Ethics and Politics* (London: George Allen & Unwin, 1954), 97.
28. *WWC*, III, 544–45.
29. *How to Stop Worrying and Start Living* (New York: Simon and Schuster, 1951), 107–108).
30. *WWC*, I, 212.
31. "Notes and Fragments," ed. R. Bucke, in *The Complete Writings of Walt Whitman*, ed. R. Bucke et al. (New York and London: G. P. Putnam's Sons,1902), IX, 117–18.
32. H. E. Cushman, *A Beginner's History of Philosophy* (Rev. ed.; Boston, New York, etc.: Houghton Mifflin, 1946), II, 119.
33. *WWC*, II, 274.
34. *Ibid.*, 61.
35. *Ibid.*, III, 251,
36. *Ibid.*, 360.
37. Quoted in Donaldson, *WW the Man*, 101.
38. *WWC*, I, 141–42.
39. *Ibid.*, II, 52.
40. *Ibid.*, IV, 198–99.
41. *The Philosophy of Necessity; or, The Law of Consequences; as Applicable to Mental, Moral, and Social Science* (London: Longman et al., 1841), I, 182–83.
42. *Some Dogmas of Religion* (London: Edward Arnold, 1930), 173.
43. "Song of Myself," Sec. 15.
44. P. B. Shelley, n. on *Queen Mab*, Sec. VI, line 198, in *The Poetical Works of Percy Bysshe Shelley*, ed. T. Hutchinson (London, New York, etc." Henry Frowde, Oxford UP, 1912), 802.
45. "Song of Myself," Sec. 33.
46. *Ibid.*, Sec. 37.
47. "You Fellons on Trial in Courts."
48. *WWC*, V, 53.
49. *Ibid.*, III, 548. A week later, discussing

his slowness in finishing the 1889 ed. of his poems, Whitman used the same anecdote: "'Some of my best friends — my own people — accuse me (have always accused me) of procrastination — the most provoking in all private annals.' He threw up his hands. 'I couldn't reply to that: I *am* slow: I could only say with Sidney Morse's nigger, who would go off on fearful sprees, have a high old time of it: "I am so because I was meant to be so!"' But after a pause, while indulging a half-audible laugh, W. said further: 'But while that is a good story they would probably meet it with another, perhaps a better, story: the story told by one of the Greek writers: the story of a master beating a slave: the slave protesting "I was ordained to do this thing: therefore, why whip me?" the reply being: "And I was ordained to give you a hell of a thrashing!" That might apply wonderfully well to my case.'"—*Ibid.*, IV, 12. Whitman here exhibits a rare and sophisticated understanding of determinism.

50. H. L. Traubel, "Round Table with Walt Whitman," in *In Re WW*, 323. Whitman's phrasing, "it must be so in the nature of things," is almost duplicated by his "necessary to be so in the nature of things" in his note on Hegel. It is interesting how, in considering determinism here and in the anecdote just quoted), Whitman in both cases uses the word "profound": "it is profound — profound indeed" and "it is a wonderfully profound thing." Compare his remark already quoted: "Freedom under law: there's no fact deeper, more engrossing than that." Cf. also his comment about "the profoundest necessity, the supremest providence" and his concluding remark, "But all this has a long tail — a very long tail!" Whitman's failure here to elaborate or explain is another indication that he chose to keep his determinism secret.

51. A. S. Wadia, *Fate and Free-Will* (London and Toronto: J. M. Dent and Sons, 1915), 145.

52. *WWC*, IV, 66.

53. *Philos. of Necessity*, I, 183. Bray was here indebted to Shelley, who, in his *Queen Mab* note on Necessity, remarks: "The conviction which all feel that a viper is a poisonous animal, and that a tiger is constrained, by the inevitable condition of his existence, to devour men, does not induce us to avoid them less sedulously, or even more, to hesitate in destroying them: but he would surely be of a hard heart who, meeting with a serpent on a desert island, or in a situation where it was incapable of injury, should wantonly deprive it of existence. A Necessarian is inconsequent to his own principles if he indulges in hatred or contempt...."— Note on *Queen Mab*, Sec. VI, line 198, in *Comp. Works*

of Shelley, ed. Hutchinson, 802. Bray's "viper" and "tiger" could have been coincidental duplications of Shelley's "viper" and "tiger." His "sedulously" can hardly have been coincidental with Shelley's "sedulously." Even more damning is the precise echo "the inevitable condition of" / "the inevitable condition of." *Mab* was published in 1813.

54. *WWC*, V, 145 (May 7, 1889).

55. *Ibid.*, III, 546.

56. *American Renaissance* (London, Toronto, New York: Oxford UP, 1964), 625.

57. Charles Bray, *Phases of Opinion and Experience During a Long Life: An Autobiography* (London: Longmans, Greene, 1885), 272 (appen.).

58. *WWC*, III, 548.

59. Mahendranath Gupta, *The Gospel of Sri Ramakrishna*, trans. Swami Nikhilananda (New York: Ramakrishna-Vivekananda Center, 1942), 211.

60. *Queen Mab*, Sec. VI, lines 207–211, in *Comp. Works*, ed. Hutchinson, 77.

61. "Notes and Frags.," Sec. 51, in *Comp. Writings*, IX, 31.

62. Quoted from the Berg Collection, New York Public Library, in Joseph Beaver, *Walt Whitman—Poet of Science* (Morningside Heights, N.Y.: King's Crown P, 1951), 137.

63. See Ch. II, n. 42.

64. "Passage to India," Sec. 5.

65. "Salut au Monde," Sec. 11.

66. *A Dissertation on Liberty and Necessity, Pleasure and Pain* (London: published by the author, 1725). Reprint (New York: Facsimile Text Society, 1930), 13.

67. *WW*, 68.

68. "To Think of Time," Sec. 7.

69. Above, n. 23.

70. "Salut au Monde," Sec. 13.

71. Above, n. 12.

72. *Crime and Criminals; an Address Delivered to the Prisoners in the Chicago County Jail* (Chicago: C. H. Kerr, 1908), pp. 3, 5. In another speech Darrow, in his inimitable manner, asserts his determinism: "Nobody nowadays believes in any such doctrine as free will; that is, nobody whose intelligence is worth talking about."— "Personal Liberty," a lecture, in *Freedom in the Modern World*, ed. H. Kallen (New York: Coward-McCann, 1928), 117. (Out of kindness to anti-determinist readers, I have buried this rash statement in the notes.)

73. "Song of Myself," Sec. 19.

74. "Song of the Open Road,"

75. Above, n. 2.

76. Above, n. 25.

77. "Song of Myself," Sec. 43.

78. *Philos. of Necessity*, I, 271.

79. "Boz and Democracy," a letter to the *Brother Jonathan*, in *Walt Whitman: Complete Poetry and Selected Prose and Letters*, ed. E. Holloway (1st ed.; London: Nonesuch P, 1938), 550.

80. "Song of Myself," Sec. 44.

81. Above, n. 25.

82. "The Sleepers," Sec. 7.

83. See Ch. IV, n. 49.

84. "Song of Myself," Sec. 42.

85. Above, n. 65.

86. "Song of the Answerer," Sec. 1. "...in my philosophy — in the bottom-meanings of 'Leaves of Grass'— there is plenty of room for all. And I, for my part, not only include anarchists, socialists, whatnot, but Queens, aristocrats." — *WWC*, V, 227.

87. *WWC*, IV, 451–52.

88. "A Backward Glance O'er Travel'd Roads," in *Leaves of Grass* (Philadelphia: David McKay, 1891–92), 429.

89. *Ibid.*, 428.

90. G. W. F. Hegel, *Lectures on the Philosophy of History*, trans. J. Sibree (London: Bell & Daldy, 1872), 26 (introd.). There is an easily overlooked key here to the Whitman-Hegel kinship: "congeries," a strange word which is probably rarely used. My italics: Hegel, "This vast *congeries* of volitions, interests and activities...." Whitman, "...the whole *congeries* of things, all history and time, and all events...." Of course, Whitman did not try to hide his debt to Hegel, but this unique echo, "congeries,"/ "congeries, is certainly suggestive of that indebtedness.

91. "Poetry To-Day in America— Shakspere [*sic*] — The Future," in *Collect*, in *Complete Prose Works* (Philadelphia: David McKay, 1892), 299 (footnote).

92. *WWC*, II, 78. A quite similar determinist view was reflected in Whitman's comment on divorce: "Divorce is not to be argued of as a thing in itself— unrelated — a flower of today. It is like the French Revolution, a result of results — the growth of soil on soil on soil on soil — layer after layer...." — *Ibid.*, VI, 156.

93. "Assurances."

94. *Phases*, 92.

95. *Philos. of Hist.*, trans. Sibree, 22 (introd.).

96. For comments on the flood and on the poem, see *WWC*, V, 257, 261, 264, 266, 267, 269, 270, 274, 278.

97. Preface, 1876, in *Collect*, in *Comp. Prose*, 284 (footnote).

98. W. H. Herndon, Ms. Letter to Mr. Lindman, Dec., 1886, quoted in J. F. Newton, *Lincoln and Herndon* (Cedar Rapids, Ia.: Torch P, 1910), 331.

99. *WWC*, IV, 148–49. Quite significantly, the words "rich" and "glow" are echoed by "rich" and "glowing" in the closing lines of "A Riddle Song." Also, "in nations of men" is an echo of "in every age and land" in those lines.

100. W. H. Herndon, *The Hidden Lincoln; from the Letters and Papers of William H. Herndon*, ed. E. Hertz (New York: Viking, 1938), 143.

101. "Notes and Frags.," in *Comp. Writings*, IX, 40.

102. Herndon letter to Lindman, in Newton, *Linc. and Hern.*, 330.

103. *WWC*, IV, 77. Cf. Charles Bray: "Under my 'Religious' phase I was not particularly happy; I had always a sense that I had 'done the thing I ought not to have done, or left undone the thing I ought to have done.' But with my 'Philosophy of Necessity' came a new era. I never fretted about the past; it *was past*, and could not have been otherwise than it had been.... I took people for what they were, and was not annoyed that they were not better; consequently I gave no admission to envy, hatred, malice or any kind of uncharitableness. I turned such feelings out of my mind, because they were both painful and unphilosophical; when fostered they are vipers sure to sting." —*Phases*, 157.

104. *Walt Whitman's America: A Cultural Biography* (New York: Alfred A. Knopf, 1995), 389–90.

105. "Whitman's Consistency," *American Literature*, VIII (1936), 250.

106. *Walt Whitman an American* (Boston: Houghton Mifflin, 1943), 169.

107. Entry, "I Sit and Look Out," in *Walt Whitman: An Encyclopedia*, ed. J. LeMaster and D. Kummings (New York and London: Garland, 1998), 298.

108. Note on *Queen Mab*, Sec. VI, line 198, in *Comp. Works of Shelley*, ed. Hutchinson, 802. Echo: Shelley, "looks ... upon" / Whitman, first line of the poem, "look out upon."

109. Cushman, *Begin. Hist. Philos.*, II, 119.

Chapter VII

1. I like the description given by Edmund Gosse, who visited Whitman in 1885: "Various boxes lay about, and one large clamped trunk and heaps, mountains of papers in a wild confusion, swept up here and there into stacks and peaks; but all the room, and the old man himself, clean in the highest degree, raised to the *n*th power of stainlessness, scoured and scrubbed to such a pitch that dirt seemed defied for all remaining time." — *Critical Kit-Kats* (London: William Heinemann, 1913), 102. Mrs. Davis was

Mrs. Mary Oakes Davis, wife of a sea captain who shortly after their marriage went down with his ship in a storm.— G. W. Allen, *The Solitary Singer* (New York: Macmillan, 1955), 518–19.

2. H. L. Traubel, *With Walt Whitman in Camden*, IV, 412. For publisher and date, see my bibliography. Hereafter *WWC*.

3. *Ibid.*, 475–76. Perhaps Spinoza was the name Whitman was trying to recall, though it may have been Schopenhauer or Hegel. Royce, elucidating Spinoza, echoes Whitman's "the idea back of ideas" with "the law of laws, the nature of natures." So maybe it *was* Spinoza Whitman had in mind. There is a clue here to the answer to Whitman's riddle in the poem "A Riddle Song," where "the real of the real" echoes "the idea back of ideas" here, and where, also, events are "justified."

4. Anicius Boethius, *The Consolation of Philosophy of Boethius*, trans. H. James (London: Elliot Stock, 1897), Bk. V. Song I, pp. 229–30. The poem is titled "Chance,." The title of Bk. V is "Free Will and God's Foreknowledge." Whitman had early knowledge of the philosophy of Boethius. In the Trent collection at Duke University, there is an article on Chaucer, pp. 158–77, from a Feb., 1849, magazine (the name of which does not appear — but note the date). At the bottom of p. 170 Whitman wrote: "Boethius's Philosopic [sic] Consolations." And at the top of p. 171 he wrote: "Boethius — year 522 — then the middle ages first became acquainted with the flattering doctrine that man, by the exercise of his reason, becomes superior to the dominion of fortune." Whitman evidently did not agree with that solution; he called it "flattering." I am indebted to my friend (and fellow graduate English student) Walt Coley for the discovery of these notes in the original in the Duke library. For Bucke's transcription of them see "Notes and Fragments," in *The Complete Writings of Walt Whitman*, ed. R. Bucke et al. (New York and London: G. P. Putnam's Sons, 1902), IX, 227.

5. "A Voice from Death." This poem has a subtitle: "(The Johnstown, Penn., cataclysm, May 31, 1889)."

6. See Ch. IV, n. 49.

7. See Ch. I, n. 9.

8. David S. Reynolds, *Walt Whitman's America: A Cultural Biography* (New York: Alfred A. Knopf, 1995), 338.

9. *Contemporaries*, in *Walt Whitman: The Critical Heritage*, ed. M. Hindus (New York: Barnes and Noble, 1971), 262.

10. "Policy Made Personal," in *Modern Critical Views: Walt Whitman*, ed. H. Bloom (New York, Philadelphia: Chelsea House, 1985), 33.

From *Leaves of Grass One Hundred Years After*, ed. M. Hindus, Stanford UP, 1955.

11. P. B. Shelley, *Queen Mab*, Sec. VI, lines 148–73, in *The Complete Poetical Works of Percy Bysshe Shelley*, ed. T. Hutchinson (London, etc.: Henry Frowde, Oxford UP, 1912), 776–77. The ensuing lines, 174–96, state unequivocally Shelley's commitment to complete determinism.

12. "Notes and Fragments," ed. R. Bucke, in *The Complete Writings of Walt Whitman*, ed. Bucke et al. (New York and London: G. P. Putnam's Sons, 1902), IX. 162.

13. Friedrich Nietzsche, *Human-All-Too-Human*, Part I, trans. Helen Zimmern, in *The Complete Works of Friedrich Nietzsche*, ed. O. Levy (Edinburgh and London: T. N. Foulis), VI (1909), Div. II, Sec. 106, p. 106.

14. "As I Ebb'd with the Ocean of Life."

15. "Notes and Frags.," in *Comp. Writings*, IX, 229. F. O. Matthiessen says Whitman "copied [this] description of style" from "a magazine article on Indian epic poetry" which he "came upon" in 1848.— *American Renaissance* (London, Toronto, New York: Oxford UP, 1964), 568.

16. "Notes and Frags.," in *Comp. Writings*, IX, 87.

17. Preface 1876, in *Inclusive Edition: Leaves of Grass*, ed. E. Holloway (Garden City, N. Y.: Doubleday, Doran, 1945), 521.

18. *Leaves of Grass, 1855 Version* (Ann Arbor Media Group [Ann Arbor, Mich.: Borders Classics, 2003]), 19. In the 1892 ed. of *Comp. Prose*, "shape" becomes "shapes," substituted here. Whitman's "spot" in "makes the present spot [sic] the passage from what was to what shall be" echoes "spot ... spot" in the preceding paragraph (on p. 18), where he proclaims his determinism with the statement often quoted herein.

19. G. W. F. Hegel, *Lectures on the Philosophy of History*, trans. J. Sibree (London: Bell & Daldy, 1872), p. 2 (introd.).

20. Hippolyte Taine, *Lectures on Art*, trans. J. Durand, 1st series: *The Philosophy of Art, The Ideal in Art* (New York: Henry Holt, 1875), 30 (introd.).

21. For information about the abridgment see *Walt Whitman, Notebooks and Unpublished Prose Manuscripts*, ed. E. Grier (New York: New York UP, 1984), III, 1075 (footnote). The abridgment ms. is in the Library of Congress.

22. *Benét's Reader's Encyclopedia* (3rd ed.; New York, etc.: Harper and Row, 1987), 954–955.

23. Hippolyte Taine, *History of English Literature*, trans. H. Van Laun (New York: Worthington, 1889). The page nos. given are for Taine's Introduction, vol. I of the two vols.

24. "A Backward Glance O'er Travel'd Roads," in *Leaves of Grass* (Philadelphia: David McKay, 1891–92), 428–29.

25. *Ibid.*, 429 and 432.

26. R. W. Emerson, "Art," in *Essays: First Series*, in *Ralph Waldo Emerson, Essays & Lectures*, ed. J. Porte (New York: Library of America, 1983), 431–32.

27. "An Old Man's Rejoinder," in *Good-Bye My Fancy*, in *Complete Prose Works* (Philadelphia: David McKay, 1892), 477.

28. *WWC*, VI, 251.

29. Ledger Wood, "The Free-Will Controversy," *Philosophy*, XVI (Oct., 1941), 397.

30. Friedrich Paulsen, *A System of Ethics*, ed. and trans. F. Thilly (New York: Charles Scribner's Sons, 1911), 458.

31. Taine, *Art*, 51.

32. *On Photography* (New York: Farrar, Straus and Giroux, 1977), 15, 21.

33. Louise Dudley and Austin Faricy, *The Humanities* (6th ed.; New York, etc.: McGraw-Hill, 1978), 151.

34. *WW's America*, 286–95. F. O. Matthiessen also noted similarities between Whitman and the "genre" painters — in his *American Renaissance* (London, etc.: Oxford UP, 1941), 598–601.

35. *History of Art* (2nd ed.; Englewood Cliffs, N. J.: Prentice-Hall; New York: Harry N. Abrams, 1977), 516.Vermeer's *The Letter*, 1666, colorplate 82, is an example.

36. Quoted from *WWC*, II, 407, in Reynolds, *WW's America*, 298.

37. *The Philosophy of Spinoza* (New York: Modern Library, 1927), lxi–lxii (introd.).

38. Quoted in Janson, *Hist. of Art*, 623.

39. *WWC*, V, 123, 133. The article was by artist Wyatt Eaton.

40. "Art," in *Society and Solitude*, in *Comp. Works*, VII (1895), 41.

41. "An American Primer," in *Poetry and Prose of Walt Whitman*, ed. L. Untermeyer (New York: Simon and Schuster, 1949), 569.

42. "Salut au Monde," Sec. 10.

43. "Song of the Redwood-Tree," Sec. 1.

44. Quoted from "The Invisible World," in *A Choice of Whitman's Verse*, 1968, in *Walt Whitman, Leaves of Grass*, ed. M. Rinde (New York: Modern Library, 2001), 749 (commentary).

45. "Beginning My Studies."

46. "Song of Myself," Sec. 24.

47. R.M. Bucke, *Walt Whitman* (Philadelphia: David McKay, 1883), 55.

48. R. W. Emerson, "Fate," in *Conduct of Life*, in *Essays: First Series*, in *Emerson, Essays*, ed. Porte, 967.

Chapter VIII

1. "On the Beach at Night Alone." With Whitman's "vast similitude" which "interlocks all" compare Emerson's "Beautiful Necessity, which secures that all is made of one piece...." — R. W. Emerson, "Fate," in *The Conduct of Life*, ed. S. Mittell (Washington, D. C.: National Home Library Foundation, 1935), 31.

2. "What Is Mysticism?" in *Reason and Responsibility*, ed. J. Feinberg (Belmont, Cal.: Wadsworth, 1985), 77–85. From *The Teachings of the Mystics*, ed. W. Stace (New York: American Library, 1960), 12–28.

3. Joseph Priestley, *The Doctrine of Philosophical Necessity Illustrated*, in *The Theological and Miscellaneous Works &c., of Joseph Priestley*, ed. J. Rutt (No place or publisher listed [Printed by George Smallfield, Hackney]), III (n.d.), 518.

4. *The Spirit of Modern Philosophy* (Boston and New York: Houghton Mifflin, 1892), 60–61.

5. H. L. Traubel, *With Walt Whitman in Camden*, IV, 475–76. For publisher and date, see my bibliography. Hereafter *WWC*.

6. *Mod. Philos.*, 62.

7. In *Complete Prose Works* (Philadelphia: David McKay, 1892), 281.

8. Friedrich Nietzsche, *Human-All-Too-Human*, Part II, trans. P. Cohn, in *The Complete Works of Friedrich Nietzsche*, ed. O. Levy (Edinburgh and London: T. N. Foulis, 1909–13), VII (1911), Div. II, Sec. 61, p. 229. Sigmund Freud must have read Nietzsche before writing, "The notion dawned on the most gifted people of antiquity that Moira [Fate] stood above the gods and that the gods themselves had their own destinies." — *The Future of an Illusion*, trans. W. Robson-Scott; rev. and ed. J. Strachey (Garden City, N. Y.: Doubleday, 1964), 25. "Editorial additions ... are printed in square brackets." — *Ibid.*, p. x (ed.'s note).

9. P. B. Shelley, note on *Queen Mab*, Sec. VI, line 198, in *The Complete Works of Percy Bysshe Shelley*, ed. T. Hutchinson (London, New York, etc.: Henry Frowde, Oxford UP, 1912), 803.

10. Benedict de Spinoza, *Ethics*, Part I, Prop. XXXIII, quoted in Stuart Hampshire, *Spinoza* (Harmondsworth, Middlesex: Penguin Books, 1951), 50. Spinoza seems to have meant that although God could not have acted otherwise, He acted through the condition of his own inherent being — not in accord with an external determining condition. Spinoza, in a letter to Oldenburg, tried to make this clear: "...I should like briefly to explain here in what sense I assert that a fatal necessity presides over all things and actions. God I in no wise subject to fate: I con-

ceive that all things follow with inevitable necessity from the nature of God...." — Baruch Spinoza, *Letters to Friend and Foe*, ed. D. Runes, trans. R. Elwes (New York: Philosophical Library, 1966), 25.

11. "As I Ebb'd with the Ocean of Life." The first three lines are from Sec. 3; the second three, from Sec. 2.

12. "Passage to India," Sec. 8.

13. These lines and the three preceding are from "A Riddle Song."

14. Friedrich Paulsen, *Introduction to Philosophy*, trans. F. Thilly (New York: Henry Holt, 1898), 216.

15. William Godwin, *Enquiry Concerning Political Justice*, ed. F. Priestley (Toronto: U of Toronto P, 1946), I, Bk. IV, Ch. VII, p. 365.

16. Surendranath Dasgupta, *A History of Indian Philosophy* (Cambridge, Eng.: Cambridge UP), III (1940), 266.

17. A. C. Ewing, *Kant's Treatment of Causality* (London: Kegan Paul et al., 1924), 170.

18. W. R. Inge, *The Philosophy of Plotinus* (3rd ed.; London, etc.: Longmans, Green, 1929), I, 181.

19. Hastings Rashdall, *The Theory of Good and Evil* (2nd ed.; London: Humphrey Milford, Oxford UP, 1924), II, 326.

20. *The Philosophy of Necessity* (London: Longman et al., 1841), I, 113.

21. Paulsen, *Introd. to Philos.*, 215.

22. Quoted, Ronald W. Clark, *Einstein: The Life and Times* (New York and Cleveland: World, 1971), 425, from *Ben-Gurion Looks Back*, London, 1961, p. 217.

23. "Starting from Paumanok," Sec. 9. Whitman's interest in the ideas of Kant is indicated in his notes for proposed lectures: "He is occupied with such problems as the nature of absolute being — Ontology. The essence and immortality of the soul — Pneumatology. The prevalence of *freedom or fate* [italics mine] in the world — Cosmology. The being of God — Speculative theology." — "Notes and Fragments," ed. R. Bucke in *The Complete Writings of Walt Whitman*, ed. Bucke et al. (New York and London: G. P. Putnam's Sons, 1902), IX, 175.

24. *An Enquiry Concerning Human Understanding*, Sec. VIII, Part I, in *The English Philosophers from Bacon to Mill*, ed. E. Burtt (New York: Modern Library, 1939), 623.

25. *Invitation to Philosophy* (Boston, New York, etc.: Houghton Mifflin, 1933), 271. Drake goes on to say: "The fact seems to be that causes are observable all about us, ["Without peeping out of the window/ One can see the Tao of heaven"] in the rough, although to find out *exactly* what the causes of events are, in fine detail, is a matter for patient scientific investigation. And to understand *why* certain causes produce certain events eludes us entirely. [Whitman's "A Riddle Song" begins: "That which eludes this verse ...." Causes are observable, but *causation* (the linkage between cause and effect) is not observable." — *Ibid.*, 273.

26. John Fiske, *Outlines of Cosmic Philosophy* (Boston and New York: Houghton, Mifflin, 1902), I, Part I, Ch. VI, p. 232.

27. *Ibid.*, 238.

28. *The Fight of a Book for the World* (West Yarmouth, Mass.: Stonecroft Press, 1926), 188.

29. *Walt Whitman: Representative Selections*, ed. F. Stovall (Rev. ed.; New York: American Book, 1939), 467 (notes).

30. "The End as Means in 'A Riddle Song,'" *Walt Whitman Review*, XXIII (June, 1977), 82–85.

31. "The Truth About 'A Riddle Song': Another Venture," *Walt Whitman Review*, XXVII (June, 1981), 78–82.

32. *Free and Lonesome Heart: The Secret of Walt Whitman* (1st ed.; New York, etc.: Vantage P, 1960), 189 (note).

33. Letter to Whitman, in Traubel, *WWC*, II, 228. When Whitman read the letter, he "put his finger down on Bucke's question mark" and mused: "Doctor has guessed — thinks he has guessed right. I wonder? I wonder?" Traubel waited for Whitman to say more and finally asked whether Whitman wanted him to answer the letter (Whitman was sick and incapable of writing). "Yes answer him," was the reply: "but answer him for yourself — don't answer him for me." Then Traubel asked, "Will *you* answer the question?" "Do I ever answer questions?" asked Whitman. He laughed quietly. "Horace, I made the puzzle: it's not my business to solve it. Doctor says he has the right answer — well, that ought to satisfy him — the right answer ought to satisfy him."

34. From "The World As I See It," from *Mein Weltbild*, in *Living Philosophies*, ed. C. Fadiman (New York, etc.: Doubleday, 1990), p. 6. Translator's name not given.

35. *The Book of Tao [Tao Teh King]*, Ch. 1, in *The Wisdom of Laotse*, trans. and ed. L. Yutang (New York: Modern Library, 1948), 41.

36. Francis Grant, *Oriental Philosophy* (New York: Dial P, 1936), 146.

37. Alexander Pope, *Selected Works*, ed. L. Kronenberger (New York: Modern Library, 1948), 95.

38. R. W. Emerson, *Journals of Ralph Waldo Emerson*, ed. E. Emerson and W. Forbes (Boston and New York: Houghton Mifflin), X (1914), 472–73. Emerson called it "the nameless Thought, the nameless Power." — "Worship," in

Conduct of Life, ed. S. Mittell (Washington, D. C.: National Home Library, 1935), 151.

39. Ch. XII, Verse 3, in *Hindu Scriptures*, ed. N. Macnicol (London: J. M. Dent & Sons; New York: E. P. Dutton, 1966), 267.

40. "Brahman," in *An Encyclopedia of Religion*, ed. V. Ferm (New York: Philosophical Library, 1945).

41. *Mandukya Upanishad*, Ch. I, Verse VII, in *The Upanishads*, trans. Swami Nikhilananda (1st ed.; New York: Harper & Brothers, n.d.), II, 236.

42. A favorite song of Ramakrishna's, quoted in Mahendranath Gupta, *The Gospel of Sri Ramakrishna*, trans. Swami Nikhilananda (New York: Ramakrishna-Vivekananda Center, 1942), 223. Ramakrishna spoke mysteriously about the indefinable it: "It is impossible to explain Brahman by analogy. It is between light and darkness. It is Light, but not the light that we perceive, not material light." —*Ibid.*, 307. Whitman echoes with "Beyond the light, lighter than light" in "Chanting the Square Deific."

43. Sec. VI, lines 197–98, in *Comp. Poetical Works of Shelley*, ed. Hutchinson, 777.

44. *The Principles of Sociology* (New York: D. Appleton), III (1907), Part VI, Ch. XVI, Sec. 660, p. 175.

45. Herbert Spencer, *First Principles* (New York: P. F. Collier and Son, 1900), Part II, Ch. III, Sec. 50, p. 142.

46. *Ibid.*, Part I, Ch. V, Sec. 31, pp. 90–91.

47. William Wordsworth, "Lines Composed a Few Miles above Tintern Abbey," in *The Poetical Works of Wordsworth*, ed. T. Hutchinson (London, etc.: Geoffrey Cumberlege, Oxford UP, 1936), 164.

48. William Hazlitt, "On the Doctrine of Philosophical Necessity," in *The Complete Works of William Hazlitt*, ed. P. Howe (London and Toronto: J. M. Dent and Sons), XX (1934), 60. The article, with different title, was first published in *The Examiner*, Dec. 10, 1815. Here (see text) Hazlitt includes the *mind* in "necessity" by holding that "thought follows thought, like wave following wave." How startlingly similar are Whitman's lines in "Out of the Cradle Endlessly [note *Endlessly*] Rocking": "Close on its wave soothes the wave behind/ And again another behind embracing and lapping, every one close." The next line is, "But my love soothes not me, not me." Is Whitman symbolically saying, "My grief is so intense that my determinism ["wave ... wave" ("Endlessly," in the title)] does not help"? Consider Whitman's expression of his kinship to the sea (its "tides").

49. "The Excursion," Bk. IX, lines 3–20, in *Works*, ed. Hutchinson, 689.

50. "A Riddle Song."

51. *Tao Te Ching*, trans. Ch'u Ta-Kao (5th ed.; London: George Allen & Unwin, 1959), Ch. XXV, p. 37. Chapter nos. vary per translations.

52. "A Song for Occupations," Sec. 2.

53. *Tao*, trans. Ta-Kao, Ch. XLVII, p. 62.

54. *Chuangtse*, Ch. 22, quoted in *Wisdom of Laotse*, trans. Yutang, 43.

55. *WWC*, VII, 156–57.

Chapter IX

1. Below, n. 3.

2. *Days with Walt Whitman* (2nd ed.; London: George Allen & Unwin, 1906), 43–44.

3. Preface, 1872, to *As a Strong Bird on Pinions Free*, in *Inclusive Edition: Leaves of Grass*, ed. E. Holloway (Garden City, N. Y.: Doubleday, Doran, 1945), 510.

4. "Passage to India," Sec. 9.

5. *Ibid.*, Sec. 5. The phrase "the true son of God, the poet" is in line 6 of this stanza.

6. Quoted in Ronald W. Clark, *Einstein: The Life and Times* (New York and Cleveland: World, 1971), 340, from Max Born, *Physics in My Generation* (London, 1956; New York, 1969), 204.

7. *Where Is Science Going?*, trans. J. Murphy (1st ed.; New York: W. W. Norton, 1932), 155–56.

8. *Spinoza* (Harmondsworth, Middlesex: Penguin Books, 1951), 157–58.

9. *A Concise Introduction to Philosophy* (4th ed.; New York: Random House, 1981), 240.

10. Sigmund Freud, *Psychopathology of Everyday Life*, Ch. XII, in *The Basic Writings of Sigmund Freud*, trans. and ed. A. Brill (New York: Modern Library, 1938), 162.

11. "Psychoanalysis," in *Current Psychotherapies*, ed. R. Corsini (3rd ed.; Itasca, Ill.: F. E. Peacock, 1984), 23–24. The quotation, slightly varied, is in Arlow's article "Psychoanalysis," in *Collier's Encyclopedia*, 1989, Vol. 19, p. 453.

12. A. S. Wadia, *Fate and Free-Will* (London and Toronto: J. M. Dent and Sons, 1915), 126.

13. *Sadhana: The Realisation of Life* (New York: Macmillan, 1914), 21. By an interesting coincidence this book is dedicated to a great admirer and friend of Whitman: Ernest Rhys.

14. H. L. Traubel, *With Walt Whitman in Camden*, IV, 220. For publisher and date, see my bibliography. Hereafter *WWC*.

15. *Ibid.*

16. Wayne Anderson, "Why Should People Choose Science Over Religion?" in *Free Inquiry*, Vol. 21, No. 4 (Fall, 2001), 59.

17. *Sadhana*, pp. 6–7.

18. *Democratic Vistas*, in *Collect*, in *Complete Prose Works* (Philadelphia: David McKay, 1892), 253.

19. *Sadhana*, 112–13.

20. Ledger Wood, "The Free-Will Controversy," *Philosophy*, XVI (Oct., 1941), 386 and 395–96.

21. *WWC*, VI, 298.

22. *Ibid.*, II, 563.

23. R. W. Emerson, "Worship," in *The Conduct of Life*, ed. S. Mittell (Washington, D. C.: National Home Library, 1935), 134–35 and 151. Emerson's determinism here (see text) is evident just after the ellipsis. When he says man "throws himself joyfully into the sublime order and [my italics:] *does, with knowledge, what the stones do by structure*," he cannot but be re-stating Spinoza's famous analogy using "a stone ... thinking and knowing," "a stone ... conscious of its own endeavor." — Letter, Oct., 1674, in *Philosophy of Benedict de Spinoza*, trans R. Elwes (New York: Tudor, 1934), 396.

24. *The World As I See It* (New York: Covici-Friede, 1934), 267–68.

25. *Cosmic Consciousness: A Study in the Evolution of the Human Mind* (12th ed.; New York: E. P. Dutton, 1946), 220.

26. Albert Einstein, *Cosmic Religion* (New York: Covici-Friede, 1931), 47–51. The essay appeared also, with variations, in *The New York Times Magazine*, in *The New York Times*, Nov. 9, 1930, Sec. 5, p. 1.

27. "Song of Myself," Sec. 20.

28. Preface to 1876 ed., in *Inclus. Ed. Leaves of Grass*, ed. Holloway, 520.

29. *Ibid.*

30. *Ibid.*

31. *WWC*, V, 318. Letter to Traubel, June 12, 1889, from London. Trans. from French by A. Basy. Earlier trans. by H. Morris was not available to the editors of *WWC*, V.

Bibliography

Aiken, Henry D. (ed.). *The Age of Ideology: The 19th Century Philosophers.* New York: New American Library; London: New English Library, 1956.

Allen, Gay Wilson. *The New Walt Whitman Handbook.* New York: New York University Press, 1975.

_____. *The Solitary Singer: A Critical Biography of Walt Whitman.* New York: Macmillan, 1955.

_____. *Waldo Emerson, a Biography.* New York: Viking, 1981.

_____. *Walt Whitman Handbook.* Chicago: Packard, 1946.

_____. "Walt Whitman's 'Long Journey' Motif." *Journal of English and Germanic Philology,* XXXVIII (Jan., 1929), 76–95.

_____ (ed.). *Walt Whitman As Man, Poet and Legend with a Check List of Whitman Publications 1945–1960 by Evie Allison Allen.* Carbondale, Ill.: Southern Illinois University Press, 1961.

Allen, Gay Wilson, and Clark, Harry Hayden (eds.). *Literary Criticism Pope to Croce.* Detroit: Wayne State University Press, 1962.

Alston, W. P., and Brandt, R. P. (eds.). *The Problems of Philosophy.* Boston: Allyn and Bacon, 1970.

Anderson, Wayne. "Why Should People Choose Science Over Religion?" *Free Inquiry,* Vol. 21, No. 4 (Fall, 2001), 58–59.

Anshen, Ruth Nanda (ed.). *Freedom: Its Meaning.* 1st ed. New York: Harcourt, Brace, 1940.

Antoninus, Marcus Aurelius. *The Thoughts of the Emperor M. Aurelius Antoninus.* Trans. George Long. 2nd ed. London: Bell and Daldy, 1869.

Aristotle. *Aristotle's Art of Poetry: A Greek View of Poetry and Drama.* Trans. Ingram Bywater. Ed. W. Hamilton Fyfe. Oxford: Clarendon, 1940.

Arvin, Newton. *Whitman.* New York: Macmillan, 1938.

Asselineau, Roger. *The Evolution of Walt Whitman.* Cambridge, Mass.: Belknap of Harvard University Press, 1960.

_____. "Whitman's Style: From Mysticism to Art." *Whitman: A Collection of Critical Essays.* Ed. Harvey Pearce. Englewood Cliffs, N. J.: Prentice Hall, 1962.

Ballou, R. O. (ed.). *The Viking Portable World Bible.* New York: Viking, 1944.

Barnard, Ellsworth. *Shelley's Religion.* Minneapolis: University of Minnesota Press, 1936.

Barrus, Clara. *Whitman and Burroughs, Comrades.* Boston and New York: Houghton Mifflin, 1931.

Bartlett, John (ed.). *Familiar Quotations.* 13th ed. Boston, Little, Brown, 1955.

Barton, William E. *Abraham Lincoln and Walt Whitman.* Indianapolis: Bobbs-Merrill, 1928.

Beaver, Joseph. *Walt Whitman — Poet of Science.* Morningside Heights, N. Y.: King's Crown, 1951.

Beck, Lewis White (ed.). *Eighteenth Century Philosophy.* New York: New American Library; London: New English Library, 1956.

Beck, Mrs. Lily (Moresby) Adams (pseud. E. Barrington). *The Story of Oriental Philosophy.* New York: Cosmopolitan Book, 1928.

Benét, William Rose (ed.). *Benét's Reader's Encyclopedia.* 3rd ed. New York: Harper and Row, 1987.

Benn, Alfred William. *The History of English Rationalism in the Nineteenth Century.* 2 vols. London: Longmans, Green, 1906.

Bennett, Paul A. *Books and Printing.* New York: World, 1951.

The Bhagavadgita. Trans. S. Radhakrishnan. New York: Harper & Brothers, 1948.

Bidney, David. *The Psychology and Ethics of Spinoza: A Study in the History and Logic of Ideas.* New York: Yale University Press, 1940.

Binns, Henry Bryan. *A Life of Walt Whitman.* London: Methuen, 1905.

Bloom, Harold (ed.). *Modern Critical Views: Walt Whitman.* New York: Chelsea House, 1985.

Boatright, Mody C. "Whitman and Hegel." *Studies in English*, No. 9, University of Texas Bulletin No. 2926, July 8, 1929, 134–50.

Boethius, Anicius. *The Consolation of Philosophy of Boethius.* Trans. H. R. James. London: Elliot Stock, 1987.

Bray, Charles. *Phases of Opinion and Experience During a Long Life:An Autobiography.* London: Longmans, Green, 1885.

_____. *The Philosophy of Necessity; or, The Law of Consequences; as Applicable to Mental, Moral, and Social Science.* 2 vols. 1st ed. London: Longman, Orme, Brown, Green, and Longmans, 1841.

_____. *The Philosophy of Necessity; or Natural Law; as Applicable to Moral, Mental, and Social Science.* 1 vol. 2nd ed. London: Longman, Green, Longman, & Roberts, 1863.

Briggs, Arthur E. *Walt Whitman: Thinker and Artist.* New York: Philosophical Library, 1952.

Browne, Sir Thomas. *Religio Medici, Letter to a Friend &c., and Christian Morals.* Ed. W. W. Greenhill. London: Macmillan, 1950.

Bucke, Richard Maurice, M. D. *Cosmic Consciousness: A Study in the Evolution of the Human Mind.* 12th ed. New York: E. P. Dutton, 1946.

_____. *Walt Whitman.* Philadelphia: David McKay, 1883.

Burtt, Edwin A. (ed.). *The English Philoso-phers from Bacon to Mill.* New York: Modern Library, 1939.

Canby, Henry Seidel. *Walt Whitman an American.* Boston: Houghton Mifflin, 1943.

Carlyle, Thomas. *An Essay on Burns.* Ed. J. W. Abernethy. ("Maynard's English Classic Series," No. 70.) New York: Maynard, Merrill, 1912.

_____. *Sartor Resartus: The Life and Opinions of Herr Teufelsdröckh.* Ed. C. F. Harrold. ("The Doubleday-Doran Series in Literature," ed. Robert Shafer.) 1st ed. Garden City, N. Y.: Doubleday, Doran, 1937.

Carnegie, Dale. *How to Stop Worrying and Start Living.* New York: Simon and Schuster, 1951.

Carpenter, Edward. *Days with Walt Whitman, with Some Notes on His Life and Work.* 2nd ed. London: George Allen & Unwin, 1906.

Chambers Biographical Dictionary. Ed. J. O. Thorne, T. C. Collocott. Cambridge: Cambridge University Press, 1984.

Chase, Richard. *Walt Whitman Reconsidered.* New York: William Sloan Associates, 1955.

Clark, Ronald W. *Einstein: The Life and Times.* New York: World, 1971.

Clemens, Samuel L. (pseud. Mark Twain). *Mark Twain in Eruption: Hitherto Unpublished Pages about Men and Events.* Ed. Bernard DeVoto. 1st ed. New York and London: Harper & Brothers, 1940.

_____. *Mark Twain's Letters.* Ed. Albert Bigelow Paine. 2 vols. New York: Harper & Brothers, 1917.

Coleman, Rufus A. "Further Reminiscences of Walt Whitman." *Modern Language Notes*, LXIII (Apr., 1948), 266–68.

Collier's Encyclopedia. Ed. W. D. Halsey, Bernard Johnson. 24 vols. New York: Macmillan Educational; London and New York: P. F. Collier, 1989.

Compton, Arthur H. *The Freedom of Man.* New Haven: Yale University Press, 1936.

Conway, Moncure Daniel. *Autobiography: Memories and Experiences.* 2 vols. Boston: Houghton Mifflin, 1904.

_____. *Emerson at Home and Abroad.* Boston: James R. Osgood, 1882.

Corsini, Raymond J. (ed.). *Current Psychotherapies.* 3rd ed. Itasca, Ill.: F. E. Peacock, 1984.

Courtney, W. L. *Life of John Stuart Mill.* London: Walter Scott; New York: Thomas Whittaker; Toronto: W. J. Gage, 1889.

Cushman, H. E. *A Beginner's History of Philosophy*. Rev. ed. Boston: Houghton Mifflin, 1946.

Darrow, Clarence Seward. *Crime and Criminals; an Address Delivered to the Prisoners in the Chicago County Jail*. Chicago: C. H. Kerr, 1908.

Darwin, Charles. *The Origin of Species by Means of Natural Selection. The Descent of Man and Selection in Relation to Sex*. (Vol. 49 in "Great Books of the Western World.") Chicago: William Benton, Encyclopedia Britannica, 1952.

Dasgupta, Surendranath. *A History of Indian Philosophy*. 5 vols. Cambridge: Cambridge University Press, 1932–55.

Davies, John E. *Phrenology, Fad and Science: A 19th Century American Crusade*. New Haven: Yale University Press, 1955.

Donald, David Herbert. *Lincoln*. London: Jonathan Cape, 1995.

Donaldson, Thomas. *Walt Whitman the Man*. New York: Francis P. Harper, 1896.

Drake, Durant. *Invitation to Philosophy*. Boston: Houghton Mifflin, 1933.

Draper, John William. *History of the Intellectual Development of Europe*. 4th ed. New York: Harper & Brothers, 1865.

Dudley, Louise, and Faricy, Austin. *The Humanities*. 6th ed. New York: McGraw-Hill, 1978.

Durant, William James. *The Story of Philosophy*. New York: Simon and Schuster, 1926.

Eddington, Sir Arthur S. *The Nature of the Physical World*. Cambridge: Cambridge University Press, 1928.

_____. "Physics and Philosophy." *Philosophy*, VIII (Jan., 1933), 30–43.

Edwards, Paul (ed.). *The Encyclopedia of Philosophy*. 8 vols. New York: Macmillan; London: Collier Macmillan, 1967.

Einstein, Albert. *Cosmic Religion, with Other Opinions and Aphorisms*. New York: Covici-Friede, 1931. [The essay "Cosmic Religion" appeared, with variations, in *The New York Times Magazine* in *The New York Times*, Nov. 9, 1930, Sec. 5, p. 1.]

_____. *Ideas and Opinions by Albert Einstein*. New trans. and rev. by Sonja Bargmann. New York: Bonanza Books, 1954.

_____. *The World As I See It*. New York: Covici-Friede, 1934.

Emerson, Ralph Waldo. *The Complete Essays and Other Writings of Ralph Waldo Emerson*. New York: Modern Library, 1940.

_____. *The Complete Works*. Ed. E. W. Emerson. 12 vols. Boston: Houghton Mifflin, 1903–1904.

_____. *The Conduct of Life*. Ed. S. F. Mittell. Washington, D.C.: National Home Library Foundation, 1935.

_____. *Emerson's Complete Works*. Riverside Ed. 12 vols. London: George Routledge and Sons, 1894–1903. [No editor given.]

_____. *Journals of Ralph Waldo Emerson*. Ed. Edward Waldo Emerson and Waldo Emerson Forbes. 10 vols. Boston: Houghton Mifflin, 1904–14.

_____. *The Letters of Ralph Waldo Emerson*. Ed. Ralph L. Rusk. 6 vols. New York: Columbia University Press, 1939.

_____. *Ralph Waldo Emerson: Essays and Lectures*. Ed. Joel Porte. New York: Library of America, 1983.

Enfield, William. *The History of Philosophy, from the Earliest Times to the Beginning of the Present Century*. 2 vols. Dublin: Printed for P. Wogan et al., 1792.

Epictetus. *Moral Discourses*. Trans. Elizabeth Carter. Ed. W. H. D. Rouse. ("Everyman's Library," No. 404.) London: J. M. Dent & Sons; New York: E. P. Dutton, 1950.

Everett, Walter Goodnow. *Moral Values: A Study of the Principles of Conduct*. New York: Henry Holt, 1918.

Ewing, A. C. *The Fundamental Questions of Philosophy*. London: Routledge & Kegan Paul, 1951.

_____. *Kant's Treatment of Causality*. London: Kegan Paul, Trench, Trübner, 1924.

Fadiman, Clifton (ed.). *Living Philosophies*. New York: Doubleday, 1990. [Contains Einstein's "The World As I See It."]

Falk, Robert P. "Walt Whitman and German Thought." *Journal of English and Germanic Philology*, XL (July, 1941), 315–330.

Feibleman, James K. *Aesthetics: A Study of the Fine Arts in Theory and Practice*. New York: Duell, Sloan and Pearce, 1949.

Feinberg, J. (ed.). *Reason and Responsibility*. Belmont, Cal.: Wadsworth, 1985.

Fergusson, Harvey. *Modern Man: His Belief and Behavior*. New York and London: Alfred A. Knopf, 1936.

Ferm, Vergilius (ed.). *An Encyclopedia of Religion*. New York: Philosophical Library, 1945.

_____. *A History of Philosophical Systems*. New York: Philosophical Library, 1950.

Fichte, Johann Gottlieb. *The Popular Works of Johann Gottlieb Fichte*. Trans. William

Smith. 2 vols. London: John Chapman, 1848, 1849.

Fisher, Mary Pat. *Living Religions.* 2nd ed. Englewood Cliffs, N. J.: Prentice Hall, 1994.

Fiske, John. *Outlines of Cosmic Philosophy.* Boston: Houghton Mifflin, 1902.

Foerster, Norman. *American Criticism: A Study in Literary Theory from Poe to the Present.* Boston: Houghton Mifflin, 1928.

Frank, Jerome. *Fate and Freedom; a Philosophy for Free Americans.* New York: Simon and Schuster, 1945.

Franklin, Benjamin. *A Dissertation on Liberty and Necessity, Pleasure and Pain.* London: Published by the author, 1725: Reprint, New York: Facsimile Text Society, 1930.

Freud, Sigmund. *The Basic Writings of Sigmund Freud.* Trans. and ed. A. A. Brill. New York: Modern Library, 1938.

_____. *The Future of an Illusion.* Rev. ed. Trans. W. D. Robson-Scott. Ed. James Strachey. Garden City, N. Y.: Doubleday, 1964.

Frost, S. E., Jr. *The Basic Teachings of the Great Philosophers.* Garden City, N. Y.: Halcyon House, 1948.

Garnett, A. Campbell. *The Moral Nature of Man; a Critical Evaluation of Ethical Principles.* New York: Ronald, 1952.

Gingerich, Solomon Francis. *Essays in the Romantic Poets.* New York: Macmillan, 1924.

Godwin, William. *Enquiry Concerning Political Justice and Its Influence on Morals and Happiness.* Ed. F. E. L. Priestley. 3 vols. Toronto: University of Toronto Press, 1946. ("Photographic facsimile of the third edition corrected.")

Gosse, Edmund. *Critical Kit-Kats.* London: William Heinemann, 1913.

Grabo, Carl. *Prometheus Unbound: An Interpretation.* Chapel Hill: University of North Carolina Press, 1935.

Grant, Francis. *Oriental Philosophy: The Story of the Teachers of the East.* New York: Dial, 1936.

Gupta, Mahendranath. *The Gospel of Sri Ramakrishna.* Trans. Swami Nikhilananda. New York: Ramakrishna-Vivekananda Center, 1942.

Halverson, William H. *A Concise Introduction to Philosophy.* 4th ed. New York: Random House, 1981.

Hampshire, Stuart. *Spinoza.* Harmondsworth, Middlesex: Penguin, 1951.

Hankins, F. H. "Individual Freedom with Some Sociological Implications of Determinism." *Journal of Philosophy,* XXII (Nov., 1925), 617–34.

Hartshorne, Charles, and Reese, William L. (eds.). *Philosophers Speak of God.* Chicago: University of Chicago Press, 1953.

Hartwick, Harry. *The Foreground of American Fiction.* New York: American Book, 1934.

Haserot, Francis S. *Essays on the Logic of Being.* New York: Macmillan, 1932.

Hazlitt, William. *The Complete Works of William Hazlitt.* Ed. P. P. Howe after the edition of A. R. Waller and Arnold Glover. 21 vols. London: J. M. Dent and Sons, 1930–34.

Hedge, Frederic H. (ed.). *Prose Writers of Germany.* 2nd ed. Philadelphia: Carey and Hart, 1849.

Hegel, Georg Wilhelm Friedrich. *Lectures on the Philosophy of History.* Trans. J. Sibree. London: Henry G. Bohn, 1857.

_____. *Lectures on the Philosophy of History.* Trans. J. Sibree. London: Bell & Daldy, 1872.

_____. *Lectures on the Philosophy of Religion.* Trans. E. B. Speirs and J. B. Sanderson. 3 vols. London: Kegan Paul, Trench, Trübner, 1895.

_____. *The Logic of Hegel.* Trans. William Wallace. Oxford: Clarendon, 1874.

Herndon, William H. *The Hidden Lincoln; from the Letters and Papers of William H. Herndon.* Ed. Emanuel Hertz. New York: Viking, 1938.

Herrick, C. Judson. *Fatalism or Freedom: A Biologist's Answer.* New York: W. W. Norton, 1926.

Hindus, Milton (ed.). *Leaves of Grass One Hundred Years After.* Stanford, Cal.: Stanford University Press, 1955.

_____, (ed.). *Walt Whitman: The Critical Heritage.* New York: Barnes and Noble, 1971.

Hobart, R. E. "Free Will as Involving Determination and Inconceivable Without It." *Mind,* XLIII (Jan., 1934), 1–27.

Hobbes, Thomas. *The English Works of Thomas Hobbes.* Ed. William Molesworth. 11 vols. London: John Bohn, 1839–45.

Holbach, Paul Henri Thiry (Baron d'). *The System of Nature; or, Laws of the Moral and Physical World.* Trans. H. D. Robinson. 2 vols. Boston: J. P. Mendum, 1889.

Holloway, Emory. *Free and Lonesome Heart: The Secret of Walt Whitman*. 1st ed. New York: Vantage, 1960.

Holman, C. Hugh, and Harmon, William (eds.). *A Handbook to Literature*. 6th ed. New York: Macmillan; London: Collier Macmillan, 1992.

Home, Henry (Lord Kames). *Essays on the Principles of Morality and Natural Religion*. 1st ed. Edinburgh: A. Kincaid and A. Donaldson, 1751.

Honderich, Ted. *How Free Are You? The Determinism Problem*. 2nd ed. Oxford: Oxford University Press, 2002.

_____, (ed.). *The Oxford Companion to Philosophy*. Oxford: Oxford University Press, 1995.

Hook, Sidney (ed.). *Determinism and Freedom in the Age of Modern Science: A Philosophical Symposium*. New York: New York University Press, 1958.

Hospers, John. "Meaning and Free Will." *Philosophy: An Introduction Through Literature*. Ed. L. Kleiman and S. Lewis. St. Paul, Minn.: Paragon House, 1992.

Hungerford, Edward. "Walt Whitman and His Chart of Bumps." *American Literature*, II (Jan., 1931), 350–84.

Inge, W. R., et al. (eds.). *Radhakrishnan Comparative Studies in Philosophy*. London: George Allen and Unwin, 1951.

Irwin, Mabel MacCoy. *Whitman: The Poet-Liberator of Woman*. New York: Published by the author, 1905.

James, William. *Essays on Faith and Morals*. New York: Longmans, Green, 1943.

_____. *Pragmatism: A New Name for Some Old Ways of Thinking*. London: Longmans, Green, 1910.

_____. *The Principles of Psychology*. 2 vols. New York: Henry Holt, 1918.

Janson, H. W. *History of Art*. 2nd ed. Englewood Cliffs, N. J.: Prentice Hall; New York: Harry N. Abrams, 1977.

Jeans, Sir James. *Physics and Philosophy*. Cambridge: Cambridge University Press; New York: Macmillan, 1943.

Joad, C. E. M. *God and Evil*. 1st ed. New York and London: Harper & Brothers, 1943.

Jones, Ernest. *Sigmund Freud: Life and Work*. London: Hogarth, 1954.

Kallen, Horace M. (ed.). *Freedom in the Modern World*. New York: Coward-McCann, 1928.

Kant, Immanuel. *Critique of Pure Reason*. Trans. "J. M. D. M." New York: American Home Library, 1902.

Kaplan, Charles (ed.). *Criticism: The Major Statements*. New York: St. Martin's, 1975.

Kaplan, Justin. *Walt Whitman: A Life*. New York: Simon and Schuster, 1980.

Kawada, Louise M. "The Truth About 'A Riddle Song.'" *Walt Whitman Review*, XXVII (June, 1981), 78–82.

Kennedy, William Sloane. *The Fight of a Book for the World: A Companion Volume to Leaves of Grass*. West Yarmouth, Mass.: Stonecroft, 1926.

Khayyám, Omar. *The Rubáiyát of Omar Khayyám, the Astronomer-Poet of Persia*. Trans. Edward FitzGerald [*sic*]. ("Complete" ed. with variants in the five original printings.) New York: Thomas Y. Crowell, 1921.

Kleiman, Lowell, and Lewis, Stephen (eds.). *Philosophy: An Introduction Through Literature*. St. Paul, Minn.: Paragon House, 1992.

Knoebel, Edgar E. (ed.). *The Modern World*. 4th ed. Vol. III in *Classics of Western Thought*. 4 vols. San Diego: Harcourt Brace Jovanovich, 1988.

The Koran: Or, Alcoran of Mohammed; with Explanatory Notes; and Readings from Salvary's Version; also Preliminary Discourse. Trans. and ed. George Sale. London and New York: Frederick Warne, 1891.

Kuebrich, David. *Minor Prophecy: Walt Whitman's New American Religion*. ("Religion in North America," ed. Catherine L. Albanese and Stephen J. Stein.) Bloomingdale and Indianapolis: Indiana University Press, 1989.

Laird, John. *On Human Freedom*. London: George Allen and Unwin, 1947.

Lao Tse. *Tao Te Ching*. Trans. Ch'u Ta-Kao. 5th ed. London: George Allen & Unwin, 1959.

_____. *The Tao Teh King*. In *The Sacred Books of China: The Texts of Taoism*. Trans. James Legge. (*The Sacred Books of the East*, ed. F. Max Muller, Vol. XXXIX.) Oxford: Clarendon, 1891.

_____. *The Wisdom of Laotse*. Trans. and ed. Lin Yutang. (First Modern Library ed.) New York: Modern Library, 1948.

Leibniz, Gottfried Wilhelm. *Philosophical Papers and Letters*. Trans. and ed. Leroy E. Loemker. 2 vols. Chicago: University of Chicago Press, 1956.

_____. *Theodicy: Essays on the Goodness of God, the Freedom of Man, and the Origin of Evil.* Trans. E. M. Huggard. Ed. Austin Farrer. New Haven: Yale University Press, 1952.

LeMaster, J. R., and Kummings, Donald D. (eds.). *Walt Whitman: An Encyclopedia.* New York and London: Garland, 1998.

Lewis, R. W. B. (ed.). *The Presence of Walt Whitman: Selected Papers from the English Institute.* New York: Columbia University Press, 1965.

Locke, John. *The Works of John Locke.* 11th ed. 10 vols. London: W. Otridge et al., 1812. [No editor is listed.]

Longman Advanced American Dictionary. Ed. Karen Cleveland et al. Harlow, Essex, Eng.: Pearson Education, 2000.

Loving, Jerome. *Walt Whitman: The Song of Himself.* Berkeley: University of California Press, 1999.

MacIver, Robert Morrison. *Social Causation.* Boston: Ginn, 1942.

Macnicol, Nicol (ed.). *Hindu Scriptures: Hymns from the Rigveda, Five Upanishads, The Bhagavadgita.* ("Everyman's Library," No. 944.) London: J. M. Dent & Sons; New York: E. P. Dutton, 1966.

Matthiessen, F. O. *American Renaissance: Art and Expression in the Age of Emerson and Whitman.* New York: Oxford University Press, 1964.

McTaggart, John McTaggart Ellis. *Some Dogmas of Religion.* London: Edward Arnold, 1930.

Mill, John Stuart. *Autobiography.* New York: Columbia University Press, 1924.

_____. *On Liberty.* In *The English Philosophers from Bacon to Mill.* Ed. E. A. Burtt. New York: Modern Library, 1939.

_____. *A System of Logic.* 8th ed. London: Longmans, Green, and Co., 1919.

Miller, Edwin Haviland (ed.). *A Century of Whitman Criticism.* Bloomington: Indiana University Press, 1969.

Miller, Perry (ed.). *The Transcendentalists: An Anthology.* Cambridge, Mass.: Harvard University Press, 1967.

More, Paul Elmer. *Hellenistic Philosophies.* Princeton: Princeton University Press; London: Humphrey Milford, Oxford University Press, 1923.

Myers, Henry Alonzo. "Whitman's Consistency." *American Literature*, VIII (Nov., 1936), 243–57.

Myerson, Joel (ed.). *Whitman in His Own Time.* Iowa City: University of Iowa Press, 2000.

Nahm, Milton C. (ed.). *Selections from Early Greek Philosophy.* 3rd ed. New York: Appleton-Century-Crofts, 1947.

Newton, Joseph Fort. *Lincoln and Herndon.* Cedar Rapids, Ia.: Torch, 1910.

Nietzsche, Friedrich. *The Complete Works of Friedrich Nietzsche.* Ed. Oscar Levy. 18 vols. Edinburgh: T. N. Foulis, 1909–13.

Nordau, Max. *Degeneration.* Trans. from 2nd German ed. New York: D. Appleton, 1895.

Oates, W. J. *The Stoic and Epicurean Philosophers.* New York: Random House, 1940.

Palmer, George H. *The Problem of Freedom.* Boston: Houghton Mifflin, 1911.

Parrinder, Geoffrey (ed.). *Religions of the World: From Primitive Beliefs to Modern Faiths.* 1st U. S. ed. New York: Grosset & Dunlap, 1971.

Parsons, Olive Wrenchel. "Whitman the Non-Hegelian." *Publications of the Modern Language Association*, LVIII (Dec., 1943), 1073–93.

Paulsen, Friedrich. *Introduction to Philosophy.* Trans. Frank Thilly. New York: Henry Holt, 1898.

_____. *A System of Ethics.* Trans. and ed. Frank Thilly. New York: Charles Scribner's Sons, 1911.

Pearce, Harvey (ed.). *Whitman: A Collection of Critical Essays.* Englewood Cliffs, N. J.: Prentice Hall, 1962.

Perlman, Jim; Folsom, Ed; and Campion, Dan (eds.). *Walt Whitman: The Measure of His Song.* Duluth, Minn.: Holy Cow!, 1998.

Planck, Max. *Where Is Science Going?* Trans. James Murphy. 1st ed. New York: W. W. Norton, 1932.

Platt, Isaac Hull. *Walt Whitman.* Boston: Small, Maynard, 1904.

Plotinus. *The Philosophy of Plotinus.* Ed. W. R. Inge. 3rd ed. 2 vols. London: Longmans, Green, 1929.

Pollock, Frederick. "Marcus Aurelius and the Stoic Philosophy." *Mind*, IV (1879), 47–68.

Pope, Alexander. *Alexander Pope: Selected Works.* Ed. Lois Kronenberger. New York: Modern Library, 1948.

_____. *The Works of Alexander Pope, Esq., in Verse and Prose.* Ed. W. L. Bowles. London: J. Johnson et al., 1806.

Popkin, Richard H., and Stroll, Avrum (eds.).

Philosophy Made Simple. 2nd ed. New York: Broadway Books, 1993.

Priestley, Joseph. *The Theological and Miscellaneous Works, &c., of Joseph Priestley.* Ed. John T. Rutt. 25 vols. in 26. [No place or publisher listed.] Printed by George Smallfiield, Hackney, 1817–32 [Individual vols. not dated.]

Pugh, C. Scott. "The End as Means in 'A Riddle Song.'" *Walt Whitman Review,* XXIII (June, 1977), 82–85.

Rajasekharaiah, T. R. *The Roots of Whitman's Grass.* Rutherford, N.J.: Fairleigh Dickinson University Press, 1970.

Ramsperger, Albert G. "Determinism." *Collier's Encyclopedia.* New York: Macmillan Educational; London: P. F. Collier, 1989.

Rankin, Henry B. *Intimate Character Sketches of Abraham Lincoln.* Philadelphia: J. B. Lippincott, 1924.

Rashdall, Hastings. *The Theory of Good and Evil; a Treatise on Moral Philosophy.* 2nd ed. 2 vols. London: Humphrey Milford, Oxford University Press, 1924.

Reed, Harry B. "The Heraclitan Obsession of Walt Whitman." *The Personalist,* XV (Apr., 1934), 125–38.

Reyburn, Hugh A. *The Ethical Theory of Hegel: A Study of the Philosophy of Right.* Oxford: Clarendon, 1921.

Reynolds, David S. (ed.). *A Historical Guide to Walt Whitman.* New York: Oxford University Press, 2000.

_____. *Walt Whitman.* "Lives and Legacies" series. New York: Oxford University Press, 2005.

_____. *Walt Whitman's America: A Cultural Biography.* New York: Alfred A. Knopf, 1995.

Royce, Josiah. *The Spirit of Modern Philosophy.* Boston: Houghton Mifflin, 1892.

Russell, Bertrand. *The Autobiography of Bertrand Russell, 1872–1914.* Boston: Little, Brown, 1967.

_____. *Bolshevism: Practice and Theory.* New York: Harcourt Brace and Howe, 1920.

_____. *A History of Western Philosophy.* New York: Simon and Schuster, 1945.

_____. *Human Society in Ethics and Politics.* London: George Allen & Unwin, 1954.

_____. *Mysticism and Logic and Other Essays.* London: Longmans, Green, 1919.

_____. *The Scientific Outlook.* London: George Allen & Unwin, 1931.

_____. *Unpopular Essays.* New York: Simon and Schuster, 1950.

Schelling, Friedrich Wilhelm Joseph. *Of Human Freedom.* Trans. James Gutmann. Chicago: Open Court, 1936.

Schopenhauer, Arthur. *The Works of Schopenhauer.* Abridged ed. Ed. Will Durant. [Trans. J. Sibree.] New York: Frederick Ungar, 1961.

_____. *The World as Will and Idea.* Trans. R. B. Haldane and J. Kemp. 3rd ed. 3 vols. London: Kegan Paul, Trench, Trübner, 1891.

Seneca, Lucius Annaeus. *Moral Essays.* Trans. J. W. Basore. 3 vols. London: William Heinemann; New York: G. P. Putnam's Sons, 1928, 1932, 1935. [Parallel text.]

Sheen, Fulton J. *Philosophy of Religion.* New York: Appleton-Century-Crofts, 1948.

Shelley, Percy Bysshe. *The Complete Poetical Works of Percy Bysshe Shelley.* Ed. Thomas Hutchinson. London: Henry Frowde, Oxford University Press, 1912.

_____. *The Works of Percy Bysshe Shelley in Verse and Prose.* Ed. H. B. Forman. 8 vols. London: Reeves and Turner, 1880.

Shephard, Esther. *Walt Whitman's Pose.* New York: Harcourt, Brace, 1936.

Smidgall, Gary (ed.). *Intimate with Walt: Selections from Whitman's Conversations with Horace Traubel, 1888–1892.* Iowa City: University of Iowa Press, 2001.

Smuts, Jan Christian. *Walt Whitman: A Study in the Evolution of a Personality.* Ed. Alan L. McLeod. Detroit: Wayne State University Press, 1973. [Written in 1894–95 and hitherto unpublished.]

Sontag, Susan. *On Photography.* New York: Farrar, Straus, and Giroux, 1977.

Spencer, Herbert. *First Principles.* New York: P. F. Collier and Son, 1900.

_____. *The Principles of Sociology.* 3 vols. New York: D. Appleton, 1907.

Spinoza, Benedict de. *The Chief Works of Benedict de Spinoza.* Trans. R. H. M. Elwes. 2 vols. Rev. ed. London: George Bell and Sons, 1891, 1898.

_____. *The Chief Works of Benedict de Spinoza.* Trans. R. H. M. Elwes. New York: Dover, 1955.

_____. *Ethic.* Trans. W. Hale White; trans. revised by Amelia Hutchison Stirling. London: Humphrey Milford, Oxford University Press, 1927.

_____. *Letters to Friend and Foe.* Ed. D. D. Runes. Trans. R. H. M. Elwes. New York: Philosophical Library, 1966.

_____. *Philosophy of Benedict de Spinoza.* Trans. R. H. M. Elwes. New York: Tudor, 1934.

_____. *The Philosophy of Spinoza, Selected from His Chief Works.* Ed. Joseph Ratner. New York: Modern Library, 1927.

_____. *Spinoza's Short Treatise on God, Man, and His Well-Being.* Trans. and ed. A. Wolf. London: Adam and Charles Black, 1910.

Spurzheim, J. G. *Phrenology, or the Doctrine of the Mental Phenomena.* 2nd American ed. 2 vols. Boston: Marsh, Capen, and Lyon, 1833.

Stace, W. T. *Religion and the Modern Mind.* Philadelphia and New York: J. B. Lippincott, 1952.

Stebbing, L. Susan. *Philosophy and the Physicists.* London: Methuen, 1937.

Stewart, Dugald. *The Collected Works of Dugald Stewart.* Ed. Sir William Hamilton. 11 vols. Edinburgh: Thomas Constable, 1854–60.

Stovall, Floyd. *The Foreground of Leaves of Grass.* Charlottesville: University Press of Virginia, 1974.

Symonds, John Addington. *Walt Whitman: A Study.* London: George Routledge & Sons; New York: E. P. Dutton, 1906.

Tagore, Rabindranath. *Sadhana: The Realisation of Life.* New York: Macmillan, 1914.

Taine, H[ippolyte] A[dolphe]. *History of English Literature.* Trans. H. Van Laun. 2 vols. New York: Worthington, 1889.

_____. *Lectures on Art.* Trans. John Durand. First series, *The Philosophy of Art, The Ideal in Art.* New York: Henry Holt, 1875. [One of 2 vols., not numbered.]

_____. *Lectures on Art.* Trans. John Durand. Second series, *The Philosophy of Art in Italy, The Philosophy of Art in The Netherlands, The Philosophy of Art in Greece.* New York: Henry Holt, 1875. [One of 2 vols., not numbered.]

Thompson, Eileen, et al. (eds.). *Prentice Hall Literature: World Masterpieces.* Englewood Cliffs, N. J.: Prentice Hall, 1991.

Tolstoy, Leo. *Power and Liberty.* Trans. Huntington Smith. New York: Thomas Y. Crowell, n.d.

Traubel, Horace L. (ed.) *Camden's Compliment to Walt Whitman, May 31, 1889.* Philadelphia: David McKay, 1889.

Traubel, Horace L. *With Walt Whitman in Camden.* Vol. I. Boston: Small, Maynard, 1906. [Mar. 28–July 14, 1888.]

_____. _____. Vol. II. New York: D. Appleton, 1908. [July 15–Oct. 31, 1888.]

_____. _____. Vol. III. New York: Mitchell Kennerley, 1914. [Nov. 1, 1888–Jan. 20, 1889.]

_____. _____. Vol. IV. Ed. Sculley Bradley. Philadelphia: University of Pennsylvania Press; London: Geoffrey Cumberlege, Oxford University Press, 1953. [Jan. 21–Apr. 7, 1889.]

_____. _____. Vol. V. Ed. Gertrude Traubel. Carbondale: Southern Illinois University Press, 1964. [Apr. 8–Sept. 14, 1889.]

_____. _____. Vol. VI. Ed. Gertrude Traubel and William White. Carbondale: Southern Illinois University Press, 1982. [Sept. 15, 1889–July 6, 1890.]

_____. _____. Vol. VII. Ed. Jeanne Chapman and Robert MacIsaac. Carbondale: Southern Illinois University Press, 1992. [July 7, 1890–Feb. 10, 1891.]

_____. _____. Vol. VIII. Ed. Jeanne Chapman and Robert MacIsaac. Oregon House, Cal.: William Bentley, 1996. [Feb. 11–Sept. 30, 1891.]

_____. _____. Vol. IX. Ed. Jeanne Chapman and Robert MacIsaac. Oregon House, Cal.: William Bentley, 1996. [Oct. 1, 1891–Apr. 3, 1892.]

Traubel, Horace L.; Bucke, Richard Maurice; and Harned, Thomas B. (eds.). *In Re Walt Whitman.* Philadelphia: David McKay, 1893.

The Upanishads. Trans. Swami Nikhlananda. 1st ed. 4 vols. New York: Harper & Brothers, n.d.

Urmson, J. O. (ed.). *The Concise Encyclopedia of Western Philosophy and Philosophers.* New York: Hawthorne Books, 1965.

Wadia, Ardaser Sorabjee N. *Fate and Free-Will.* London and Toronto: J. M. Dent and Sons, 1915.

Waterman, William Randall. *Frances Wright.* New York: Columbia University Press, 1924.

Weatherford, Roy C. "Determinism." *The Oxford Companion to Philosophy.* Ed. Ted Honderich. Oxford: Oxford University Press, 1995, pp. 194–95.

_____. *The Implications of Determinism.* London: Routledge, 1991.

Weinberg, Arthur (ed.). *Attorney for the Damned.* New York: Simon and Schuster, 1957.

Wellek, Rene, and Warren, Austin. *Theory of Literature.* New York: Harcourt, Brace, 1949.

Whitman, Walt. *Catalogue of the Whitman Collection in the Duke University Library.* Ed. Ellen Frances Frey. Durham, N. C.: Duke University Library, 1945. [Part of the Trent collection.]

_____. *Complete Poetry and Collected Prose [Leaves of Grass (1855); Leaves of Grass (1891–92); Complete Prose Works (1892); Supplementary Prose].* Ed. Justin Kaplan. New York: Library of America, 1982.

_____. *Complete Prose Works.* Philadelphia: David McKay, 1892.

_____. *The Complete Writings of Walt Whitman.* Ed. Richard M. Bucke, Thomas B. Harned, and Horace L. Traubel with additional bibliographical and critical material by Oscar L. Triggs. 10 vols. New York: Knickerbocker, 1902.

_____. *A Concordance of Walt Whitman's Leaves of Grass and Selected Prose Writings.* Ed. Edwin Harold Eby. Seattle: University of Washington Press, 1955. [Originally published in five fascicles: I, A-He, 1949; II, He-Pa, 1950; III, Pa-Sw, 1952; IV, Sw-Z and prose A-Fa, 1953; V, prose, Fa-Z, 1954.]

_____. *An 1855 Notebook Toward the Second Edition of "Leaves of Grass."* Ed. Harold W. Blodgett and William White. Carbondale: Southern Illinois University Press, 1959. [Original in the collection of Charles E. Feinberg of Detroit.]

_____. *Inclusive Edition: Leaves of Grass.* Ed. Emory Holloway. Variorum Readings by Oscar Lovell Triggs. Garden City, N. Y.: Doubleday, Doran, 1945.

_____. *Leaves of Grass.* Boston: Thayer and Eldridge, 1860–61.

_____. *Leaves of Grass.* Philadelphia: Rees Welsh, 1882.

_____. *Leaves of Grass.* Philadelphia: David McKay, 1891–92. ["Authorized edition." Sometimes called the "deathbed edition."

Unless otherwise specified, all quotations of poetry are taken from this, the 1891–92 edition.]

_____. *Leaves of Grass.* Ed. David McKay. Philadelphia: David McKay, 1900.

_____. *Leaves of Grass.* Ed. (notes by) Meir Rinde. New York: Modern Library, 2001. [Reprint of "deathbed" ed., with commentaries.]

_____. *Leaves of Grass and Other Writings.* Ed. Michael Moon. New York and London: W. W. Norton, 2002.

_____. *Leaves of Grass, 1855 Version.* Ann Arbor Media Group. Ann Arbor, Mich.: Borders Classics, 2003.

_____. *Notebooks and Unpublished Prose Manuscripts.* Ed. Edward F. Grier. 6 vols. New York: New York University Press, 1984.

_____. *The Poetry and Prose of Walt Whitman.* Ed. Louis Untermeyer. New York: Simon and Schuster, 1949.

_____. *The Uncollected Poetry and Prose of Walt Whitman.* Collected and ed. by Emory Holloway. 2 vols. Garden City, N.Y.: Doubleday, Page, 1921.

_____. *Walt Whitman: Complete Poetry and Selected Prose and Letters.* Ed. Emory Holloway. 1st ed. London: Nonesuch, 1938.

_____. *Walt Whitman: Representative Selections, with Introduction, Bibliography, and Notes.* Ed. Floyd Stovall. Rev. ed. New York: American Book, 1939.

Wood, Ledger. "The Free-Will Controversy." *Philosophy*, XVI (Oct., 1941), 386–97.

Wordsworth, William. *The Poetical Works of Wordsworth.* Ed. T. Hutchinson. London: Oxford University Press, 1936.

Wright, Frances. *A Few Days in Athens, Being the Translation of a Greek Manuscript Discovered in Herculaneum.* New York: Peter Eckler, 1822.

Index